YO-CJH-592

MANAGEMENT OF RURAL CHANGE IN KOREA:
THE SAEMAUL UNDONG

Management of Rural Change in Korea:
The Saemaul Undong

by
In-Joung Whang

The Institute of Social Sciences
Korean Studies Series No.5

Seoul National University Press

Copyright © 1981 by *In-Joung Whang*
Published by Seoul National University Press
Printed by Sam Hwa Printing Co. Seoul, Korea
(1963. 6. 15 Reg. No. 1-256)
First Printing

Management of Rural Change in Korea

In-Joung Whang

Seoul National University Press
Seoul, Korea

To my lovely two daughters and son:
Hie-nam, Hie-shin and Youn-sung.

FOREWORD

To characterize the rapid change Korea has undergone during the last decade as fundamental or historical is based on the fact that the change included and in a sense centered around a significant transformation in the organization and operation of rural life. Much praise and acclaim have been accorded to the Korean economic development in general and the rural development in particular. At the same time, some sharp criticisms have been voiced mostly by domestic critics on the effectiveness and equity of the modes and consequences of such economic and rural changs. It is surprising indeed that, while the praises and blames were heard loud and often, only a few attempts have been made to analyze systematically the nature and process of the development in Korea, particularly the changes in the rural setting. While the *Saemaul Undong* has caught the imagination and interest of social planners in many countries, we have not been able to produce a work in international language which could supply a coherent analysis of the various facets of rural change in Korea. The present volume by Dr. In-Joung Whang represents a successful effort to meet the demands in the international community for a scholarly exposition on the management of rural change in Korea.

Having served on the faculty of Seoul National University, United Nations Asian Center for Developmental Administration in Kuala Lumpur and Korea Rural Economic Institute, Dr. Whang is certainly one of the most eminently qualified scholars to perform the task on hand, and this volume should contribute to not only the comparative analysis of rural changes but also the art of policy planning for the management of rural innovation. It is our belief that the publication of Dr. Whang's study on the rural change in Korea could mark a beginning for a new phase in the comparative study of rural development in Asia and other developing areas.

                                Hongkoo Lee
                                Director
                                Institute of Social Sciences

August, 1981

ACKNOWLEDGEMENTS

There are many factors which stimulated and encouraged me to undertake this work. In chronological order, my academic interests in the management of rural innovation emerged from my earlier study on the management of family planning which indeed is concerned with the process of innovation at the *individual level*. In pursuit of my own inquiries into the management of innovation, rural development became an additional challenge to a student of interdisciplinary policy sciences as it involves the management of synchronized innovations at the *individual* as well as *organizational levels*. My interest in this field was further provoked by a series of curiosities and challenging questions raised through constant contacts with scholars and administrators from abroad whom I have met during my service with the United Nations Asian and Pacific Development Administration Center (formerly, ACDA) in Kuala Lumpur and during their visits to Korea after my return home.

In carrying out this work, I have benefited from a number of people who have helped me in several ways. My first indebtedness is to Dr. Hahn-Been Lee, Univercity Professor of Ajoo University (formerly, Deputy Prime Minister) for the kind guidance which he has provided me as well as for his continuous encouragement of my research in the field of development and innovation. I also wish to thank Mr. Bo-Hyun Kim, President of the Korea Rural Economic Institute, for his generous allowance of time for me to complete this work. I am very grateful to Professor Hongkoo Lee, Director of the Institute of Social Sciences, Seoul National University for his encouragement of my research in the field as well as for his kind agreement to publishing this book in the Korean Studies Series. My thanks also should be addressed to Professor Yunshik Chang, University of British Colombia, Canada for his kind reading of the early draft and his constructive comments. There are countless others to whom I am equally indebted.

For trust in my ability to produce something worthwhile, I shall always be indebted to Mr. Chong-Min Park who helped me in preparation of this manuscript in book form and also for his arduous service in proofreading. I owe a debt of gratitude to Mr. Jae-Woong Shim who helped me in collecting and analyzing data during the field survey and interview conducted in 1979. Finally I am also indebted to Jung-Soo Han for her kind service in typing in spite of busy preparations for her happy marriage. For all the help and encouragement I have received, I am extremely grateful.

In-Joung Whang

Jinhung
August, 1981

CONTENTS

Foreword vii
Acknowledgements ix
Contents xi
List of Tables, Forms and Charts xv

PART I: INTRODUCTION

Chapter 1.
Introduction 2
Chapter 2.
A Conceptual Framework of the Saemaul Undong 9
   1. Unit of Rural Community for the Saemaul Undong
   2. Participatory Community Structure and Leadership
   3. Perceptual and Attitudinal Change of Rural People
   4. A Wide Range of Development Projects
   5. Extensive Role of Government in Support of the Saemaul Undong
   6. Nationwide Mobilization of Political and Social Support
   7. Summary: A Model of Integrated Rural Development

Chapter 3.
Performance of the Saemaul Undong, 1970–79 22
    1. Expansion and Diffusion of the Saemaul Undong
    2. Amount and Pattern of Investment in Saemaul Projects
    3. Mobilization of Financial Resources

PART II: STIMULATORS AND CHANGE AGENTS

Chapter 4.
Political Commitment and Government Support 38
    1. Introduction
    2. Commitment of the Political Leadership
    3. Government Support and Assistance
    4. Development Implications of Commitment

Chapter 5.
Village Leaders: Background and Performancee 57
    1. Leadership Pattern of Saemaul Leaders
    2. Socio-economic Background of Saemaul Leaders
    3. Role Performance of Saemaul Leaders
    4. Motivational Level and Behavioral Pattern of Saemaul Leaders
    5. Summary

Chapter 6.
Mode of People's Participation and Role of Women in the Saemaul Undong 90
    1. Extent of People's Participation
    2. Factors Affecting People's Participation
    3. Socio-economic Prerequisites for People's Participation
    4. Role of Women in Rural Change
    5. Implications of People's Participation for Rural Development

PART III: ORGANIZATION, MANAGEMENT, AND TRAINING

Chapter 7.
Organization and Planning of the Saemaul Undong 114

    1. Major Tasks of the Saemaul Undong
    2. Organization in Support of the Saemaul Undong
    3. Implications of Village-Level Organization
Chapter 8.
Management Techniques for Saemaul Projects 125
    1. Introduction
    2. Management Techniques in the Rural Context
    3. Specific Management Techniques Applied to Saemaul Projects
    4. Conclusions
Chapter 9.
Monitoring and Evaluation of Saemaul Projects 138
    1. Introduction
    2. Monitoring Systems of Saemaul Projects
    3. On-Going Evaluation
    4. Assessment of the Monitoring Systems
Chapter 10.
Saemaul Training in Rural Development: Concepts and Approach 158
    1. Training Needs for Integrated Rural Development
    2. Korean Approach to Rural Development Training
    3. Managerial Implication of the Saemaul Training
    4. Conclusions

PART IV: IMPACT AND RESULTS

Chapter 11.
Impact on National Economy and Rural Employment 178
    1. Impact on National Economy
    2. Impact on Village Economy
    3. Rural Employment Strategies Underlined in the Saemaul Undong
    4. Summary and Conclusions
Chapter 12.
Impact on Values and Perceptions of Rural Farmers 207
    1. Introduction
    2. Value-Orientation of Rural People
    3. Attitudinal Pattern of the Rural People

PART V: SUMMARY AND POLICY IMPLICATIONS

Chapter 13.
Factors of the Success and Their Transferability 238
    1. Performance and Impact of the Saemaul Undong
    2. Factors Contributing to the Success of the Saemaul Undong
    3. Extent of Transferability

Chapter 14.
Future Courses of the Saemaul Undong: Policy Implications 256
    1. Development Strategies of Korea for the 1980's
    2. Development Potentials of the Saemaul Undong
    3. Future Courses of the Saemaul Undong for the 1980's
    4. Supplementary Measures: Conclusions

Appendix One 269
Bibliography 271
Index 281
About the Author.....................................286

LIST OF TABLES, FORMS AND CHARTS

Table:

3-1	Expansion and Diffusion of the Saemaul Undong, 1971–78	23
3-2	Accomplishments of Saemaul Projects per Village, 1970–79	27
3-3	Investment in Saemaul Projects, 1973–78	28
3-4	Allocation of Resource by Category, 1973–78	29
3-5	Government Support for Saemaul Projects, 1971–78	32
3-6	Financial Sources of Saemaul Investment, 1971–78	33
3-7	Increase in Saemaul Investment, 1971–78	35
3-8	Sources of Government Assistance, 1971–78	36
4-1	Themes and Issues Raised in Press Conferences	43
4-2	Degree of President's Interests in Rural Development	44
4-3	Government Expenditures for the Saemaul Undong	51
5-1	Distribution of Sample Leaders by Region, 1970–79	58
5-2	Incumbency of Leaders and Village Development	59
5-3	Saemaul Leaders by Incumbency	60
5-4	Election Methods of Saemaul Leaders	60

5-5	Leaders' Evaluation of Saemaul Training	62
5-6	Ages of Saemaul Leaders	63
5-7	Age Distribution: People *vs.* Leaders	63
5-8	Educational Level: People *vs.* Leaders	65
5-9	Former Occupation of Saemaul Leaders	66
5-10	Duration of Village Life: People *vs.* Leaders	67
5-11	Life Experience in Other Villages: People *vs.* Leaders	68
5-12	Self-estimation of Gross Income: People *vs.* Leaders	69
5-13	Ownership of Farm Land: People *vs.* Leaders	69
5-14	Military Service of Saemaul Leaders	71
5-15	Initiators of Saemaul Projects	74
5-16	Contributors to Project Implementation	75
5-17	Promoters of Cooperation and Unity	76
5-18	Source of Information about Projects	77
5-19	Saemaul Leaders as Advocator of New Techniques	78
5-20	Pattern of Village Leadership: People *vs.* Leaders	80
5-21	Pattern of Village Leadership: Common *vs.* Outstanding Villages	81
5-22	Cooperative Relationship between Saemaul Leaders and Village Heads	82
5-23	Motivation of Saemaul Leaders	82
5-24	Devotion of Saemaul Leaders	83
5-25	Satisfaction of Saemaul Leaders	84
5-26	Morale and Working Spirit of Saemaul Leaders: Opinions of Local Officials	85
5-27	Social Recognition of Saemaul Leadership	87
5-28	Personal Character Traits of Saemaul Leaders	88
6-1	People's Contribution to the Saemaul Undong	92
6-2	Number of Farm Households by Size of Land Ownership	98
6-3	Number of Enrolled Students	100
6-4	Rate of School Attendance and Illiteracy	101
6-5	Expansion of Saemaul Women's Associations	105
11-1	Rural and Urban Household Income, 1970–78	180
11-2	Private Savings and Saemaul Funds	181
11-3	Requirements for Village Reclassification	183

List of Tables xvii

11-4	Project List for Village Reclasisfication, 1976	184
11-5	Reclassification of Villages	185
11-6	Contribution of Saemaul Factories to Export	185
11-7	Average Farm Household Income in 36 Sample Villages	187
11-8	Composition of Farm Household Income (36 Sample Villages)	188
11-8	Rate of Increase in Income by Source, 1976–78 (36 Sample Villages)	189
11-10	Agricultural Mechanization in 36 Sample Villages	190
11-11	Composition of Farm Household by Income Source (36 Sample Villages)	191
11-12	Pattern of Land Utilization of Average Household (36 Sample Villages)	193
11-13	School Attendance Ratio	194
11-14	Electronic Appliances of Rural Households	195
11-15	Domestic Electronic Appliances Adopted by 36 Sample Villages	195
11-16	Economically Active Population	197
11-17	Saemaul Wage-earning Projects, 1974–79	198
11-18	Impact of Saemaul Factories	199
11-19	Average Farm Household Income by Source	200
11-20	Structure of Off-farm Income	201
12-1	Necessity of New Variety Development: Outstanding *vs.* Common Villages	211
12-2	Willingness to Try New Varieties	212
12-3	Views of Government Officials on the People's Attitudes toward Change	214
12-4	Use of Money	215
12-5	How often People Think about the Future	217
12-6	Future Planning of Rural People: Observed by Government Officials	217
12-7	Prospect of Farmers Future Life	219
12-8	Achievement Motivation of Rural People: Observed by Government Officials	219
12-9	Planning for Farming	220
12-10	Estimating Cost and Income of Farming	221
12-11	Necessity of Technical Improvement	223

xviii

12-12 Desire to Change Vocation........................224
12-13 Necessity of Technical Improvement:
 Developing *vs.* Developed Villages 224
12-14 Desire to Change Vocation: Developing *vs.*
 Developed Villages 225
12-15 To Whom to Sell Land When Moving out:
 Common *vs.* Outstanding Villages 226
12-16 Cooperative Attitudes of Rural People:
 Opinions of Local Officials.....................227
12-17 Relationship between Rural People: Common
 vs. Outstanding Villages 228
12-18 To Whom to Sell Land When Moving Out:
 Developing *vs.* Developed Villages 228
12-19 Response of Neighboring Village People If You
 Participate in that Village Meeting..............229
12-20 Views on Intervillage Joint Projects................230
12-21 People's Attitude toward Intervillage joint Projects:
 Opinions of Government Officials...............231
12-22 Acceptance of Villagers' Recommandations by
 Local Officials 232
12-23 Attitude of Local Officials to People 234
12-24 People's Manner Against Officials: Officials' View ..234
13-1 Social Background of Village Leaders..............241

Chart:
7-1 Organizational Arrangement for the Saemaul
 Undong......................................120
9-1 Monitoring Systems of Saemaul Projects by Level ...141

Form:
9-2 People's Participation by Activity 143
9-3 Daily Progress Report of Saemaul Projects 145
9-4 Field Visit Report at the Initial Stage...............149
9-5 Monitoring of Progress in Saemaul Undong
 (Field Visit) 150
9-6 Project Monitoring Report (Field Visit) 151

PART I
INTRODUCTION

Chapter 1

INTRODUCTION

Rural communities in most developing countries in the world are characterized by a deeply rooted "vicious circle of poverty," rural unemployment and underemployment, a large illiterate population little experienced in modern organization, little access to modern technology and a fatalistic view of the natural and social environments. Rural poverty as well as rural unemployment are the major concerns of rural development programs and policies in most developing countries. For reduction of rural unemployment and poverty, different sectors of rural life should be considered together as a package. Rural life is affected by various factors such as political and social institutions and organizations, rural economic structure, rural credit and finance, tenancy and land tenure systems, transport and communication, administrative infrastructure, community organizations and institutions, rural technology, agro-based rural industries, rural employment, health and nutrition, education and vocational training, dominant values and community norms, and so on (Ahmad 1975).

Rural development, therefore, involves a complex process of changes in rural sub-systems and their interaction, leading to desired improvements in rural income, employment opportunities, income distribution, rural welfare, and other aspects of rural life. It is in this context that an integrated rural development (IRD) is a powerful concept in approach to rural development. However, there is no concensus on the concept as it may be viewed from different perspectives:

(a) IRD is a radical concept. It is, in fact, an ideology which carries implied criticism of existing institutions and socio-economic policies in the poor countries. It is multi-disciplinary in approach and multi-sectoral in operation. Hence, it is hard to comprehend and implement (FAO 1977, 9).

(b) IRD is a growth strategy for a particular target population —the rural poor. "It involves extending the benefits of development to those whose future lies in the pursuit of a livelihood in rural areas. These include small-scale farmers, tenants and the landless." Rural poverty is the immediate objective. Because the rural poor tend to be the most deprived of all sectors of the community, they have very limited access to services such as health and education. In addition, they have very limited access to modern inputs for agricultural development. Unless special programs are developed to correct existing bias, "their poverty will become self-reinforcing and will increase even if economies grow" (IBRD 1974, 1).

(c) The concept of IRD requires "a fundamental review of policies and approaches for socio-economic progress in the rural sector." It is implied that in addition to changes concerned with production methods, changes also take place in the socio-political infrastructure. Policies to achieve such changes involve a comprehensive package by inter-locking factors—socio-cultural, political, economic and technical—all closely interrelated within an overall institutional framework (FAO 1977, 10).

From the above discussion, it is viewed that IRD is an equity-oriented growth startegy as well as an approach to rural development. The essence of IRD strategy now may be summarized as "(1) adoption of a rural development philosophy which leads to modernization and integration of the rural masses into society as a whole, giving them more equitable access to productive resources, employment and income, and (2) recognition by governments that strong political will on a continuing basis is a prerequisite to change. Without this quality of integration there will be no meaningful improvement of the quality of life of the rural people" (FAO 1977, 11).

The concept of IRD is further clarified in terms of its operational implications which are as follows (Whang 1978c, 2–5):

(a) "IRD could be viewed as a package program of various rural development services and activities of government which are closely interrelated. This involves a conventional notion of horizontal integration, regardless of its operational level, among various programs.

(b) While horizontal integration is emphasized for functional complementarity between different sectoral programs, vertical integration is also to be introduced to improve the relationship between agencies at different levels—federal, state, and local.

(c) In addition to horizontal and vertical integration, the integration between the government machinery and rural people should be emphasized with a view to promoting the positive participation of rural people in the decision-making process, especially at the local government level. Local needs for rural development at the village level should be reflected, through people's participation, into the package of government supports.

(d) It is also viewed as a nation-wide process of social change stimulated or guided by government, because IRD requires broadly based societal support to development projects.

(e) IRD includes the optimum utilization and mixture of all the resources and instruments relevant to rural development, including institutional infrastructure, manpower resources such as extension workers, teachers, etc., technical resources, and material as well as financial resources.

(f) IRD is an integrated process of changes in values and perceptions of rural people, an increase in dynamism of rural organization, and concomitant changes in village economy and community structure. IRD consists of a process of fundamental change in people's motivation and also in their world outlook and perceptions which should be conducive to organizational performance and also lead to socio-economic development of the rural community."

The list of rural development projects and activities derived from the concept of IRD tends to be similar among developing countries. They include, for example, development of high-yielding varieties, irrigation projects, soil improvements, social and physical infrastructures, agro-based industries, marketing, etc. However, it is presumed that these projects and activities will contribute to the eventual reduction of rural poverty and unemployment as well as to the improvement in income and standard of living in rural areas. It may be true if they are properly performed. Nevertheless, this assumption seems quite critical, especially when we consider that the performance of IRD programs would require a deliberate change in various aspects of a rural community. The projects and activities necessary for rural development have been relatively well conceived by the governments of developing countries regarding what should be done for rural development in their respective countries. However, how one can successfully implement these projects within the given social, political and administrative constraints of rural communities has been little discussed. It should be remembered that rural development cannot be achieved simply by the maximum influx of resources into rural communities without the proper response or broadly-based community initiative of rural people.

By virtue of conceptual categorization, there are two distinctive strategies of government for rural development: maximum intervention *vs.* minimum intervention. Governments of developing countries intervene in the process of rural development by utilizing either of two instruments for intervention—that is, government financing and state authority (Whang 1970b, 174-176). Maximum intervention strategies are those in which government directly invests available capital in rural areas through government-decided schemes of resource allocation, and also regulates important aspects of rural life by means of state authority. Minimum intervention strategies imply government promotion and inducement of desired measures and changes in rural areas indirectly through supportive policies and technical and financial incentives, and also through communication and social education activities. In categorical terms, the experience of the Asian countries is largely that of minimum intervention strategies (Wanasinghe 1977).

In accordance with stategies of minimum intervention and stimulation, the Korean Government introduced the Saemaul Undong (new community movement) in 1970 and vigorously implemented it during the last decade. It now tends to be recognized as a Korean model of rural development although it has been experimental in its nature because it was not based on academic research nor theoretical reference. The strategies and program contents of the Saemaul Undong have been adapted to Korean society and culture through the continued process of trial and error. The nation-wide Saemaul Undong was initiated and advocated by the late President Park Chung-Hee with his own personal zeal for rural modernization. From the grass-root level also successful experimentation with the ideas involving the people's own risks and motivations has provided a realistic base for the nation-wide advocation. The implementation of Saemaul Undong programs was fraught with many problems and required a multi-disciplinary and, in many ways, an innovative approach. It required a nation-wide mobilization of relevant talent and energy, efficient large-scale management and also coordination of conflicting interests and forces among various sectors and segments of the population. Deliberate government efforts were, therefore, necessary to provide the required financial, technical and organizational inputs essential for the effective implementation of Saemaul Undong programs. Mobilization of the skills and resources relevant to the Saemaul Undong but scattered among specialized ministries and agencies of the government itself calls for a major effort.

It is in this context and against this background that a series of questions were raised regarding the managerial aspects of the Saemaul Undong with a view to drawing some lessons from Korea's recent experience in integrated rural development and her experimentation with a nation-wide rural development movement. The Saemaul Undong has been continuously enlarged during the last decade in terms of variety of activities and projects, work performance, the number of persons participating, the resources mobilized, and so forth. A decade is a significant period during which changes in major aspects of rural communities could be manifest.

What are the managerial implications of the Saemaul Undong

in terms of action imperatives from the government point of view? To what extent did the Saemaul Undong permeate into the rural communities in terms of its work performance? Who are those involved in the nation-wide movement who really made it work in the rural context of Korean society? What roles did the top political leadership play in the complex process of rural change? To what extent did government support make the movement a success? How was the farmers' cooperation promoted and to what extent did the rural people participate in the Saemaul Undong? What was the overall management system for the planning and implementation of Saemaul Undong? How were the rural development programs and activities monitored and evaluated, and on what criteria? How did they foster the village-level leadership and train the human resource for the Saemaul Undong? What impact did it make on individuals, organizations, environments and physical infrastructures of rural communities? What are the future implications of the Saemaul Undong after its vigorous implementation for the last ten years? To what extent is the Saemaul Undong transferable to other developing countries for rural development?

These seem to be legitimate questions for the systemic analysis of the overall management process of rural change introduced by vigorous implementation of the Saemaul Undong in Korea. The purpose of this book is to make a descriptive analysis of the Saemaul Undong from the managerial perspective with a view to identifying the actual mechanisms of the nation-wide rural development movement and to finding some policy implications for the future.

What information and research methods are mobilized for this study? An interdisciplinary approach would naturally require different research methods depending on the nature of the issues. The methods utilized for this work include field survey, interview, content analysis, mailing questionnaire, in addition to document analysis and literature survey. Especially for the analysis of socio-economic background of village leaders as well as their role in rural development, critical information was collected through interview with former and current leaders of 36 villages selected through stratified sampling (Appendix One). The total number of leaders in these villages was 88 (Chapter 5). In parallel with this, another interview survey was conducted in the same 36 villages for collecting data on socio-economic background as well as values and perceptions of farmers. The total number of interviewees was 1,497 persons (Chapter 12). This survey provided additional information for comparative analysis between village leaders and farmers with regard to their social background and value systems. Additionally, a mailing questionnaire survey was utilized with regard to opinions of local government officials to collect supplementary data on perceptual patterns and motivational levels of both sample leaders and village people. The officials were chosen from among those at the Gun (county) and Myeon (township) levels who had close contact with village people and leaders in support of the Saemaul Undong in the 36 villages. Of those canvassed, 288 officials made replies to the questionnaire (Chapters 5 and 12). More specific methods and procedures for collecting data will be discussed in the respective chapters.

This book is organized into five parts consisting of the conceptual framework of the Saemaul Undong, major change agents and stimulators, management systems, results and impact, and policy implications. Some of the chapters in this volume were published before by academic journals and presented in other academic meetings and media. Although a considerable part of possible overlap was eliminated through the editing process, it seems inevitable that a slight overlap in information be retained in order to make concepts more clear and allow a systematic analysis of particular issues.

Chapter 2

A CONCEPTUAL FRAMEWORK OF THE SAEMAUL UNDONG

What is the Saemaul Undong? It is a nation-wide movement that has been primarily active in rural areas to improve the welfare of rural people. Therefore it is defined in terms of its nature and characteristics from a rural development perspective. Rural development is here viewed as a deliberate process in which different kinds of action agents and personnel are mobilized to eventually bring about fundamental changes in various aspects of rural communities, ranging from individual farmers to organizations and the environment. Therefore, an analysis of rural development requires an analysis of the unit of action, and then discussion about the systemic aspects of rural communities which are relevant to the identification of changes in the context of rural development of Korea.

1. Unit of Rural Community for the Saemaul Undong

What is the unit of rural community in the context of the Saemaul Undong which is suitable to coordination and integration of rural development inputs from different sources for desired changes in rural life?

The optimal unit of rural community may be theoretically defined by an economic criterion based on the principle of *economy of scale*. However, a more important consideration may be the issue of whether the unit is suitable for the management of the Saemaul Undong for self-reliant development of rural communities. The managerial criterion is such that the size of the community unit should match the perceptions of community identity among rural people enhancing their sense of common interest, mass participation and support mobilization, and the exercise of community-based leadership. These variables are crucial and fundamental constraints which should be born in mind with respect to strategies of sustained and self-reliant rural development. Rural development requires far-reaching change in the values and attitudes of community people toward their rural life and society. Rural development cannot be achieved solely through pursuing calculated economic rationality. In fact, the appropriate unit of rural community for integrated rural development programs will differ from country to country since the traditions, cultures and social structures of rural communities have been formed in different ways depending on individual and/ or group perceptions of the scope of one's "community".

Based on the above perspective, from the very beginning of the Saemaul Undong the rural village has been the primary unit. The rural village is a naturally identified primary unit of rural community in Korea characterized by the pursuit of traditionally common interests, physically close interaction, and cooperative action among villagers. In later stages, however, when the village economy has grown bigger with more and stronger linkages to external units and systems through marketing arrangements, it will be desirable and possible to expand the unit of rural community up to the township (Myeon) level through the integration of several neighboring villages.

2. Participatory Community Structure and Leadership

In order to facilitate the maximum contribution of their energies and resources to rural development, community members should participate in decision-making processes (Haq 1976). The extent of people's participation in community decision making will depend on their level of education and motivation as well as the organizational characteristics of the rural community. The higher the educational level of community people, the more extensive their participation in decision-making with respect to community activities is likely to be. However, under the present circumstances of village farmers in most rural Asian villages, it is unlikely that the educational level of the villagers will be improved within a short period of time. If the community is organized in a more egalitarian way in terms of the ownership of land and other productive assets, and the distribution of benefits from cooperative action, then the level of participation and commitment of community members tends to be higher. In the present situation, however, agrarian reform with respect to land ownership and the village power structure will also require a long gestation period if it is ever to be effective in encouraging wider participation. In fact, in most Asian villages there are likely to be tensions and conflicts between landowners, tenants, and laborers resulting from differences in their wealth, status, power, and economic interests. Because of its social and political as well as ideological implications, agrarian reform may be difficult to implement in some Asian countries within a short period of time. In Korea, however, it seems fortunate to successfully implement the Land Reform of 1949–52 which eventually provided a different basis for rural development from those of several other Asian countries (Lee SW 1978).

The extent of people's participation in community decision-making in the Saemaul Undong also depends on the dynamics of community-based leadership: the ability, vision, government contacts, and understanding of individuals in the community. If leaders in a village are really influential and dominant, according to literatures, they will be able to persuade and encourage many villagers to join the community decision-making process and to participate in cooperative action for their common interest (Cheema 1977). Indeed, one of the critical roles of community leadership in rural development is to induce and stimulate the participation of village members in decision-making to a maximum extent and to make individuals firmly committed to this involvement (Inayatullah 1976).

The personalities of Saemaul leaders are diverse, ranging from traditional elites to change agents. Traditional elites, however, have often proved to be less effective in performing required leadership roles while change agents who play crucial developmental roles, are chosen from among leaders of farmers' organizations, village cooperatives, youth clubs, women's clubs, etc. Characteristically, they are regarded by their fellow villagers as being more modernized in terms of their mode of behavior, life style, level of income, and perceptual patterns. They also tend to be relatively open-minded with regard to innovative ideas and have some experience in modern organizations. In the case of Saemaul Undong they are former military officers and semi-government clerks, i.e. persons trained in leadership and modern organization to some extent and therefore somewhat confident about the applicability of their experiences to their contemporary community settings. These persons also tend to search for new and efficient management styles which break with tradition.

Therefore, the identification and development of community leadership is viewed by policy makers as an important instrument which directly or indirectly influences the level of community participation as well as the level of motivation and commitment of rural people to improving their rural life. Indeed, the Saemaul Leadership Training Course at Suwon has served as the major instrument for fostering both change and change-agents in the rural villages of Korea.

3. Perceptual and Attitudinal Changes of Rural People

It seems difficult to expect rural development to take place within a short period of time. It usually takes a decade or more. Moreover, sustained change and development in a rural community requires concomitant changes in the values and attitudes of community people with respect to their lives, community environments, and the future. It has been often said that the cognitive system of individuals as well as their value systems, attitudes, and motivation are important independent variables in bringing about desired change and development in a community (Weber 1958; DeVries 1961).

Some of the values and attitudes required for the profound changes in villages toward self-reliant development are related to a self-help spirit, hard work, motivation, actual commitment to the community through positive participation in decision-making processes, cooperation, an orientation to the future and confidence in innovation. Beyond that, the perceptions of individuals in rural villages with respect to input availability and output market, new organization and rural institutions, new technology and their own community image tends to influence the performance level of rural communities.

In order to inculcate values, attitudes and perceptions of individuals, government can utilize two distinctive channels: formal education programs and nonformal education activities which may be undertaken as a supplement to formal education. Formal education contributes to the formation of values, perceptions and behaviors in the children and youth of rural communities. However, it usually takes a long period of time, at least a decade or a generation, to become influential in community activities and rural lives. Moreover, a serious obstacle to progress is the fact that most village people have little access to formal education. Therefore, short-term alternatives should be considered in order to bring about desired change in the attitudes and behavior of rural people in addition to long-term educational programs. A series of short-term but recurrent activities for public information, education and communication (IEC) with respect to various aspects of rural development (such as family planning communication activities, agricultural extension, rural health and sanitary education, etc.) belongs to the category of non-formal education of rural people. This category also includes special programs which are organized for the improvement in technical know-how as well as the inculcation of development values and attitudes of children and youth in rural villages who cannot continue their school education.

A wide range of social education and communication activities either sponsored by voluntary organizations or encouraged by the government provide opportunities for introducing change in the way of thinking of the rural people. Technical training for rural people arranged through agricultural extension projects or by other types of community workers would often influence their behavioral change with respect to new seeds and technology, mode of cooperative action among farmers, rural cooperatives and institutions. Such changes take place only when they are connected with learning of new farming methods and other developmental activities. Policy-makers in charge of rural development might have to pay close attention to this means of introducing desired change in the behavior and attitudes of community people. However, it is stipulated that the impact upon values and attitudes of village people through this type of arrangement is in fact limited because of the advanced age of the clients and the short period of time allocated for special training objectives. In most cases where training of village farmers through extension workers or community development activities have been tried, constant reinforcement and long-term commitment to the training tend to be lacking on the part of government. In other words, this type of training cannot be successful in forming development values of rural people unless systematic and consistent follow-up is built into the training program as part of the total package. In fact, only the Comilla experiments in the late 1960's (Raper 1970; Haq 1973) and the Saemaul training in Korea are viewed as successful cases (Chapter 10).

Community leaders directly or indirectly influence behavior and attitudes of village people through their constant contact with them. Therefore, an intensive Saemaul training course was organized for reorientation (or retraining) of Saemaul leaders in order to stimulate their leadership development mechanism. Organization of a deliberate, systematic training program for development of community leadership was infused with a view to eventually influencing the behavior and attitudes of village people toward developmental community action. In fact, Korea's experiment in this area has shown successful results. The community leadership development during the last decade has also provided the "younger" generation with better education i.e. those mostly in their 40's who have a middle-high school education; and as a result, they have taken over the roles of older farmers, especially the leadership roles, in many rural villages (Chapter 5; Boyer and Ahn 1977).

4. A Wide Range of Development Projects

Another feature of the Saemaul Undong is the variety of development projects planned and implemented at the village level. Saemaul projects are typically planned and organized by village people although sometimes initiated by Saemaul leaders or government officials. As has already been noted, the role of change-agents and people's participation in the process of rural development is crucial in the case of the Saemaul Undong.

Saemaul projects range from projects for improvement in physical environment such as farm roads, village entrance roads, sanitary water systems, rural electrification, village halls, construction of small bridges and small-scale irrigation systems to income generation projects such as special crops, livestock, marketing arrangements, etc. One interesting point is the fact that approximately 70% of the total resources required for these projects over the last decade was contributed by rural people in the form of donations of labor, land, and recently, even cash (MOHA 1979a). In this respect, the managerial capabilities of Saemaul leaders must be given special credit.

Again, a prime mover of rural development in Korea has been the increase in agricultural income. The growth of the village economy depends on the expansion of the market for village products as well as the availability of necessary technical and financial inputs. The exploitation of new markets and additional demand for rural products has helped to energize the whole system of rural communities. Market expansion also influences the reorganization of the community in terms of the mode of people's participation in community decision-making, the pattern of cooperation among village people, positive demand for specific government assistance and support, etc. Therefore, the establishment of linkages for the identification of changing markets as well as efficient delivery systems of rural products will become important tasks for community leaders in Korea.

It is recognized that linkage establishment depends on the institutional arrangements of the government as well as on a number of government support policies. These are based partly on government study of the market situation and partly upon community requests. Therefore, the way in which community leaders aggregate and articulate requests for linkage establishment must be of special concern in training community leaders. This is especially true in the case where self-reliant development is the ultimate objective of the rural development program (Haque, *et al.* 1975). Community leaders should have constant access to reliable information sources with respect to changing demands and the availability of necessary inputs, including institutional support and assistance. This is an important subject in terms of community leadership development, that is quite apart from their management capabilities.

5. Extensive Role of Government in Support of the Saemaul Undong

One of the crucial inputs into the Saemaul Undong is the package of government supports. Under the present circumstances of rural villages in most Asian countries, in fact, rural development can hardly take place without the financial and technical support of their governments (Chee and Khong 1977). In this respect, Korea is no exception. Government support for the Saemaul Undong covers various kinds of services and assistance intended to introduce system change in rural villages. Among these are the development of community-based leadership, restructuring of community organizations for greater people's participation, spiritual revolution for self-help movement, people's motivation and commitment, facilitation of developmental roles of financial and other rural institutions, and nationwide mobilization of resources and support.

The government deliberately prepares a plan for the sequential arrangement of various types of support and assistance over a certain period of time. This contributes to building up a certain momentum which ultimately enables the rural community to achieve self-reliant development. Indeed, government support for the Saemaul Undong has been consistent with respect to both the various activities and goals it has sought to implement over time from the beginning of its support until the stage of strategic withdrawal. Constant evaluation of the capacity of a particular rural village (or community) for self-reliant development has been built into the process of government mobilization of support and assistance. It, in fact, requires a high level technical competence on the part of government officials, especially at the local level, in terms of collecting and analyzing information on the many facets of transformation which occur in a particular rural community.

It is clear that an effective system of government support at the local government level is an essential requirement for the successful implementation of the Saemaul Undong, because local governments in Korea have a certain amount of authority when it comes to applying local criteria to policy guidelines of the central government in order to fit them into the village situation. Historically, local governments in Korea have been instruments of the central government in charge of controlling local resources, and oriented to law and order. Support of rural development for meeting developmental needs of rural communities seemed to be a new concept to them. The functions of the local government at the district level, however, have become reoriented toward rural development. Local governments tend to be easily accessible to the community people. They would encourage community leaders to extensively participate in the process of governmental policy making. They are able to identify community needs and efficiently deliver government services to rural villages. The organization of local governments have also been restructured so as to introduce a functional transformation from control and regulation to development support administration.

With regard to the delivery system of rural development support, local governments pay great attention to the coordination and integration of various kinds of development projects with respect to the required development inputs. These include financial and technical, human and materials, public and private, organizational and individual resources at the level of the rural village. Although coordination and integration at this level is a function of community leadership, the package of government supports is one which is coordinated between agencies which provide different types of rural development assistance and services. The package is also integrated into the total scheme of village development activities. In other words, various kinds of government support are coordinated within the government to avoid confusion, unnecessary duplication and conflict in the implementation process at the village level. Also the package of services and assistance from government agencies fits into the total scheme of the Saemaul Undong within a specific time framework in order to provide the proper supplementary and complementary services. These services naturally include the total mobilization of government sponsored field workers in the rural villages, such as extension workers, family planning workers, community development workers, voluntary organization personnel, owners and managers of private agro-industries, and so on. In case of the Saemaul Undong, these functions have been performed by county-level local administrators in collaboration with township officials.

The smooth performance of the change-promoting and change-protecting functions of local government for the Saemaul Undong is based on an improved relationship between government officials and community people. Historically, the attitude of government officials toward community people was bureaucratic, colonialistic, and regulatory and, therefore, community people were accustomed to perceiving them as exploiters. This mutual discord created a source of distrust between the two sides. The perceptual gap between government officials and community people regarding their respective roles and mutual relationships has created a lack of government credibility which incidentally became a serious obstacle to the introduction of government-mediated innovation in rural villages in Korea during the 1950's. A perceptual change toward interdependence as well as attitudinal change toward cooperation and collaboration between the two sides is now one of the critical indicators of improvement in the local support system of the Saemaul Undong.

In this connection, it is noted that the evaluation of officials' performance in terms of increase in rural production or improvement in the rural life of the communities to which government services have been delivered, has almost been institutionalized. This is especially meaningful because the administrative input and supportive services for the Saemaul Undong are predominantly under the control of local government officials.

The utmost importance of local government support to rural communities is related to the managerial capability of local governments for the delivery of required services and assistance to the right clients in the right way at the right time. The managerial competence of top level administrators in the local government is a function of their knowledge and management skills, which are related to information analysis, decision-making, planning and design of delivery systems, inter-agency communication and coordination, mobilization of resources and support from political leadership as well as from the central government, leadership capability and the ability of monitoring the performance of rural development support programs.

The managerial competence of local officials in Korea during the 1970's has improved mainly through the extensive management training throughout the 1960's and 70's. The competence of officials at the field workers' level is a function of both certain skills and the capability to build a fresh image of "service men or women" who are able to efficiently deliver required services, easily contact and communicate with community people, project a homophilous feeling with rural people, and stimulate, motivate and encourage community people. This ability of course is complemented by their competence in technical subject matters. Those field workers who frequently contact community leaders are able to understand the tasks of community leaders and their needs for assistance in their respective areas. The managerial and technical competence of the local government system tends to bring about a synergetic effect because government officials at the district office become highly motivated to the achievement of certain results in rural transformation.

6. Nationwide Mobilization of Political and Societal Support

Change-introducing development projects under the Saemaul Undong require the commitment of top political leadership. As rural development implies profound changes in the major aspects of a rural village, top leadership commitment to the movement is of essential importance to its success. In the case of the Saemaul Undong the strong commitment of the top political leadership has been reflected in a favorable allocation of resources to the rural sector and necessary changes in the legal as well as administrative framework.

The support of top political leaders has been very helpful to rural development especially because both political leaders and the society as a whole have supported the ideas and changes implied in the Saemaul Undong. A supportive mood among the political as well as social elite with regard to implementation of the Saemaul Undong has been extremely helpful. The mobilization of societal support for the Saemaul Undong as a kind of social movement reinforces the values and ideas of rural development. In this process, it is wise to get leaders of political parties, members of congress, high-level civil servants, religious leaders, leaders of voluntary organizations, managers of big business corporations, university professors, journalists, and the other intellectual elite to understand the ideas and changes implied in the Saemaul Undong by getting them to participate in the training course together with Saemaul leaders and to become actively involved in the movement. Their perception of rural problems and their understanding of the philosophies and strategies of the Saemaul Undong are conducive to a favorable allocation of resources and mobilization of adequate policy support from the government as well as other social sectors.

In view of the Korean experience, it may be said that the Saemaul Leaders' Training Course addressed to both political and other social elite has made a significant contribution to the success of the Saemaul Undong. There seems to be no doubt that to date the training has served as a mechanism for (a) reinforcing support of the Saemaul Undong at the grass-roots level, (b) promoting wider social recognition of rural workers and Saemaul leaders as development agents, and (c) helping to further social control of local government services.

7. Summary: A Model of Integrated Rural Development

From the above discussion, it can be stated that the Saemaul

Undong is a Korean version, uniquely adapted to Korea's own societal and cultural context, of integrated rural development in light of its major inputs, process, results and impact. The major inputs into the Saemaul Undong are (a) highly motivated village people, (b) community-based leaders who play the role of change agents in rural villages, (c) efficient local officials who are experienced in providing development services, and (d) the commitment and support of top political leadership as well as the urban intellectual elite. In this sense, the Saemaul Undong is regarded as a *nation-wide* social movement, which requires large-scale mobilization of institutional, manpower and technical resources from every sector of the country.

The process of rural development promoted by the Saemaul Undong is characterized by the fact that Saemaul development projects are organized and implemented through close interaction and cooperation between government agencies and rural people. The close *coordination* and *integration* of different functions and agencies are essential to the success of the Saemaul Undong, since their efforts cover various projects and activities which include: improvements in physical and social infrastructures, income boosting projects, leadership formation, village reorganization for people's participation and changes in the values and attitudes of farmers.

In light of its results and impact, the Saemaul Undong may be viewed as an *integrated process* of three significant changes: changes in the values and attitudes of individual farmers, dynamics of participatory organization and leadership development, and concomitant changes in village economies and rural infrastructure. This series of changes is the most significant prerequisite for self-reliant development in rural communities.

Chapter 3

PERFORMANCE OF THE SAEMUAL UNDONG, 1970-79

The better understanding of the ideas and essential concept of the Saemaul Undong requires a close examination of its actual performance over the last decade from its inception to the present in terms of the expansion and accomplishments of the numerous Saemaul activities and programs.

1. Expansion and Diffusion of the Saemaul Undong

To what extent did the rural Saemaul Undong expand over the last decade? In quantitative terms, as shown in Table 3-1, the number of participating villages in the Saemaul Undong increased from 33,267 in 1971 to 36,257 villages in 1978, the latter figure including some 1,492 cities and suburban villages. Meanwhile, total labor participation increased some 37.6 times, from 7.2 million man-days in 1971 to 271 million man-days in 1978. In the rural Saemaul projects alone, the total participation amounted to 184 million man-days in 1978 which represents an increase of 25.5 times over the 1971-78 period.

The rapid diffusion of the Saemaul Undong may be grasped by

Table 3-1. Expansion and Diffusion of the Saemaul Undong, 1971-78

	Unit	1971	1972	1973	1974	1975	1976	1977	1978
No. of Participating Village	each	33,267 (33,267)	22,708 (22,708)	34,665 (34,665)	34,665 (34,665)	36,547 (34,665)	36,557 (35,031)	36,557 (35,031)	36,257 (34,815)
No. of Participants	million man-days	72 (72)	320 (320)	693 (675)	1,069 (373)	1,169 (489)	1,175 (351)	1,372 (451)	2,709 (1,836)
No. of Projects	1,000	385 (385)	320 (320)	1,093 (1,093)	1,099 (415)	1,598 (696)	887 (630)	2,463 (2,200)	2,667 —
Total Investment	billion won	12.2 (12.2)	31.3 (31.3)	98.4 (98.4)	132.8 (122.2)	295.9 (286.3)	322.6 (317.5)	466.5 (439.1)	634.2 (603.5)
No. of Participants per Village	man-days	216 (216)	1,409 (1,409)	1,999 (1,948)	3,082 (1,077)	3,198 (1,413)	3,215 (1,003)	3,753 (1,288)	7,472 (5,274)
No. of Projects Implemanted per Village	each	12 (12)	13 (13)	32 (32)	32 (12)	44 (20)	24 (18)	67 (63)	74 —
Investment Amount per Village	1,000 won	367 (367)	1,378 (1,378)	2,839 (2,839)	3,831 (3,526)	8,096 (8,259)	8,825 (9,063)	12,764 (12,535)	17,492 (18,110)
Investment Amount per Project	1,000 won	32	98	90	121	185	364	189	238

*The numbers in parenthesis indicate corresponding figures for rural areas.
Source: Ministry of Home Affairs, *Saemaul Undong: From Its Inception Until Today*, respectively 1973, 1975, 1977, and 1978.

noting the number of Saemaul projects implemented over the same period. The projects numbered only 385 thousand in 1971. But by 1978 the number had increased to 2,667 thousand (or 26.9 times). This extraordinary increase was reflected in the rural Saemaul Undong which increased from 385 thousand projects in 1971 to 2,200 thousand projects in 1977 (1978 statistics are not available), an increase of 5.7 times. In the scale of investment as well, there was significant growth. The total investment in 1971 was 12.2 billion won but by 1978 it had reached 634.2 billion won –an increase of 52 times in current price. The total investment in the rural Saemaul Undong increased from 12.2 billion won in 1971 to 630.5 billion won in 1978, a 51.7 fold increase. Calculated in 1971 constant price, this means a 19 fold increase in the real total investment in the Saemaul Undong, an increase which is mainly attributable to multiplied government investment. In 1971, government investment totalled only around 4 billion won but in 1978 the amount was 130.3 billion won in 1971 constant price, which translates to a real increase of 44 times. Such a drastic expansion of the Saemaul Undong indicates the extensive support as well as strategic emphasis of the government on the rural development effort.

The expansion of the Saemaul Undong and its overall rural impact is further demonstrated by several other indicators. The number of total participants per village went up from 216 man-days in 1971 to 3,755 in 1978–17.4 times more. In the rural village alone, a 24.4 times increase was recorded between 1971 and 1978 while the number of projects carried out per village increased some 5.7 times, from 12 in 1971 to 68 projects in 1978. There was a 5.3 times increase in the farming villages alone between 1971 and 1977 (1978 statistics are not available). On the average, the amount of capital investment per rural villages was 370 thousand won in 1971, a figure which later increased to 18 million won in 1978 (or 49 times more in current prices). In 1971 constant price, this means a real increase by 18 times.

Investment per project also more than doubled between 1971 and 1978, increasing from 32 thousand won to 221 thousand won (82 thousand won in 1971 constant price).

The programs of the Saemaul Undong are reflected not only in the visible achievements quantified above, but also in the even larger sphere of projects undertaken, all of which demonstrate how the Saemaul Undong has grown in its scope and impact on rural development.

Up to 1973, the Saemaul movement was largely carried out in rural areas, but since 1974 it has been extended to urban areas including industrial plants and schools, and even to the military bases. The factory Saemaul Undong and school Saemaul Undong are both important examples of the urban Saemaul movement.

2. Amount and Pattern of Investment in Saemaul Projects

As mentioned above, the total investment in Saemaul projects increased 19 times between the years 1971 and 1978 while government investment in the Saemaul Undong increased by 44 times. This dramatic increase in government investment not only reflects the keen interest of the government in rural development but also the extent to which the effectiveness of the Saemaul Undong was socially recognized.

The extent of societal support for the Saemaul Undong and the degree of actual input and participation of the people may be visualized by noting the 19 fold increase in financial outlays for the Saemaul Undong as compared with the growth in the total fixed capital of the overall national economy. The latter increased by only three times in 1970 price from 680 billion won in 1971 to 1,803 billion won in 1978.

The increase in investment in the various types of Saemaul projects has a number of implications. The Saemaul projects consist of several categories, such as welfare-environment projects, production infrastructure projects, income-increasing projects, spiritual enlightenment projects and urban and factory Saemaul projects.

The welfare-environment projects include expansion and pavement of village roads, sewage improvement, pavement of laundry areas, beautification of village environments and main roads, installation of potable water supply facilities, development of small towns, construction of community halls, public baths, children's playgrounds, and electrification of rural villages.

Production infrastructure projects include, among other things, expansion of farm roads, construction of bridges, expansion of village entrance roads, improvements in small reservoirs, erection of reservoir banks and dikes, rearrangement of water-ways, village warehouse construction, farm reconciliation, small-scale irrigation, and water pump installation.

Income-increasing projects include green houses, preservation and processing facilities, raising dairy cattle, farming machinery, oyster farming, marketing facilities, special crops, mushroom farming on a cooperative basis, reforestation and village bank operation.

Spiritual enlightenment includes Saemaul training of those who are actively involved in as well as those who support the Saemaul Undong at all the levels. The urban and factory Saemaul Undong covers various activities including beautification of living and working environment, improvement in labor-industry relations, improvement in labor conditions, improvement in product quality, the campaign for observance of traffic order, community libraries and others.

As for the coverage of the investment in the Saemaul Undong, Table 3-2 demonstrates the accomplishments of some major projects in the categories of production infrastructure and welfare-environment improvement.

There are no statistics available for the investment amount by category of project in 1971 and 1972. As shown in Table 3-3, the investment in production infrastructure amounted to 61.8 billion won in 1973, about 64% of the total investment for the year. In 1978 the amount was 61.2 billion won in 1973 constant price. Therefore, there was little change in category of investment over the period. On the other hand, investment in welfare-environment projects increased by about 4.4 times in real terms while investment in income-increasing projects posted a 19 fold increase during the same period. The investment in urban and factory Saemaul projects remained stable in real terms during the 1974–77 period but in 1978 decreased to about 21% of the 1974 figure. Investment in spiritual enlightenment projects increased by about 7.6 times during the 1973–78 period.

This shift in the pattern of resource allocation indicates the

Table 3-2. Accomplishments of Saemaul Projects per Village, 1970-79

Projects	Unit	Completed by 1979
Rural Roads		
Village Roads	Km	1.24*
Farm Feeder Roads	Km	1.26
Bridge Construction	No.	2.10
Irrigation Facilities		
Small Reservoirs	No.	0.31
Small Irrigation Channel	No.	0.81
Raceway	M.	120.4
Embankment of Rivers	M.	263.3
Communal Facilities		
Village Halls	Bldg.	1.03†
Public Warehouses	Bldg.	0.56
Public Workshops	Bldg.	0.13
Public Compost Pits	No.	2.01
Common Use Barns	Bldg.	0.12
Rural Electrification and Communication Networks		
Electrification	% to all households	98.9
Telephone	% to all villages	100.0
Rural Water Supply and Sanitary Improvement		
Water Supply	No.	0.52
Public Wells	No.	3.45
Public Bath Houses	No.	0.20
Public Laundry Places	No.	1.91

*Total number of Villages as of 1979 was 34,871.
†In some cases, an administrative village consists of more than two natural villages. Therefore there could be more than two village halls in an administrative village.
Source: Sung-Hwan Ban, "Development of the Rural Infrasturcture and Saemaul Undong," presented at International Research Seminar on the Saemaul Movement, 7-13 December, 1980, p. 8.

changing emphasis of the Saemaul projects. At first, production infrastructure projects claimed the largest portion of available resources, as they required the investment of bulky capital. Later on, however, more emphasis was placed on income generation. To understand the implications of this shift in investment pattern, it is necessary to analyze the allocation of investment capital by category of projects over the period. Available data during the

Table 3-3. Investment in the Saemaul Projects, 1973-78[1]

Unit: billion won

		1973[2]	1974[2]	1975	1976	1977	1978
Production infrastructure	A[3]	61,767	56,451	63,684	90,180	135,772	130,662
	B	61,767	44,596	40,503	40,509	65,578	61,150
		(100.0)	(72.2)	(65.6)	(80.2)	(106.2)	(99.0)
Income increase	A	5,936	33,783	187,480	154,067	182,624	242,646
	B	5,936	26,689	119,237	84,583	88,207	113,568
		(100.0)	(449.6)	(2,008.7)	(1,424.9)	(1,486.0)	(1,913.2)
Welfare-environment	A	27,636	28,771	30,507	67,572	110,043	244,575
	B	27,636	22,729	19,402	37,097	53,151	114,470
		(100.0)	(82.2)	(70.2)	(134.2)	(192.3)	(414.2)
Spiritual enlightenment	A	772	3,237	4,635	5,676	10,664	12,583
	B	772	2,557	2,948	3,116	5,151	5,889
		(100.0)	(331.2)	(381.9)	(403.6)	(667.2)	(762.8)
Urban-factory	A	—	10,548	9,589	5,157	27,429	3,725
	B	—	8,333	6,099	2,831	13,248	1,743
			(100.0)	(73.2)	(34.0)	(159.0)	(20.9)
Totals	A	96,111	132,790	295,895	322,652	466,532	634,191
	B	96,111	104,904	188,189	277,136	225,335	296,820
		(100.0)	(109.1)	(195.8)	(184.3)	(234.5)	(308.8)

The numbers in parenthesis indicate index.
1) Investment statistics for 1971 and 1972 were not available.
2) Reclassified in accordance with the criteria of the period 1975-78.
3) A: Current price
   B: 1973 constant price (calculated by GNP deflator).
Source: Ministry of Home Affaris, *The Saemaul Undong: From its Inception Until Today*, 1978.

period between the years 1973 and 1978 are shown in Tables 3-3 and 3-4.

Total investment made in 1973 was 96.1 billion won of which 64% (or 61.8 billion won) was used for production infrastructure projects. For welfare and environment projects 29% of the total (or 27.6 billion won) was invested. This indicates that during the the early stage, projects such as production infrastructure and environment improvement projects were stressed because they yielded tangible and visible results. The implementation of such projects tended to make village people identify with the results of their cooperation, active participation and self-help efforts which, of course, helped to cultivate developmental values among them.

Table 3-4. Allocation of Resource by Category, 1973-78

Unit: %

	1973	1974	1975	1976	1977	1978	'73-78
Production Infrastructure	64.6	42.5	21.5	27.9	29.1	20.6	27.6
Income Increasing	6.2	25.4	63.4	47.8	39.1	38.3	41.4
Welfare-Environment	28.8	21.7	10.3	20.9	23.6	38.5	26.1
Spritual Enlightenment	0.8	2.4	1.6	1.8	2.3	2.0	1.9
Urban-Factory	—	8.0	3.2	1.6	5.9	0.6	3.0
Totals	100.0	100.0	100.0	100.0	100.0	100.0	100.0

Source: Ministry of Home Affairs, *The Saemaul Undong: From its Inception Until Today*, 1978.

Since any rural development effort which does not aim at increasing rural income is difficult to continue, income boosting projects later became the focus of concern. The total investment in 1974 amounted to 132.8 billion won out of which 56.5 billion won (42.5%) went into production infrastructure projects, 33.8 billion won (25.4%) into income-increasing projects, 28.8 billion won (21.7%) into welfare-environment projects and 10.6 billion won (8.0%) went into urban and factory Saemaul projects.

Judging by the investment pattern of 1974, it is obvious that investment in production infrastructure was less emphasized than in 1973 while investment in income-generating projects increased greatly. It is clear that the period up until 1973 was considered a foundation period during which the government stressed production infrastructure projects, while the period between 1974–1976 was a self-propelling period during which stress was put on income increase of the rural populace.

Total investment reached 295.9 billion won during 1975, which was 2.2 times that of the previous year in current price. Of that amount, 63.7 billion won (21.5%) was allocated to production infrastructure projects, 197.5 billion won (63.4%) to income-increasing projects (including 79.9 billion won in wage-earning projects), 30.5 billion won (10.3%) to welfare-environment projects, 3.2 billion won (1.6%) to spiritual enlightenment projects, and 9.6 billion won (3.2%) to urban and factory Saemaul projects. The portion of investment allocated to income-increasing projects was relatively higher than in the previous year, while both production infrastructure and welfare-environment projects received smaller investment portions. This is because Saemaul projects began to emphasize income-increasing projects after 1975. In that particular year, greater effort and investment were put into increasing food grain production. Similarly, income-increasing special projects, special support for outstanding villages, income-boosting projects for developed villages, and income-increasing model village projects were increasingly emphasized in terms of resource allocation.

Total investment during 1976 was 322.7 billion won which was only a 9% increase over the previous year. Of that amount, 90.2 billion won (27.9%) was allocated to production infrastructure projects, 154.1 billion won (47.8%) to income-increasing projects, 67.6 billion won (20.9%) to welfare-environment projects, 5.7 billion won (1.8%) to spiritual enlightenment, and 5.2 billion won (1.6%) to urban and factory Saemaul projects. As in the previous year, investment in income-increasing projects took the biggest portion during 1976 but that amount had actually decreased from the previous year. This is attributable to the fact that investment in wage-earning projects decreased to 2.7 billion won in 1976, 4.28 billion won less than in 1975. But investment in other income-increasing projects exceeded that of 1975, indicating the government's major emphasis on income increasing projects since 1975.

During 1977 total investment reached 456.5 billion won, a 45% increase over the previous year. During that year, 135.8 billion won (29.1%) was invested in production infrastructure projects, 182.6 billion won (39.1%) in income-increasing project, 110 billion won (23.6%) in welfare-environment programs, 10.7 billion won (2.3%) in spiritual enlightenment projects, and 27.4 billion won (5.9%) in urban and factory Saemaul projects. The investment in income-increasing projects was again the largest portion in 1977 as it was in 1975 and 1976. It is particularly noteworthy that the portion of investment in welfare and environment improvement projects increased to a 24% share of the total investment which is almost equivalent to the investment portion of income increasing projects (29%). This dramatic increase in investment in environment projects was due to the large scale investment projects launched during that year for the purpose of rural village renewal and squatter improvement. Those particular projects were designed to cope with increasing demands from the rural people for a better living environment.

Total investment in the Saemaul Undong during 1978 was 634.2 billion won, which represented a 35.9% increase over the previous year. This figure was 130.7 billion won (20.6%) in production infrastructure projects, 242.7 billion won (38.3%) in income-increasing projects, 244.6 billion won (38.5%) in welfare and environment improvement projects, 12.6 billion won (2.0%) in spiritual enlightenment projects, and 3.7 billion won (0.6%) in urban Saemaul projects. During that particular year, investment in the welfare and environment improvement field exceeded that in the income-increasing and production infrastructure field. One reason for this is that during that year, the rural housing improvement project, which had been under way since 1977, was expanded to other areas such as fishing villages and cities.

As seen above, the emphasis of the Saemaul Undong in its early stage was on production infrastructure projects, later in the mid-1970's, it was on income-increasing projects, and more recently, emphasis has been on welfare and environment projects, which include village renewal projects.

3. Mobilization of Financial Resources

How was such an enormous amount of capital mobilized? As pointed out earlier, the Saemaul Undong was comprised of village level development projects organized and implemented through the rural people's cooperation, diligence and self-help effort. Nevertheless it was the initial government support that ignited the rural people's will and zeal to develop the projects into a full-fledged nationwide movement.

Table 3-5 shows that financial support for the Saemaul projects from both central and local governments increased at a higher rate than the development expenditures of the general government sector. The expenditures of the general government allocated to national economic development increased by about 7.4 times during the period of 1971–1978, while the government budget in support of Saemaul projects increased by 82 times during the same period, both in current prices. The implications of such a dramatic increase in Saemaul support are quite significnat in view of the fact that the general government budget itself increased 6.4 fold during the same period. This indeed indicates that the government made a very favorable allocation of its financial resources toward rural development. The material as well as technical supports of the government were clearly effective in inducing the voluntary contribution of idle labor, materials, land, small amounts of cash for rural village development projects. Thus a multiplying effect was brought about by government assistance.

Table 3-5. Government Support for Saemaul Projects, 1971-78

Unit: billion won

Year	Development Expenditures from General Gov't Sector	Government investment in Saemaul Projects*
1971	117.4(21.4)	4.1(n.a.)
1972	240.2(36.2)	3.6(–12.7)
1973	176.8(–26.4)	17.1(378.4)
1974	301.1(70.3)	45.5(165.4)
1975	522.3(73.5)	165.3(263.4)
1976	669.5(28.2)	165.1(–0.1)
1977	729.9(9.0)	246.0(49.0)
1978	873.0(19.6)	338.4(37.7)

Nunbers in parentheses indicate increased percentage from the previous year.
* Government support includes financial loans.
Source: Economic Planning Board, *Major Economic Indicators*, 1979.

Table 3-6 shows that the total investment in the Saemaul Undong during the whole period of 1971–1978 amounted to 1,991 bil.ion won of which 28% (or 55.2 billion won) was made by the government and 71.3% (or 1,420.9 billion won) was invested by the rural people and the remaining 1.0% (or 19.1 billion won) was raised by donations from non-village individuals or private organizations. Of the total 12.2 billion won invested during 1971, the government contribution was 4.2 billion won (34%), while

Table 3-6. **Financial Sources for Saemaul Investment, 1971-78**

Unit: million won

Year	Total Investment (A)	Government (B)	Rural* People (C)	Other Donations (D)	A/B (%)	C/B (%)	C+D/B (%)
1971	12,200 (100.0)	4,100 (33.6)	8,100 (66.4)	—	297.6	197.6	—
1972	31,594 (100.0)	3,581 (11.3)	27,348 (86.6)	665 (2.1)	882.3	762.3	782.3
1973	96,111 (100.0)	17,133 (17.8)	76,850 (80.0)	2,128 (2.2)	561.0	448.5	461.0
1974	132,790 (100.0)	30,780 (23.1)	98,738 (74.4)	3,272 (2.5)	431.4	320.8	331.4
1975	295,895 (100.0)	124,499 (42.1)	169,554 (57.3)	1,842 (0.6)	237.7	136.2	137.7
1976	322,652 (100.0)	88,060 (27.3)	227,440 (70.5)	7,152 (2.2)	366.4	258.3	266.4
1977	466,532 (100.0)	138,057 (29.6)	325,033 (69.7)	3,442 (0.7)	337.9	235.4	237.9
1978	634,191 (100.0)	145,703 (23.0)	487,835 (76.9)	653 (0.1)	435.3	334.8	335.3
'71-78	1,991,965 (100.0)	551,913 (27.7)	1,420,898 (71.3)	19,154 (1.0)	360.9	257.5	260.9

*Includes loans by the government and other organizations.
Source: Ministry of Home Affairs, *The Saemaul Undong: From its Inception Until Today*, respectively 1973, 1975, 1977, and 1978.

the rural populace contributed 8.1 billion won (66%).

During 1972 the investment in Saemaul projects was 31.6 billion won of which 11% was contributed by the government while 87% was contributed by the rural populace. Donations from other private sources amounted to 2.1%. The decrease in the government share of investment sources was attributable to the fact that the government support was given only to those 16,600 villages where project performances were outstanding during 1971. This is in keeping with the principle of "the better village the first support" to encourage the less productive villages to participate. Not long after, six thousand villages joined in the Saemaul Undong using their own resources.

During 1973, government support accounted for 18% of the total 96.1 billion won invested while the investment by the rural people accounted for 80%, with 2% orginating from other sources.

Of the total investment of 132.8 billion won during 1974, 23% came from the government, 74% from the rural people and 2.5% from other sources. This means a slight increase from the previous year in the government proportion of the total investment. Government investment was 42% of the total 296.9 billion won invested during 1975, while the rural people contributed 57% of the total. The increased government investment during that year was caused by the new emphasis of the government on various income-increasing projects as pointed out earlier. In 1976 total investment reached 322.7 billion won, of which 27% came from the government, 71% from the rural dwellers and 2% from others. Investments made by the rural people themselves during 1977 and 1978 were 69.7% and 76.9% respectively.

Saemaul projects gained momentum at the early stage by virtue of strong government support and assistance but were later expanded through efforts on the part of the rural people. Thus, the financial burden of the people increased. This can be observed in the index of increase in the government share versus that of the people's contributions. Table 3-7 indicates that government support increased by about 12 times between 1971 and 1978 while that of the rural people increased about 20 times. In other words, the self-helping efforts of the people expanded at a faster pace than the increase of government support during this period.

An analysis of the financial sources of investment exposes the leading forces of the Saemaul Undong. 34% of the total investment in the first year 1971 was contributed by the government. However, this proportion decreased to 11% in the next year, even though the total amount of government assistance increased, showing the magnitude of the increasing role of the private sector in the Saemaul projects. In 1971, government investment induced double scaled investment from the private sector and subsequently in the rural development part, total investment reached three times that of the government.

In 1972, government investment resulted in seven times more induced investment from the private sector, 4 times that of 1973

Table 3-7. Increase in Saemaul Investment, 1971-78

Unit: million won in 1971 price

Year	Total Investment	Gov't Budget	Rural* People	Others
1971	12,200	4,100	8,100	—
	(100.0)	(100.0)	(100.0)	
1972	27,714	3,141	23,989	583
	(227.2)	(76.6)	(296.2)	(100.0)
1973	78,844	14,055	63,044	1,745
	(646.3)	(342.8)	(778.3)	(289.5)
1974	76,624	17,761	56,975	1,888
	(628.1)	(433.2)	(703.4)	(323.8)
1975	134,988	56,797	73,351	840
	(1,106.5)	(1,385.3)	(905.6)	(144.1)
1976	127,531	34,806	89,897	2,827
	(1,045.3)	(848.9)	(1,109.8)	(484.9)
1977	174,209	51,552	121,372	1,285
	(1,427.9)	(1,257.4)	(1,498.4)	(220.4)
1978	211,962	48,698	163,047	218
	(1,737.4)	(1,187.8)	(2,012.9)	(37.4)

*Includes loans by the government and other organizations.
Figures in parentheses indicate index.
Source: Ministry of Home Affaris, *The Saemaul Undong: From its Inception Until Today*, respectively 1973, 1975, and 1978.

as seen in Table 3-5. During the whole period of 1971–1978, government investment in the Saemaul projects amounted to 551.9 billion won in current prices. The government support eventually induced 1,402.9 billion won worth of investment from the private sector which made for a grand total investment of 1,999.2 billion won in the Saemaul projects.

The major fund sources of the government sector are the central and local government budgets. The breakdown between the two financial sources is shown in Table 3-8. At the initial stage of the Saemaul Undong, central government support accounted for the major part of the budget (100% in 1971) but in 1974 when the movement entered the stage of self-propelling development, the local governments' responsibility for fund-raising increased to 56% of the total government support. This enhanced role of the local governments in financing Saemaul projects until 1978,

Table 3-8. Sources of Government Assistance, 1971-78

Unit: million won

Year	Totals	Central Gov't	Local Gov't	Subsidy
1971[1]	4,100 (100.0)	4,100 (100.0)	—	
1972	3,581 (100.0)	2,000 (55.9)	1,581 (44.4)	—
1973[2]	17,133 (100.0)	—	—	—
1974	30,708 (100.0)	12,089 (39.2)	17,329 (56.3)	1,362 (4.5)
1975	124,499 (100.0)	60,661 (48.7)	63,838 (51.3)	—
1976	88,060 (100.0)	48,437 (55.0)	39,623 (45.0)	—
1977[2]	138,057 (100.0)	59,875 (43.4)	72,323 (52.3)	5,859 (4.3)
1978	145,703 (100.0)	65,398 (44.9)	77,283 (53.0)	3,022 (2.1)

[1] No data as for each sources available.
[2] Includes loans and subsidies by other organizations.
Source: Ministry of Home Affairs, *The Saemaul Undong: From its Inception Until Today*, respectively, 1973, 1975, 1976, 1977, and 1978.

and is attributable to the fact that the movement was at first carried out by the Ministry of Home Affairs but later was shifted to local governments at the Do (province) and Gun (county) levels.

From the above discussions, it is clear that the government strategy for mobilizing financial resources for the Saemaul Undong was to motivate the rural people to voluntarily contribute their own labor, land, cash and other resources to the maximum extent, as opposed to being fully subsidized or receiving donated material assistance. The strategy was successful in making rural people bear the responsibilities and risks. They thus became more active in pushing forward the projects with collective self-help spirit. This is part of the reason why the Saemaul Undong was so successful in Korea during the 1970's, while physically similar but strategically different efforts made in other countries, as well as in Korea, failed during the 1960's.

PART II
STIMULATORS AND CHANGE AGENTS

Chapter 4

POLITICAL COMMITMENT AND GOVERNMENT SUPPORT

1. Introduction

The purpose of this chapter is to examine the extent of government commitment to rural development and to review mechanisms and dynamics of government commitment to the promotion of rural development in Korea. After being implemented for a decade, the conceptual framework of Saemaul Undong can be identified as having the following features (Chapter 2):

(a) A package program of various rural development services and activities of government;
(b) An emphasis on both horizontal and vertical integration of the interrelated functions of government;
(c) A close working relationship between government machineries and rural people at the grass-root level with positive participation of people;
(d) The mobilization of wider societal support for rural development including support from urban, industrial, and the intellectual elite;
(e) The utilization of all available resources and instruments

in the rural sector including institutional, manpower and technical resources; and

(f) An integrated effort for planned change in values and attitude of people, for dynamic change in rural organization and leadership, and for improvements in village economies and infrastructures.

It has often been mentioned that the Saemaul Undong of Korea is to date one of the most successful cases of integrated rural development. The Saemaul Undong has made an enormous impact upon villages in Korea, at three levels: changes in values and perceptions of rural farmers toward developmental values (Chapter 12); modes of village organization and development of community-based leadership (Chapter 5); and improvements in rural infrastructures and village economies (Chapter 11). How did the Korean government make the Saemaul projects achieve satisfactory results in terms of rural development? So far this question has been little discussed. In this respect, it should be born in mind that rural development cannot take place simply by planning or the formal announcement of rural development programs and policies *without* continued support and real commitment from the government to rural development in the country (Adelman and Morris 1967, 78–81). It is almost a truism to point out that the extent of commitment of the political leadership and government of a country to rural development is a significant determinant of its success in raising the standard of rural living. This is particularly true in contemporary developing countries in which socio-structural, cultural, and attitudinal barriers to rural change are sufficiently strong.

What indicators define the extent of government commitment to rural development in the Korean context? Government commitment means the public promise of government to undertake to make certain types of commitments to rural development. It includes the manifested interest of government in rural development which leads to specific action programs for the realization and completion of their explicitly or implicitly announced promise, policies or programs. In Korea, the Saemaul Undong itself demonstrates the great concern of government as well as its commitment to rural development.

The extent of government commitment to rural development is determined by the state authority as well as by the finance of government. As institutional setting for government power and authority are not behaviorally elaborated yet in most developing countries, the state authority tends to be exercised by the top political leadership. Therefore, in this chapter, the extent of government commitment to rural development in Korea will be analyzed in terms of two major elements: (a) political leadership commitment made on the basis of state authority; and (b) finance-backed government support and assistance such as financial, material, technical and institutional assistance.

The data for the analytic description of this case were collected through content analysis of presidential speeches, government documents, literature on the subject matter and interviews with relevant personnel.

2. Political Leadership Commitment

To what extent did political leadership make a commitment to rural development in Korea? Political leadership commitment tended to be made by explicit expressions of the leadership's personal interests and concerns about rural development in formal or informal statements, by manifested action such as specific instructions regarding program design or resource allocation and field visits for identification of problem and/or monitoring of program performance, and by exercising personal influence on the power elite in various sectors of society in favor of rural development.

Traditionally the presidency of the government has been the major source of political power in the context of Korean politics during the 1970's. Therefore, the commitment of the top political leadership to rural development will be analyzed in terms of the personal commitment to rural development by the late President Park who was incumbent during the period 1962–79.

A. *Rural Background of the Personality*

The late President Park was born and grew up in the rural sector. The ruling party led by him was based on the popular vote of rural farmers, while the opposition party was based on the support of the urban sector. His personal as well as political background might motivate him to make a strong commitment to rural development. The rural poverty in Korea had been one of his major concerns during his presidency, as the poverty in rural villages had been little improved until his initiation of the Saemaul Undong. It was especially so during the 1970's when the popular support for the presidency tended to be challenged and skeptical, partly because as a consequence of rigorous implementation of the First and Second Five-Year Plans rapid industrialization preceeded rural development. The deteriorating rural situation widened the gap between industry and farm, and became a major cause of the rapid rural-to-urban migration. Regardless of the level of his motivation, his strong personal as well as institutional support and commitment to rural development were reflected in his inauguration of the Saemaul song and the Saemaul flag. The song has been popular among various categories of people. During working hours the Saemaul flag has been hung together with the national flag at all kinds of office buildings throughout the country.

B. *Personal Interests and Concerns*

Already it has been pointed out that Saemaul Undong was personally initiated by the late President Park. The leadership commitment to rural development was also demonstrated by the contents of statements made on rural issues and by the frequency of these speeches.

The President often stressed the philosophy and importance of rural development in order to mobilize societal support and to encourage people's participation in Saemaul Undong. He did this on various occasions, for example, at the New Year Press Conference and National Conference of Saemaul Undong Leaders and at the Seoul National University Graduation Ceremony. Through his speeches, he also elaborated on the standard of government support and promised specific assistance, as shown by the following statements:

"The decisive factor is how the farmers and fishermen respond, and how actively they participate in the program. The key factor is whether they are inspired by a desire to help themselves, whether they make a systematic effort to help themselves, and whether they are really fired by a productive spirit. Provided they have the confidence that they can achieve better living if only they strive hard enough, we can achieve rural modernization and upgrade the living standard of farmers and fishermen." (Congratulatory Message at the Second Special Competition of Farmers and Fishermen in Income-Boosting Skills, November 11, 1970).

"But the fundamental problem is the lack of voluntary effort on the part of the local inhabitants themselves to improve their environment and better their living standards. . . . The important factor is that there should be a sincere desire to improve things at the grass-roots level. The village will be up and thriving in a span of two or three years.

Without such a spontaneous determination to improve, the village will not improve in five thousand years, but continue in the vicious circle of poverty and sloth. But if there is such a fervent desire, especially on the part of the village youth, and if only a little help is forthcoming from the government, then this village will make progress in two or three years. . . .

The basic lack is one of leadership at the village level. The local administrative officers at the village level should provide such leadership—should try to get the local leaders together, and try to enlighten them first. . . " (Message to the Conference of Provincial Governors on Drought Counter Measures, April 22, 1970)

"The Government. . . is going to assign top priority to those areas or regions which demonstrate the strongest spirit of self-help, cooperation, participation, solidarity and simple hard work, so that these communities will grow faster than others and serve as a model for all the rest to emulate.

The basis of this movement is a spiritual awakening on the part of rural inhabitants, who will discard the mentality of abject dependence on external support. . . .

You (city mayors and county chiefs) must uphold the Saemaul spirit as the basic guideline of national development, and do your best for its universal dissemination. You must in particular seek our young and ambitious workers, and train them as potential leaders in the rural development program." (Message to Comparative Administration Conference of City Mayors and County Chiefs, September 17, 1971)

In this connection, the frequency of President's statements on rural issues seemed to be relevant to the analysis of the degree of his interests. Generally the New Year Press Conference with the President used to cover major issues reflecting his interests. During the last decade, 82 themes and issues were raised throughout ten conferences. Table 4-1 indicates the distribution of themes and issues by 11 categories. It is interesting to find that beside the political and international affairs, one of the most frequently raised categories of issues and themes is rural and agricultural development. It scores the same as industrial development and trade.

Table 4–1. Themes and Issues Raised in Press Conferences

Unit: No. of Themes

Category of Policy Matters	Themes
Political and International Affairs:	
National Security	18
South-North Talk	4
International Relations	11
Domestic Politics	13
Economic Affairs:	
Economic Matters in General	6
Agricultural and Rural Development	7
Industrial, Trade, Resource	7
Socio-cultural Affairs:	
Anti-corruption	5
Education and Culture	4
Labor and Social Welfare	4
Conservation of Natural Environment	3
Total	82

Source: content analysis of New Year Press Conferences with President, during the period 1970–79.

The degree of the late president's personal interest is measured here in terms of the portion of total speech time spent for statements on rural development on a particular occasion, which assumes that the more interest in a particular subject, the more time spent for speech on the subject.

In this paper, the New Year Press Conference and the Budget

Speech are chosen for content analysis since they are the most comprehensive of his speeches. As speech time tends to be proportional to the number of letters mobilized in the speech, the analysis is made on the basis of number of letters. According to Table 4-2, it is found that the interests of the President in issues and policies of rural development was high throughout the period of the 1970's. On the average, the President allocated about 9% of the total speech time for projection of the future image of rural society, government policies and support for rural development, farmers' role and village leadership, etc. In view of the numerous issues to be covered at both occasions, the time shared for rural problems seems to be quite substantial.

Table 4-2. Degree of President's Interests in Rural Development

Unit: No. of letters (%)

year	New Year Press Conference (1) Total	Rural Development	Annual Budget Speech (2) Total	Rural Development	Both (1) + (2) Total	Rural Development
1970	21,864	2,568(11.7)	7,848	216(2.8)	29,712	2,784(9.4)
1971	33,768	2,808(8.3)	9,192	552(6.0)	42,960	3,360(7.8)
1972	34,200	3,120(9.1)	6,192	264(4.3)	40,392	3,384(8.4)
1973	35,856	4,656(13.0)	9,864	768(7.8)	45,720	5,424(11.9)
1974	29,856	1,032(3.5)	14,784	1,296(8.8)	34,640	2,328(6.7)
1975	44,376	3,936(8.9)	11,256	840(7.5)	55,632	4,776(8.6)
1976	36,912	2,640(7.2)	10,800	624(5.8)	47,712	3,265(6.8)
1977	28,320	2,232(7.9)	10,176	696(6.8)	38,496	2,928(7.6)
1978	31,080	4,848(15.6)	10,800	600(5.6)	41,880	5,448(13.0)
1979	38,304	4,584(12.0)	14,160	1,152(8.1)	52,464	5,736(11.0)
Total	334,536	32,424(9.7)	105,072	7,008(6.6)	429,608	39,433(9.2)

Source: content analysis of New Year Press Conferences and Annual Budget Speeches of President, during the period 1970-79.

The President also expressed his great concern about rural development by personally visiting rural villages. His frequent field visits also served as a mechanism for identification of problems, and provided opportunities to make specific instructions and guidelines for program design as well as for monitoring program performance. As a matter of fact, the frequent field visits were once dramatized by the term of "administration by identification," meaning that every important decision regarding rural development would be made mostly after his personal identification and confirmation of the factual circumstances. He also participated with farmers every year in the plantation of rice and its harvesting.

President Park's personal interest in and concern for rural development tended to be institutionalized in terms of the organizational setting and reporting system. The president used to personally award prizes to the two best Saemaul leaders at the monthly meeting with economic ministers of his cabinet where the Monthly Economic Situation Report was presented to the President. It is also interesting to note that the President himself personally made a speech at the Annual National Conference of Saemaul Undong Leaders in which he encouraged, motivated and stimulated Saemaul Leaders from all the villages of the nation to make their best endeavor for rural betterment.

> "All these outstanding results are a crystallization of the sweat and labor of all the Saemaul leaders and the rural population who have worked in unity and were inspired by the Saemaul spirit of diligence, self-help, and teamwork. In my view, the Saemaul movement. . . is the driving force behind the conquest of difficulties and the creation of a new chapter of national history. . . . The responsibilities and missions assigned to you (Saemaul leaders) are heavy and important beyond comparison." (Message at National Conference of Saemaul Leaders, December 18, 1974)

The personal interest and commitment of the President to rural development tended to be followed up with the assistance of a secretariat. The head of the team held a position equivalent to the rank of Vice Minister. The special Assistant for Rural and Agricultural Development, who was a scholar as well as a movement-organizer, also assisted the President.

C. *Personal Influence and Public Education*

Using his formal authority, the late President Park also intentionally exercised his influence to get the power elite to form favorable attitudes toward, and to give moral support and commitment to, rural prosperity. As a consequence, Saemaul Undong has also been practiced with modification in other sectors such as in urban and industrial communities, schools and the military, with a view to supporting the original version of Saemaul Undong. Due to the influence of the President, a social mood was created which was favorable to rural development, so that the ruling elite including religious leaders, business elite, journalists, and other intellectual elite were motivated to participate in the Saemaul Leaders Training Course. They were trained together with village leaders from the countryside.

"The Saemaul movement is not intended for farmers alone; . . . nationwide bases. University students and intellectuals should also voluntarily join in, and play the leading role in this movement." (Address at Seoul National University Graduation Ceremony, February 26, 1972)

D. Reorientation of Government

The political leadership commitment tended to be reflected in the reorientation of government priority, policy direction, resource allocation and official attitude.

"Rural housing will be improved gradually to the standards prevailing in advanced countries. This will go far toward modernizing the living environment of farmers. A full-scale effort in this direction will be mounted this year, when 75 billion won will be disbursed to finance the construction of 50,000 units of modernized rural housing." (New Year Press Conference, January 18, 1978)

"You will come to realize that over 90 percent of my words are about the development of spiritual resources, not about economic matters or material things. I also wish to emphasize that the real hero of a rural community is the man who devotes his sweat and blood, without words, to the task of developing his home town or village. Our society is in need of many such community heros. National construction or development cannot be achieved by those who make fine speeches but do not fit actions to their words." (Message to the Conference of Provincial Governors, July 30, 1971)

One of the movement's remarkable effects is the reorientation of government administrators toward inter-ministerial or interagency coordination which is an administrative prerequisite for the success of change-introducing development projects involved in Saemaul Undong.

"All problems arising within your respective areas of jurisdiction should be tackled under the joint responsibility of all government agencies concerned, with the city mayor or the county commissioner taking primary responsibility, and with the local tax office, the police station or other related agencies providing whatever assistance or cooperation may be called for. . . . It seems to me things would not have come to a head had the chiefs of responsible local government agencies cooperated with each other more closely. In the future, the local city mayor or county commissioner should take the lead in solving all local problems of importance, after sufficient prior consultation with the heads of related government agencies, and seeking the understanding and cooperation of the local inhabitants. Once the policy is set, the matter should be pushed vigorously under joint responsibility." (Message to Comparative Administration Conference of City Mayors & County Chiefs, September 17–18, 1971)

3. Government Support and Assistance

The commitment of the top political leadership and, in turn, the reorientation of the system of government to rural development would be reflected in all kinds of governmental assistance and support to rural villages. To what extent did governments, central and local, provide the necessary support and assistance to rural development? The extent could be defined in terms of the appropriateness as well as the varieties of services. The analytical discussion of both relies on kinds of indicators or variables chosen to measure these factors.

In this chapter, government support and assistance to rural development will be analyzed from a general systems perspective (Perrow 1970, 50–91; Katz and Kahn 1966, 24–29): (a) *structure*, which includes organizational and institutional arrangement within the government system and also particularly a local government support system in terms of functional and structural innovations; (b) *resources* made available for rural development, which include budgetary and financial support and also manpower development for improving both village capacity and officials' capability; (c) *output,* which covers rural support projects, programs and policies; and (d) *process* or *technology,* which means strategies adopted by the government for development support.

In the review and evaluation of the government support system for rural development, *responsiveness* and *creativity* of the government system beyond its *efficiency* will be applied as criteria (Selznick 1957, 134–154). The significant and relevant indicators are selected and evaluated on the basis of such criteria.

A. *Organizational and Institutional Reform*

The planning and management of activities in support of rural development require organizational and institutional reform as a manifested consequence of real commitment by the government. In the central government, the Saemaul Undong Bureau, which is responsible for development of overall strategies and policies regarding the Saemaul Undong, was newly established within the Ministry of Home Affairs. At the provincial level, the Saemaul Planning Division was newly established in the provincial government to support and guide the activities of local governments at the county level. A Deputy County Chief was newly appointed to every county office with the sole responsibility of managing specific support and assistance to Saemaul Undong. An administrative unit was also added within each township office to assume duties for the planning and guidance of Saemaul projects in rural villages within its jurisdictional boundary.

In addition to the setting of line organization, the government also made special arrangments for the planning and coordination of Saemaul projects. This included (a) the Saemaul Central Consultative Council, chaired by the Minister of Home Affairs and with approximately twenty members including several vice ministers and heads of national federations of cooperatives and other agencies related to rural development; (b) the Saemaul Provincial Consultative Council, chaired by the governor, and whose members include university professors and heads of regional offices of the central ministries; (c) the Saemaul County Consultative Council, chaired by the County Chief and members of relevant officers; (d) the Saemaul Township Promotion Committee, chaired by the Myeon Chief and whose members include Saemaul leaders; and finally (e) the Village Development Committee, chaired by the Saemaul leader and 5 members selected from among the villagers. This series of councils and committees from the central level down to the village level was set up with a view to facilitating coordination between ministristries and agencies concerned with rural development and to providing diversified perspectives for solid planning of Saemaul projects. It is noted, in this connection, that Saemaul leaders participate as members in both county and township-level councils, to positively represent their interests and ideas.

Another interesting point is that the responsibilities for implementation of Saemaul projects are assumed by the deputy chiefs of local government for their respective levels of administration, while the chief of local governments at any level is responsible for planning, resource commitment and setting guidelines. It is assumed that such an arrangement will promote efficient coordination between related agencies and functions.

B. Local Government System

The improvement in local government support seems to be an essential requirement for the successful implementation of Saemaul projects. Historically, the local government system in Korea was oriented to law and order and served as an action instrument of the central elite for the control over local resources. However, the reorientation of the local government system toward rural development was enforced for the Saemaul Undong and thus they became more accessible to the community people during the 1970's. Village leaders were encouraged to positively participate in the government decision-making process.

The organizational reform of local governments become more conducive to the performance of development support administration at the community level. Although the coordination and integration of resources and inputs for rural development is primarily a role of community leadership, the package of government support is one which is coordinated between different agencies of government and integrated into the total scheme of village development. The coordinating effort of local governments makes avoidable unnecessary duplication and conflicts in the village level activities and helps in providing services complementary to each other.

The efficiency of the local government system in support of the Saemaul Undong is boosted by the improvement in mutual relationship between local governments and their constituents. The existing mutual discord due to the traditionally bureaucratic and colonial attitude of local officials toward people has been gradually evaporated by the consistent drive of development support on the part of local governments. The government's credibility indeed provided a perceptual basis for government-mediated rural innovations in the process of Saemaul Undong. It is noteworthy in this connection, that the promotion of local officials on the basis of the evaluation of their work performance for Saemaul projects is almost institutionalized.

The managerial capability of local government is another dimension of development support administration. The managerial competence in senior officials in terms of planning of service delivery, monitoring of work performance, communication and coordination and other techniques was improved through the extensive management training throughout the 1960's and 1970's.

In this respect, the remarkable discipline of local government officials in the process of their service delivery should be noted. The timely and accurate delivery of materials and services to villages according to the planned schedule is an indicator of outstanding performance and commitment of local administrators which partly contributes to the credibility of government. The commitment of local government is also reflected in arrangements for special assignment of local officials. Each staff member is assigned to take a responsibility for efficient implementation of Saemaul projects in a village. This arrangement is an extended version of the "administration by identification" approach. In addition to their competence in technical subject matters with which they deal, the competence of field workers also includes certain skills and the capability to build a fresh image of "service men" to efficiently deliver required services, to easily contact and communicate with community people, to project a homophilous feeling with rural people, and to stimulate, motivate, and encourage community people. The managerial and technical competence of the local government system tends to bring about a synergetic effect as the government officials at the county office are highly motivated and committed to the achievement of certain results in rural transformation.

C. Budgetary Support

Although it is claimed that Saemaul Undong has been implemented with people's strong motivation, zeal, participation and contribution in kind, one of the significant inputs is undoubtedly a package of government support and assistance. The extent of actual commitment of government in terms of assistance and support is explicitly manifested in the allocation of budgetary resources. According to Table 4-3, the development expenditure out of the General Government Sector Budget has increased by 7.8 times in terms of current prices during the period of 1971–78. During the same period, budgetary expenditures of both central and local governments in support of rural Saemaul projects has increased about 82 times. Thus the ratio of government expenditure in support of Saemaul projects has been increased over the period. During 1978, government support to Saemaul Undong reached the scale of ₩338 billion which was equivalent to 38% of development expenditures of the General Government Sector Budget (Whang 1980a, 41–43).

Table 4-3. Government Expenditures for the Saemaul Undong

Unit: billion won

Year	Development Expenditures of Central Government*	Expenditures for Saemaul Projects†
1971	111.7	4.1
1972	240.2	3.6
1973	176.8	17.1
1974	301.1	45.5
1975	522.3	165.3
1976	669.5	165.1
1977	729.9	246.0
1978	873.0	338.4

Sources: *Economic Planning Board, *Major Economic Indicators*, 1978, pp. 90–91.
†Ministry of Home Affairs, *Saemaul Undong*, 1978.

D. Manpower Development

Another significant input supporting Saemaul Undong in Korea is the consistent and extensive arrangements for training both private and government manpower resources. The government has organized a Saemaul Leaders Training Center at the central level and similar institutes in each province. According to a recent study (Whang 1980a, 118–120), 54 Saemaul leaders out of 63 leaders interviewed had been trained once or more, the nine exceptions were newly-recruited leaders who had not had a chance to join the training course. The majority of them (85%) considered the training course relevant to their role performance. Another study (Chae 1978b, 120) also indicates a similar finding.

The Saemaul training course was designed especially for changing values and the world outlook of Saemaul leaders. For this purpose it adopted special training methods. The special arrangement of government to get social elite to voluntarily participate in the training program also represents the special concensus as well as the total commitment of government to the program, since encouraging such participation is politically risky.

In addition to the training program for Saemaul leaders, similar programs were organized for government officials. There are, for example, Saemaul training courses at the Central Officials Training Institute and the Local Administration Training Institute. The consistent conduct of training courses during the past ten years has not only influenced the attitudinal change of administrators but has also motivated administrators to work closely with village farmers. The courses also helped them to understand the philosophy and strategy of rural development in the Korean context and to develop close perceptual ties with rural villagers. According to one study (Shin 1979, 331), it is found that approximately 15 thousand middle-high level officials of central government were trained in the Saemaul course conducted by the Central Officials Training Institute alone during the period of 1972–79.

E. Operational Strategies

Strategies for efficient support toward self-reliant development of rural villages could be analyzed in terms of standards of operation in rural support administration, methods and criteria for the allocation of available resources, and technology related to stimulation and inducement.

At the initial stage of Saemaul Undong, the government classified rural villages into three categories on the basis of the degree of development: underdeveloped, developing and developed villages. The classification provided a psychological basis for competition between villages in promoting their village improvement. It also provided a criterion by which government could apply different packages of support and assistance to villages depending on their level of development. In this respect it should be noted that the priority of government support is given to more developed villages rather than less developed ones. This principle of "the better village the first support" became an effective stimulator of people's motivation to better achievement in Saemaul projects. Although the psychology of excess competition tends to be an obstacle to implementation of inter-village Saemaul projects which have recently developed as a new thrust of Saemaul Undong, the competition mood between neighboring villages substantially contributed to the success of Saemaul Undong at the early stages.

Another point to be made is the strategic shift of priority in supporting projects. During the period of 1970-73 the priority of government commitment was given to the area of improvement in rural infrastructures, namely to environmental improvement projects such as the construction of small bridges, a village entrance road, farm roads, electrification, sanitary water supply, etc. However, since 1974 the priority was shifted to the income-boosting projects of farmers including special crops, livestock, and marketing facilities (Whang 1980a, 48-62). The priority of government support to improvements in rural infrastructure had a strategic implication in view of the fact that people's participations in cooperative action for rural infrastructures would bring about tangible and visible results immediately after their contribution. This serves as a mechanism of learning by doing so as to reinforce their developmental values. Such experimentation especially at the initial stage had enhanced a sense of participation and confidence. It also made rural people recognize the values of self-help, diligence, cooperation and participation (Whang 1980a, 200-201).

Specific commitment of government is also reflected in the incentive system to make rural people participate. Since an enforcement scheme was believed to have limited value in motivating people, a variety of incentives were provided both for villages and individual leaders. The initial incentive, at the village level was to provide government support in kind, for example, cement and steel. The government donation of materials to villages, for example the donation of 335 bags of cement to each village, tended to induce a positive response from the village people in the form of their participation in decision-making with regard to what to do with the cement and also their positive cooperation to achieve the results. This is a process of induced change in rural villages in which the village people tended to face problems related to identity crisis, leadership capability, organizational and managerial competence and other issues related to dynamic changes in rural villages (Park JH 1977, 13–26).

The incentive at the individual level was the award system which has been utilized frequently to encourage village leaders and outstanding farmers. This includes medals and special presidential awards (in cash) given to Saemaul leaders for demonstration of excellent Saemaul spirit.

Lastly, it is noted that the government deliberately prepared a plan for the sequential arrangement of various types of assistance and support over time to build a certain momentum which enabled the rural community to become capable of self-reliant development. Indeed, government support for the Saemaul Undong has been consistent between different activities and between goals and instruments over a period of time from the beginning of its support until the stage of strategic withdrawal of the support. Constant evaluation of the capacity of a particular rural village (or community) for self-reliant development has been built into the process of government mobilization of support and assistance.

F. Supporting Policies and Programs

In connection with the firm commitment of government to rural development, specific policies and programs should be mentioned. One of the significant policies is the high-rice-price policy which has been predominant during the 1970's. The policy has boosted farmers' incomes substantially. While the policy is currently being criticized because of the accumulation of a deficit and because the government purchase of rice tends to create inflationary pressure, the high price policy nevertheless encouraged farmers to work harder and to participate in rural development activities.

The government commitment was also manifested in the heavy investment in research and development in the agricultural sector, particularly the development of high-yielding varieties (HYV). Indeed, the development as well as nationwide diseemination of HYV of rice eventually made Korea self-sufficient in rice. The dissemination of new rice seeds and the intensification of Saemaul Undong seemed to be a mutually reinforcing process of change in the rural economy.

The government also provided some follow-up measures to the innovation process. For example, the Saemaul Technical Service Corps was organized with participation by scientists in various fields, such as agriculture, food processing, cottage factories, engineering, health, etc.

4. Developmental Implications of Commitment: Conclusions

Change-introducing projects require commitment of top political leaders. As rural development implies profound changes in major aspects of rural village, top leadership commitment to the Saemaul Undong is of essential importance to its success. Actual commitment of top political leadership tends to affect resource allocation as well as the legal/administrative framework in favor of the rural sector. The support and commitment of top political leadership also influenced the ruling elite to form favorable attitudes toward rural development and to commit themselves to the Saemaul Undong. The societal support tends to reinforce the values and ideas of rural development. The active involvement of the elite in the Saemaul Undong and their understanding of its philosophies and strategies tend to be conducive to the mobilization of adequate support from the government as well as other social sectors. The strong commitment of the top political leadership to the success of Saemaul Undong tends to remove bureaucratic inertia which could be obstacles to efficient coordination and to administrative innovations at the local level.

The Saemaul Leaders Training Course addressed to village leaders as well as ruling elites has significant implications in terms of dissemination of rural innovations and mobilization of relevant resources and instruments.

Another aspect of commitment is naturally reflected in the package of government support. Under present circumstances in most Asian countries, including Korea, rural development requires not only financial and technical assistance delivered directly to rural villages but also a series of supporting policies and programs. The integrity of government commitment was also recognized by consistent training programs, organizational rearrangement and operational strategies.

It is found that government commitment has a synergetic effect on rural development. The deliberate, consistent and solid package of government support and commitment tends to have multiple impacts on rural innovation. An adequate level of government assistance and support to villages tends to stimulate a positive response from rural people, in view of their greater contributions and their extensive participation. Nevertheless, it should be born in mind that the universal application of government support and stimulation tends to be accompanied by undesirable consequences because of the lack of flexibility to fit into the village-specific situations.

Government commitment is essential to the success of the Saemaul Undong in view of the mobilization and allocation of all types of resources in favor of the rural sector. It is, nevertheless, felt that without the positive participation of people in the decision-making process and their active cooperation in the project implementation, the government support alone would not bring about effective results in rural development (Park JH 1978). The mutual stimulation between government machinery and rural people is the key to the Saemaul Undong's success.

Chapter 5

VILLAGE LEADERS: BACKGROUND AND ROLE PERFORMANCE

Through what process and mechanism was village leadership identified and fostered in rural areas? What social and economic backgrounds did the village leaders have? What roles have they played in the process of the Saemaul Undong and what are the characteristics of their behavioral patterns and motivational levels?

To date there is limited information on the social background of village leaders and their leadership formation available for this kind of analysis. Therefore, this analysis is based on information collected through interview surveys with former and current Saemaul leaders at 36 villages selected through stratified sampling. The total number of leaders in the 36 villages was 88 out of which only 63 were available for interviews due to death, moving away, or travel.

For comparative purposes, the socio-economic background of 1,497 village people who lived in the same 36 villages were also analyzed (Chapter 12). The comparative analysis was originally planned from the beginning when the survey design was made. In other words, the same questions regarding leaders' opinions on their own roles and behavioral patterns were asked to ordinary village people as a complementary device for improving the objectivity of the data. Opinions of government officials at Gun and Myeon offices who were in charge of the Saemaul Undong in the 36 villages were also studied through a mailing survey in order to collect supplementary data on perceptual patterns as well as motivational level of the sample leaders. Of those canvassed, 288 local officials made replies to a well-designed mailing questionnaire.

As shown in Table 5-1, a total of 88 persons have served as Saemaul leaders in 36 surveyed villages over the past 10 years. On the average, 2.4 leaders per village served the nationwide movement during that period. Chungcheongbug-Do and Gyeongsangbug-Do (provinces) have had 16 leaders respectively, and average three leaders per village during the same period. In Chungcheongnam-Do and Gyeongsangnam-Do there have been 13 leaders respectively, which breaks down to two leaders per village.

Table 5-1. Distribution of Sample Leaders by Region, 1970-79

Region	No. of Villages	No. of Leaders	No. of Leaders interviewed	Out-migration	Death	Travel	Leaders per Village
Chungcheongbug-Do	6	16	11	3	–	2	2.7
Chungcheongnam-Do	6	13	11	1	–	1	2.0
Jeonrabug-Do	6	15	11	1	1	2	2.5
Jeonranam-Do	6	15	10	–	–	5	2.5
Gyeongsangbug-Do	6	16	9	1	1	5	2.7
Gyeongsangnam-Do	6	13	11	1	–	1	2.0
Total	36	88	63	7	2	16	2.4

Source: Whang (1980a, 116).

The high percentage of leaders who left for urban areas, 7 out of the total 88 shows that the Saemaul leaders were no exception to the recent trend of exodus from rural areas.

1. Leadership Patterns of Saemaul Leaders

A. *Incumbency of Saemaul Leaders*

The number of leaders during the past 10 years differs widely among the villages. In six villages out of the 36 surveyed, only one leader in each served for the entire period of the last decade while in other cases as many as 5 leaders had served in each village during the same period. But a majority of villages had about 2 or 3 leaders during the period, which means the average incumbency of the Saemaul leaders was 4 or 5 years. It is clear from Table 5-2 that the more rapidly a village develops, the longer the incumbency of the Saemaul leaders. In other words, the turnover rate of Saemaul leaders in outstanding villages was lower than in common villages where development has been more sluggish.

Table 5-2. **Incumbency of Leaders and Village Development**

Unit: village

No. of Leaders	Common Villages	Outstanding Villages	Total
1	2	4	6
2	4	10	14
3	5	6	11
4	3	1	4
5		1	1
Total	14	22	36

Source: Whang (1980a, 116).

Leaders usually worked continuously and consistently in those rapidly developing villages where the presidential award encouraged the village people as well as the leaders to be more enthusiastic and more motivated toward better achievement. Having won an award based on an objective evaluation of their performance may have enhanced the confidence of the people in their village leadership. Table 5-3 shows that 17 out of 63 leaders served as leaders for more than 5 years, and 11 for 4–5 years. On the other hand, leaders with less than 1 year of service numbered 15, out of which 8 assumed their duties in 1979. This indicates that the turnover rate of the Saemaul leadership has been growing recently.

B. Election of Leader

Table 5-4 shows that 35% (or 22 leaders) of 63 leaders interviewed were chosen by a general vote by the village people while 29% (18 leaders) accepted the position at the request of the village people. Sixteen percent (10 leaders) were nominated either by the

Table 5-3 Saemaul Leaders by Incumbency

Unit: person

Incumbency Period	Common Villages	Outstanding Villages	Total
Below 1 year	9	6	15
1-2 years	3	7	10
2-3 years	1	4	5
3-4 years	1	4	5
4-5 years	3	8	11
Over 5 years	8	9	17
Total	25	38	63

Source: Whang (1980a, 117).

village head or by a group of leading villagers and 13% (8 leaders) was elected by the village development committee, 5% (3 leaders) were nominated by the government (Gun or Myeon office), and three percent (2 leaders) volunteered to do the job.

There is a significant difference in the pattern of selection of leaders between the common and the outstanding villages. The number of leaders who were elected by a general vote of either the village people or the village development committee is greater in the case of outstanding villages than in the case of common ones. This fact supports the hypothesis that democratic leadership based

Table 5-4. Election Methods of Saemaul Leaders

Unit: person (%)

Election Method	Common Village	Outstanding Village	Total
Volunteered	2(8.0)	–	2(3.2)
Elected by village Development Committee	1(4.0)	7(18.4)	8(12.6)
Elected by General Vote	7(28.0)	15(39.5)	22(34.9)
Nominated by Government	1(4.0)	2(5.3)	3(4.8)
Nominated by Village Head or Leading People	6(24.0)	4(10.5)	10(15.9)
At Request of Villagers	8(32.0)	10(26.3)	18(28.6)
Total	25(100.0)	38(100.0)	63(100.0)

Source: Whang (1980a, 118).

on the consensus of the people is extremely effective in managing development projects at the village level in terms of fostering successful achievement. The process by which village people themselves actively participated and evaluated their achievements in terms of visible results served as a form of training for them in political development "from the bottom."

C. Identification and Fostering of Village Leadership

One important aspect of this empirical study of Saemaul leaders is related to the Saemaul leadership training programs. How has this program evolved over the period under study and to what extent was it effective in developing leadership? Out of the 63 leaders, 22 (35%) received training at the Central Training Institute in Suwon and 32 (50%) were trained at local training centers. In other words 85% of the leaders were trained through formal training programs. And of the 15 new leaders with less than one year's service, 9 were yet to be trained. Thus, the training programs for fostering Saemaul leadership were very active. In fact, such programs have been implemented very intensively over the past ten years to exert a decisive influence on leadership formation in rural villages.

To what extent was the leadership training conducive to the performance of their tasks? As shown in Table 5-5, 85% (46 leaders) replied that their training was very helpful to their work performance while only 2% answered they got little help from the training.

Which courses in the training program were most effective in fostering village leadership? Twenty-three leaders (or 43%) of the 54 trained leaders regarded spiritual training as being the most helpful. Eleven leaders (21%) viewed case studies as most helpful in motivating and dissemination of innovative ideas and 9% perceived that lectures by invited speakers were useful.

The average incumbency of the Saemaul leaders was between 4 and 5 years, and the longer their incumbency, the more rapid their village developed. It is also very interesting that in villages with leaders chosen through a democratic process, the Saemaul Undong was more successful to the extent that such villages often became winners of the presidential prize. It is found that the

Table 5-5. Leaders' Evaluation of Saemaul Training

Unit: person (%)

Responses	Persons
It was very helpful for the job	30(55.5)
It was comparatively helpful	16(29.6)
Not so helpful but good	7(13.0)
Little help for the job	1(1.8)
Total	54(100.0)

Source: Whang (1980a, 119).

leadership training programs were effective devices for fostering community leadership and most leaders responded very positively to the training programs.

2. Socio-economic Background of Saemaul Leaders

An attempt is made in this section to analyze the leaders' socio-economic background as well as their values and perception. From this an understanding of the relationship between their performance and rural development may be gained.

In general, analysis of the socio-economic background of leaders is useful for understanding leadership patterns (Mattews 1954; Singer 1964; Frey 1965; Edinger & Searing 1967, 428–445). For this purpose, age, educational level, job situation, previous job experience, income level and military service have been taken into consideration.

A. Age

The average age of the interviewed leaders was 45. A majority (25%) of leaders (or 16 including those who had already retired) were between 40 and 44. The next group (22%) was comprised of individuals between 45 and 49 (14 leaders) while 18% of the leaders (or 11 leaders) belonged to age group between 50–54; and 13% between 35 and 39. This means that about 48% of the leaders were in their 40s (Table 5-6).

Both present and former Saemaul leaders were most numerous between the ages 40 and 49. About 70% of the incumbent leaders belonged to the age group 25–49 while 65% of former leaders be-

Table 5-6. Ages of Saemaul Leaders

Unit: Person (%)

Age Group	Present Leaders	Former Leaders	Total
25–29	2(5.6)	1(3.7)	3(4.8)
30–34	2(5.6)	–	2(3.2)
35–39	4(11.1)	4(14.8)	8(12.7)
40–44	9(25.0)	7(25.9)	16(25.4)
45–49	8(22.2)	6(22.2)	14(22.2)
50–54	7(19.4)	4(14.8)	11(17.5)
55–59	4(11.1)	2(7.4)	6(9.5)
Over 60	–	3(11.2)	3(4.7)
Total	36(100.0)	27(100.0)	63(100.0)

Source: Whang, (1980a, 121).

longed to this group. This does not necessarily mean that the leaders' ages are decreasing because the ages of former leaders were taken at the time of survey and not during their incumbency. Therefore, it may be assumed that leaders in almost the same age group have performed their roles for the past 10 years. Although Saemaul leaders have been changed over every 4 years on the average, leadership of approximately the same age has been consistently exercised throughout the entire period under this study. Assuming that retired leaders have stayed in their rural villages and continued to play leadership roles there, a comparison was made between the average age of the Saemaul leaders and the rural people in Table 5-7. It appears that the Saemaul leaders were four years younger on the average than the general public in the villages.

Table 5-7. Age Distribution: People vs. Leaders

Unit: person (%)

Age Group	Rural People	Leaders
20–29	94(6.3)	3(4.8)
30–39	248(16.6)	10(15.8)
40–49	473(31.6)	30(47.7)
50–59	401(26.8)	17(26.9)
Over 60	268(17.9)	3(4.8)
No response	13(0.9)	—
Total	1,497(100.0)	63(100.0)
Average age	49 years	45 years

Source: Whang (1980a, 122).

However in view of the mode and median ages, Saemaul leaders were actually representative of the general people. It is interesting here to note that leaders in their 40s have performed a positive role in the rural areas of Korea where traditionally the idea of giving priority to the elders is still predominant and therefore younger people are not as influential as their elders.

B. Educational Level

Twenty three (or 37%) out of the total of 63 Saemaul leaders were middle school graduates and twenty Saemaul leaders (32%) were high school graduates. The number of college-educated (either completed or not) leaders was only two (3%). The fact that more than one third of the leaders were educated at a level beyond high school demonstrates the overall enhancement of educational level of the rural people. It is also noteworthy that rural dwellers with higher education were more interested in the role of Saemaul leaders than before as the social recognition of Saemaul leadership became more widely recognized among them.

The comparison between the village people and the leaders in their educational level (Table 5-8) shows that almost 70% of the people were educated at the elementary level or lower, while on the contrary, 72% of leaders were educated at a level beyond middle school which includes high school and college. It implies that those educated at a relatively high level were elected as Saemaul leaders because they were thought to have the ability to communicate, persuade, organize and mobilize their fellow villagers, all of which are vital skills for their job performance.

On the other hand, the fact that Saemaul leaders were more educated than the common villagers implies that they were probably wealthier in terms of property and income level and, thus, they were probably viewed as more capable and more motivated to perform work for the village development.

It was also found that the present leaders (at the time of the survey) were more educated than the former leaders. The portion of those educated at the high school level or above from among the present leaders was 42% while it was 26% in the case of former leaders.

It is interesting to note that even though both the present and

Table 5-8. **Educational Level: People vs. Leaders**

Unit: person (%)

Level of Education	Rural People	Saemaul Leaders
Illiterate	353(23.6)	2(3.2)
Under elementary school	675(45.1)	16(25.4)
Under middle school	256(17.1)	23(36.5)
Under high school	150(10.0)	20(31.7)
Under junior college	15(1.0)	—
Above college	29(1.9)	2(3.2)
No response	19(1.3)	—
Total	1,497(100.0)	63(100.0)

Source: Whang (1980a, 124).

former leaders belonged largely to the same age group, the present leaders were by large more educated than the former leaders. The reasons for this may include: (a) there is a tendency that the higher a leader's educational level is, the longer he tends to serve in the leader's position; (b) it is a recent trend that people with higher education tend to be elected Saemaul leaders; and (c) those with a high level of education tend to participate more actively in the Saemaul Undong at least in recent years.

C. Present and Former Occupations of the Leaders

Most Saemaul leaders who responded to the interview survey were engaged in agriculture except for two who were no longer in the leader's position. It is quite natural that farmers were selected as Saemaul leaders as long as their most important job was to organize and carry out community projects for rural development. As for retired leaders, they were eligible for positions in such public organizations as Agricultural Cooperatives, but in practice they did not take that option frequently. Therefore, most of the former leaders were apt to help incumbent leaders in the capacity of supporting resource persons for the successful implementation of Saemaul Undong in their villages. Since most leaders were engaged in farming, their interests were congruent with those of the rural villagers (of whom 82% were farmers). Nevertheless they were obliged to also be responsible for reflecting the interests of non-farming villagers (18% of the sample population) in the Saemaul Undong in various ways.

On the other hand, Table 5-9 shows that 67% of the 63 leaders (42 persons) had no experience in occupations other than farming while 33% had previously worked at public organizations, technical positions, business or as a military officer.

Table 5-9. Former Occupations of Saemaul Leaders

Unit: person (%)

Jobs	Incumbent Leaders	Former Leaders	Total
Farming	19(52.8)	23(85.2)	42(66.7)
Public Sector	5(13.9)	3(11.1)	8(12.7)
Teacher	—	1(3.7)	1(1.6)
Company Employee	2(5.6)	—	2(3.2)
Business	3(8.3)	—	3(4.8)
Engineer (Lower Class)	4(11.1)	—	4(6.3)
Labourer	2(5.6)	—	2(3.2)
Military	1(2.7)	—	1(1.5)
Total	36(100.0)	27(100.0)	63(100.0)

Source: Whang (1980a, 125).

Of the 36 incumbent leaders, 17 (47%) had worked at the government or public organizations such as Agricultural Cooperatives but only 4 out of 27 former leaders (or 15%) had had experience in other jobs. It implies that the social mobility (Moore 1963) of incumbent Saemaul leaders was much higher than that of the former leaders. This indicates that rural people have recently realized, even though it has been through a process of trial and error, that the Saemaul leaders should be equiped with the ability to accept or induce innovation as well as have a sense of modernity and creativity.

The high trend of social mobility and change-orientation of the leaders' perception is more obvious when compared to that of the general public. Only 66% of the leaders had engaged in farming since childhood while 81% of the village people had been farmers all of their lives (Whang 1980a, 126). This fact implies that the leaders, through their experience in other vocations, were probably more motivated to better themselves and more oriented toward innovation than the common villagers. This characteristic might, therefore, have become an important qualification for rural leaders recently.

D. Affiliation with Their Own Villages

Apart from the social mobility observed among Saemaul leaders, geographical mobility is another important aspect in any analysis of their background. According to general theories of development, the higher one's geographical mobility is, the higher their change-orientation and motivational level (McClelland 1961) and thus the more qualified for a leadership role. However, an actual survey came up with the opposite result. It is found that almost 75% of the Saemaul leaders had been members of their own villages since their grandfathers' generation while only 53% of the village people had been there that long. Similarly, only 75% of the village people had been members of the same village since their parent's generation while 92% of the leaders had been there since their parents' generation (Table 5-10). This means that the leaders were not selected from among the newly arriving people but rather, were taken from among those who had been there at least since their parents' generation.

This analysis implies many interesting things if we presume that the length of residence corresponds to the degree of devotion a leader has for his village. As shown in Table 5-11, only 16 leaders (25%) had ever lived in other villages before, but 47 (75%) had never lived outside their own villages. Compared to other non-leaders, it is obvious that the Saemaul leaders displayed very low geographical mobility. This may also indicate that they have a greater affection for their village which might spur their zeal

Table 5-10. Duration of Village Life: People *vs.* Leaders

Unit: person (%)

Period	Rural People	Leaders
Before grandfarther's generation	799(53.4)	47(74.6)
Since parent's generation	329(22.0)	11(17.5)
In his generation (over 10 yrs.)	242(16.2)	5(7.9)
In his generation (under 10 yrs.)	110(7.2)	—
Temporary residence	6(0.4)	—
No response	11(0.8)	—
Total	1,497(100.0)	63(100.0)

Source: Whang (1980a, 127).

Table 5-11. Life Experience in Other Places: People *vs.* Leaders

Unit: person (%)

Responses	Rural People	Leaders
None	963(64.3)	47(74.6)
Other farming village	280(18.7)	7(11.1)
Gun or Eub (town capital)	132(8.8)	5(7.9)
Small, medium cities	34(2.3)	—
Big cities*	43(2.9)	3(4.8)
No response	45(3.0)	1(1.6)
Total	1,497(100.0)	63(100.0)

* Seoul, Pusan, Taegu, Taejon and Kwangju.
Source: Whang (1980a, 128).

for village development. According to that interpretation the longevity of geographical affiliation with their own villages was probably viewed as a source of credibility when it came to assuming village leadership.

However, among the incumbent leaders, many have had experience with living in big cities like Seoul, Pusan, Taegu, Taejon and Kwangju. This may suggest that even though the Saemaul leaders were expected to have lived in the village for a long time, people also realized the necessity for their having varied experience from more advanced areas when it comes to organizing and implementing Saemaul projects.

E. *Income Level and Living Standards*

Income level has a decisive impact on the mode of thinking among people and their attitude since it forms one's perception of personal status, especially in the less-differentiated rural communities. An important indicator in this regard was obtained by having the leaders evaluate their own financial status in terms of low-medium-high levels, although this method runs the risk of being too subjective. Therefore, this study tried to classify incomes, through only roughly, of the leaders in 1978 based on their self estimation.

As shown in Table 5-12, 70% of the sampled 1,497 people belonged to the below 2 million won income bracket while only 43% of the Saemaul leaders fell within that group. The gross income of farm households throughout the nation in 1978 was 1.88

million won. Those above the national average comprised 28% of the total in the case of general villagers while among the leaders the figure was 52%. From this finding it is clear that the village leaders have substantially more income than the general people in the rural sector.

Table 5–12. Self-estimation of Gross Income: People *vs.* Leaders

Unit: person (%)

Gross Income during 1978	Rural People	Leaders
Less than 1 million won	709(47.4)	9(14.3)
Between 1~1.5 million won	338(22.6)	18(29.6)
Between 1.5~2 million won	195(13.0)	15(23.8)
Between 2~2.5 million won	83(5.5)	5(7.9)
Between 2.5~3 million won	54(3.6)	6(9.5)
Above 3 million won	99(6.6)	7(11.1)
No response	19(1.3)	3(4.8)
Total	1,497(100.0)	63(100.0)

Source: Whang (1980a, 129).

Table 5-13 indicates the land ownership scale in relation to income level. The Saemaul leaders have more farm land than other rural dwellers. Those among the rural people who have more than the national average of 1 *ha* comprised only 17% of the total 1,497 while among the leaders the figure was 32% of the 63 persons interviewed.

It is interesting to note that 52% of the Saemaul leaders earned more income than the national average gross income of farm house-

Table 5–13, Ownership of Farm Land: People *vs.* Leaders

Unit: person (%)

Land Ownership	Rural People	Leaders
None	193(12.9)	5(7.9)
Less than 0.5 ha	613(40.9)	14(22.2)
Between 0.5–1 ha	443(29.6)	22(34.9)
Between 1–1.5 ha	158(10.6)	10(15.9)
Between 1.5–2 ha	55(3.7)	6(9.5)
Above 2 ha	35(2.3)	4(6.4)
No response	—	2(3.2)
Total	1,497(100.0)	63(100.0)

Source: Whang (1980a, 130).

holds, but on the other hand only 32% of them had more land than the average cultivation acreage. This means that the productivity of the leaders' farmland is higher than that of the villagers which is in part attributable to the fact that 58% of the leaders were engaged in livestock husbandry, gardening, silk-worm farming and other income-increasing activities.

The present leaders were rather well-to-do compared to former leaders in their own estimation of their incomes, since 64% of the incumbent leaders and 48% of former leaders said they earned more than 1.5 million won gross income in 1978. The recent trend of electing financially rich farmers as leaders is consistent with the increasing level of education of the leaders.

The higher level of income of the leaders was also visible in their greater utilization of modern conveniences. The leaders owned far more consumer durables such as TV sets, electric irons, electric cooking pans, electric fans, audio systems, tape recorders, refrigerators and motocycles. These are known to serve as status symbols in the rural communities.

F. Military Service

All but eleven of the Saemaul leaders (or 17.5%) who are over 50 years of age served in the military. As shown in Table 5-14, one leader served in the army as an officer while 46 leaders (or 74%) served as privates or staff sergeants.

Because all male citizens are required to serve in the military for a certain period of time, most men are presumed to have served in the army even though there is no survey of the general people in this regard. It was found that Saemaul leaders have in many ways adopted the military subculture in the process of organizing village resources and manpower, and project selection as well as its implementation. In selecting the project, they encouraged full discussion as soldiers do at military staff meetings, but once decided, the project was pushed forward in a military manner. There also seemed to be very smooth communication and broad understanding between the rural people and Saemaul leaders.*

---

* On the positive impact of the military subculture on administrative efficiency, see Hahn-Been Lee (1966, 203–238) and L. Pye (1962, 89–90).

Table 5-14. Military Service of Saemaul Leaders

Unit: person (%)

Responses	Current Leaders	Former Leaders	Total
None	4(11.1)	7(25.9)	11(17.5)
Reservist	3(8.3)	2(7.4)	5(7.9)
Private	22(61.1)	18(66.7)	40(63.5)
Staff Sergeant	6(16.7)	—	6(9.5)
Officer	1(2.8)	—	1(1.6)
Total	36(100.0)	27(100.0)	63(100.0)

Source: Whang (1980a, 132).

In this respect, it is generally accepted that the quantitative expansion and qualitative improvement of the Korean army since the Korean War incidentally altered organizational dynamics at the village level so as to become a fundamental factor in the success of the Saemaul Undong. Military service also partly fostered the social education of the rural people and indirectly contributed to training the village leadership (Chapter 6).

G. Summary

The socio-economic background of the Saemaul leaders was analyzed by studying their age, educational level, career, residence history and income level.

In age, the Saemaul leaders were four years younger on the average than the general rural populace but nevertheless they were still in the same representative age group, their 40s, as other rural dwellers. Moreover, both the former and incumbent leaders were around the same age.

In both educational and income levels, the leaders were in a far higher bracket than other rural dwellers. The incumbent leaders were both more educated and enjoyed more prosperity and income compared to former leaders. This means that the people tended to select such persons as leaders because those in better financial status and with more education were considered better fit for leadership and beyond that such persons were thought to be more interested in actively participating in community development activities.

Most leaders have been living in the same villages since their grandfathers' or fathers' generations. In other words, they may be viewed as representatives of their families by being elected as leaders. They were all engaged in farming but most of them had worked in public organizations, engineering jobs or other businesses. This implies that their social mobility was greater than that of other rural dwellers and thus they were more strongly oriented toward innovation, modernity, and achievement.

Another characteristic of the leaders except for very elderly people is that most of them fully understand the efficiency of science and technology and modern organization through their experience in the military subculture. Indeed, they tend to follow the methods and behavior of the army in organizing and mobilizing the rural people. Because they retain such behavior and goal-oriented attitudes, they are apt to make action-oriented plans in order to effectively carry out Saemaul projects.

3. Role Performance of Saemaul Leaders

Village leadership in the Saemaul Undong must be somewhat different from that in formal organizations such as the army, business enterprises, and government bureaucracy. Certain characteristic of rural dwellers as well as other constraints which determine the leadership role in rural communities are as follows:

a) There is no hierarchical relationship among rural people who participate in the Saemaul Undong. Both the leaders and the people are on a relatively equal basis. There is no legal basis by which a Saemaul leader can instruct people or enforce order when managing a project.

b) Participation in the Saemaul Undong is based on volition. Villagers can either participate or refuse to become involved. Often people reluctantly join in the project because of different personal interests, but such non-spontaneous methods always fail to bear any continuous or practical fruit in the Saemaul Undong.

c) Jobs related to the Saemaul Undong cannot be the major occupation of rural people as they are usually engaged full-time in agriculture, commerce, industry or some form of service business. In this sense, the Saemaul Undong is different from formal bureaucratic organizations since they cannot devote an excessive number of hours to it alone.

d) Rural people have many things in common and yet they are heterogeneous when compared to the members of formal organizations who are chosen according to a certain standard designed to meet the organization's goals.

Therefore, the successful exercise of village leadership for the Saemaul Undong requires the strong and spontaneous support of the people in order to effectively organize these non-hierarchical, voluntary groups whose members are busy with their own jobs.

Ideally a Saemaul leader should perform his role in the rural development process as: (a) a planner (or initiator of new projects); (b) implementor of projects (or organizer and mobilizer of resources); (c) coordinator (or persuader if necessary); (d) educator; and (e) advocator of new technology (Esman 1978, 47–56).

There are many ways to evaluate the roles of the leaders involved in the Saemaul Undong. To make an objective evaluation, participatory observation and interviews with the leaders comprise the most important avenue of investigation. In this study, however, the opinions of rural people are also analysed in order to supplement the information. Specifically 1,497 villagers in the 36 villages were asked to answer a question regarding what was the major role of the Saemaul leader in planning and implementing the village's most successful Saemaul project.

A. *The Role of Planner (or Initiator)*

As shown in Table 5-15, only 14% of the rural people responded that Saemaul leaders had either planned or initiated the particular Saemaul project.* On the other hand, 22% said that the local government such as the Gun or Myeon office played the role of initiator while 33% thought the people themselves played that role. About 18% thought some leading village figures (opinion leaders) did it and 9% answered that the village chief initiated it. If we consider the real process by which villagers' ideas come to the fore, that is, through their Saemaul leaders or the village development committee, most projects were by large planned or initiated by the rural people. In other words, only 23% of the

---

* That is, the most successful project as identified by the respondent through a shadow question preceeding the other questions analysed in Table 5-15.

respondents answered that the local government initiated the project.

Table 5-15. Initiators of Saemaul Projects

Unit: person (%)

Initiators	Common Villages	Outstanding Villages	Total
Instructed by Gun, Myeon	112(19.2)	225(24.6)	337(22.5)
Vilg. Comtt. members	122(20.9)	154(16.8)	276(18.4)
Village head	49(8.4)	78(8.5)	127(8.5)
Saemaul leader	65(11.1)	145(15.9)	210(14.0)
Village people	208(35.7)	279(30.5)	487(32.5)
Others	3(0.5)	20(2.2)	23(1.5)
No response	24(4.1)	13(1.4)	37(2.6)
Total	583(100.0)	914(100.0)	1,497(100.0)

Source: Whang (1980a, 136).

The percentage of cases in which projects were initiated by the Saemaul leaders was slightly higher in outstanding villages than in common villages. But the Saemaul leaders still appeared to be very passive in planning and initiating new projects. The fact that outstanding villages received many more instructions from the local governments (25%) than the common villages (19%) may imply that the more closely guided a project is, the higher is the possibility of successful implementation. This may be so because government support usually comprises the government instructions. It may be concluded then that the Saemaul leaders as individuals have played only a small role as planners or initiators over the past ten years. However, as members of the village development committees or together with other village elite, Saemaul leaders have played an important role (41%).

The high percentage of response indicating that the local government has played an important role as initiator of projects also indicates the extent of the government's interest and concern with the Saemaul Undong and the degree of government support and influence exerted on village development.

B. The Role of Implementor

An important role of rural Saemaul leaders is that of implementor of projects. Without a formal means justifying this role, a leader has to rely on the customary relationships among the village members. As a project manager, he tries to complete the project through mobilizing, persuading and organizing the rural people, while at the same time negotiating with the local government for necessary material support for the projects. Table 5-16 shows responses to the question "Who do you think has devoted the greatest effort to the successful completion of the Saemaul project?"

Table 5-16. Contibutors to Project Implementation

Unit: person (%)

Most Devoted Persons	Common Village	Outstanding Village	Total
Local officials	41(7.0)	42(4.6)	83(5.5)
Vilg. Commtt. members	100(17.2)	114(12.5)	214(14.3)
Village chief	98(16.8)	211(23.1)	309(20.6)
Saemaul leader	113(19.4)	287(31.4)	400(26.7)
Village people	205(35.2)	233(25.5)	438(29.3)
Others	3(0.5)	14(1.5)	17(1.1)
No response	23(3.9)	13(1.4)	36(2.5)
Total	583(100.0)	914(100.0)	1,497(100.0)

Source: Whang (1980a, 138).

Saemaul leaders were second only to the rural people themselves in terms of how much devotion they have displayed for Saemaul projects. In the outstanding villages, the leaders' role in the success of the project was more highly evaluated (31%) than that of the general people's (25.5%). On the other hand, only 19% of people in common villages admitted that the project succeeded thanks to the leaders while 35% responded that they themselves were responsible for it. This difference implies that in order to accelerate village development, so as to receive a presidential award, a village must have an active Saemaul leader who will play his role as implementor.

C. The Role of Coordinator

Another important role of a Saemaul leader is to coordinate people when there is a conflict of interests so as to garner their mutual cooperation. How well did Saemaul leaders play their roles as coordinators in the representative Saemaul project of the villages? Table 5-17 shows responses to the question "Who do you think has promoted cooperation and unity among the people during the process of project implementation?" It is found that people rated the village chief as more active than the Saemaul leaders in playing the role of coordinator. In terms of percentage, the role of coordinator was played mostly by the village chief (32%), Saemaul leader (30%) and development committee members (26%).

Table 5-17. Promoters of Cooperation and Unity

Unit: person (%)

Chief Promoter of Coordination	Common Villages	Outstanding Villages	Total
Gun, Myeon official	36(6.2)	34(3.7)	70(4.7)
Vilg. Commtt. members	147(25.2)	248(27.1)	395(26.4)
Village chief	206(35.3)	273(29.9)	479(32.0)
Saemaul leader	156(26.8)	293(32.1)	449(30.0)
Others	13(2.2)	34(3.7)	47(3.1)
No response	25(4.3)	32(3.5)	57(3.8)
Total	583(100.0)	914(100.0)	1,497(100.0)

Source: Whang (1980a, 139).

In outstanding villages, 32% of the villagers responded that the Saemaul leaders played the main role of coordinator but 30% of them responded that the village head instead played that role. The difference between these two figures does not seem to be statistically significant. Nevertheless, the fact that the Saemaul leaders in common villages were less frequently identified as the chief promoters of cooperation may suggest that the more positive the co-ordination role played by Saemaul leaders, the higher the possibility of success for the village's Saemaul projects.

D. The Role of Educator

It is a very important role of the Saemaul leader to understand and motivate the rural people with regard to the ideas and objectives behind Saemaul projects. This survey posed indirect questions to the village people in order to evaluate the performance of the leaders as educators. Table 5-18 shows responses to the

Table 5-18. Source of Information about Projects

Unit: person (%)

Major Informers	Common Villages	Outstanding Villages	Total
Gun, Myeon officials	46(7.9)	82(9.0)	128(8.6)
Opinion leaders	124(21.3)	178(19.5)	302(20.2)
Village chief	189(32.4)	246(26.9)	435(29.1)
Saemaul leader	186(31.9)	361(39.5)	547(36.5)
Others	10(1.7)	19(2.1)	29(1.9)
No response	28(4.8)	28(3.1)	56(3.8)
Total	583(100.0)	914(100.0)	1,497(100.0)

Source: Whang (1980a, 140).

question "Who do you think played the most important role in informing the objectives of and necessity for implementing the successful Saemaul project in your village?" Of the 1,497 respondents, 37% answered that the Saemaul leaders did that job. About 29% answered that the village heads played that role. In other words, Saemaul leaders and village chiefs together played the role of educator.

As shown in Table 5-18, people in outstanding villages thought that the Saemaul leaders had performed the role of educator much better (40%) than the village heads (27%). This confirms the argument that for the success of Saemaul projects at the village level, it is essential for Saemaul leaders to inform people and make them understand the background, purpose, and methods of the Saemaul projects.

E. The Role of Advocator of New Technology

An important role of the Saemaul leader as the major agents for rural modernization is to spread new farming techniques to the villagers. In this survey, a question was asked not to the leaders themselves but to the people: "Do you and your neighbors learn many new farming techniques from the Saemaul leader?" As shown in Table 5-19, about 74% gave positive answers to that question. More than half of the 1,497 villagers said either "We learned very much" or "We learned comparatively much." The role of the Saemaul leaders as advocators of new farming techniques appeared almost the same in both outstanding and common villages. This implies that this role is not necessarily a decisive factor in the success of the movement. It is because the Saemaul Undong has not been an agricultural modernization program through innovations in farming techniques but rather an integrated rural development strategy in which the values and perceptions of the people are subject to change, and idle labor force are mobilized for capital formation in the rural sector.

Table 5-19. Saemaul Leaders as Advocator of New Techniques

Unit: person (%)

Responses	Common Villages	Outstanding Villages	Total
We learn:			
Very much	130(22.3)	198(21.7)	328(21.9)
Comparatively much	184(31.6)	279(30.5)	463(30.9)
Not much, not little	121(20.8)	193(21.1)	314(21.0)
Not so much	79(13.6)	183(20.0)	262(17.5)
Almost nothing	53(9.1)	56(6.1)	109(7.3)
No response	16(2.6)	5(0.6)	21(1.4)
Total	583(100.0)	914(100.0)	1,497(100.0)

Source: Whang (1980a, 141).

The fact that a high percentage of rural people learned new farming technology from Saemaul leaders, despite the fact that there had been little input in the leadership training course on that particular subject, may reflect the strong need for improvement in farming techniques among villagers. The leaders' experience in livestock husbandry and high-income crop farming, which was considerable according to the analysis of their social background, was probably helpful to other village members. This phenomenon, moreover, seems to have been reinforced after the Saemaul Undong began to stress income-increasing projects. In view of this trend, the role of advocator of new techniques will become increasingly important for Saemaul leaders, and as a result it will be necessary to take this into account in the curriculum of leadership training programs in the future.

F. Summary of the Leaders' Role

Of the five major roles of Saemaul leaders—initiator, executor, educator, advocator and coordinator—the leaders in general most actively performed the role of initiator except in the case of those projects carried out with the strong support and control of the government. In particular, the leaders' role as a project initiator was very conspicuous in outstanding villages. In this context, the cooperation and support of the village head was a decisive factor. In outstanding villages, Saemaul leaders appeared to have played bigger roles than the village heads. Nevertheless, it is clear that only with the cooperation and positive support of the village head could Saemaul leaders perform their roles without much difficulty. What then is the relationship between the two types of leaders? This will be discussed in terms of behavioral patterns of Saemaul leaders.

4. Motivation Level and Behavioral Pattern of Saemaul Leaders

So far the socio-economic background of Saemaul leaders and the pattern of their services and role performance have been analysed. The following section is devoted to studying the extent to which they contributed to the development of villages, their motivational level, and their behavioral pattern in exercising their leadership. In collecting relevant information, the opinions of the rural people and local government officials at Gun and Myeon offices were taken into consideration in addition to interviews with leaders themselves.

A. Leadership Pattern

The relationship between a leader and the people of a village used to be defined in terms of two polar concepts: democratic and dictatorial. This study put these two concepts at either end of a continuum and tried to located the leaders according to their dictatorial, mixed or democratic patterns of behavior.

Those respondents who answered that the Saemaul leaders decide in consultation with influential villagers (semi-democratic) or on the basis of village meetings (democratic) comprised 76%

Table 5-20. Pattern of Village Leadership: People vs. Leaders

Unit: person (%)

Leadership Pattern	Rural People	Saemaul Leader
Leader decides alone (dictatorial)	115(7.7)	1(1.6)
Mainly decided by leader although discussed at meetings (semi-dictatorial)	222(14.8)	2(3.2)
Mostly decided after discussions bet. leader and leading villagers (semi-democratic)	358(23.9)	26(41.3)
Mostly decided at village meeting (democratic)	776(51.8)	31(49.2)
No response	26(1.8)	3(4.7)
Total	1,497(100.0)	63(100.0)

Source: Whang (1980a, 143).

of the 1,497 rural dwellers interviewed.

On the other hand, 90% of the 63 Saemaul leaders interviewed answered that they decide either at the village meeting or in consultation with influential villagers. Both general people and Saemaul leaders admitted that village leadership was exercised in a democratic way in pursuance of Saemaul projects and in turn such statistical information reflected the extent of people's participation.

Table 5-21 shows that 54% of people in outstanding villages thought their Saemaul leaders were democratic in implementing the projects while 49% of people in common villages thought the same way. Although the statistical significance of this difference is weak, it implies that people in outstanding villages are somewhat more likely to perceive their village leadership as more democratic than those in common villages. People in outstanding villages perceive their leaders as carrying out Saemaul projects in close cooperation with fellow villagers.

This is partly attributable to the guidelines of the Saemaul Undong which stress democracy under the slogan "Saemaul Undong is the vehicle for promoting Korean democracy." The guidelines appear to have had a strong impact on forming a democratic foundation at the grass-root level by requiring that (a) all people should participate, (b) leader should be elected by the will of the people, (c) decisions should be agreed upon by all peo-

Table 5-21. Pattern of Village Leadership: common vs. outstanding villages

Unit: person (%)

Leadership Pattern	Common Villages	Outstanding Villages	Total
Leader decides alone	45(7.7)	70(7.7)	115(7.7)
Mainly decided by leader although discussed at meetings	70(12.0)	152(16.6)	222(14.8)
Mostly decided after discussions bet. leader and leading villagers	169(29.0)	189(20.7)	358(23.9)
Mostly decided at village meeting	284(48.7)	492(53.8)	776(51.8)
No response	15(2.6)	11(1.2)	26(1.8)
Total	583(100.0)	914(100.0)	1,497(100.0)

Source: Whang (1980a, 144).

ple and (d) projects should be selected so as to benefit the whole village (Kim JH 1977, 45–50).

B. Relationship between Saemaul Leader and Village Head

In the previous chapter, it was presumed that the success of the Saemaul Undong heavily depended on cooperation between the Saemaul leaders and the village heads. It is interesting then to explore exactly what kind of relationship exists between these two leading personalities in the villages. Again to avoid the risk of subjectivity, this study asked opinions of the rural people and of the government officials who have been in contact with them.

As shown in Table 5-22, 53% of the people thought cooperation between the Saemaul leaders and village heads was very good and about 37% thought it was good. On the other hand, out of the 288 local officials at the Gun and Myeon levels, 27% answered that the leaders maintained very good cooperation and 64% said they had good cooperation. Although the percentage of responses differed, the prevailing opinion in this regard was that both the Saemaul leaders and village heads enjoy a good cooperative relationship.

If the response of the people is classified according to outstanding vs. common villages, the cooperative attitude was far more significant in outstanding villages. As shown in Table 5-22, 57% of those respondents in outstanding villages answered that cooperation between the Saemaul leaders and the village heads

Table 5-22. Cooperative Relationship between Saemaul Leaders and Village Heads

Unit: person (%)

Cooperative Relationship	Rural People Common Villages	Rural People Outstanding Villages	Rural People Total	Government Officials
Very good	275(47.2)	516(56.5)	791(52.8)	79(27.4)
Good	215(36.9)	341(37.3)	556(37.1)	185(64.3)
Not so good	52(8.9)	36(3.9)	88(5.9)	21(7.3)
Little cooperation	10(1.7)	15(1.6)	25(1.7)	3(1.0)
No response	31(5.3)	6(0.7)	37(2.5)	—
Total	583(100.0)	914(100.0)	1,497(100.0)	288(100.0)

Source: Whang (1980a, 145).

was excellent while only 47% answered similarly in common villages. This implies that the better the relationship between the Saemaul leaders and village heads, the greater the chances are of success for Saemaul projects.

C. *Motivational Level of Leaders*

To analyse the degree of devotion and enthusiasm of Saemaul leaders, rural people were asked to answer a question regarding what was the hidden motivation of the leaders in accepting their unpaid position. It seems to be hardly justifiable to ask people about someone else's motivation for such an analysis. However it assumed that the observation of the people would have considerable validity because of their constant contact with Saemaul

Table 5-23. Motivation of Saemaul Leaders

Unit: person (%)

Responses	Common Villages	Outstanding Villages	Total
For the well-being of people	453(77.7)	700(76.6)	1,153(77.0)
For his own prestige	36(6.2)	72(7.9)	108(7.2)
To enjoy privileges	36(6.2)	42(4.6)	78(5.2)
Others	26(4.5)	91(10.0)	117(7.8)
No response	32(5.4)	9(0.9)	41(2.8)
Total	583(100.0)	914(100.0)	1,497(100.0)

Source: Whang (1980a, 146).

leaders in the course of their daily lives in the rural villages.

As shwon in Table 5-23, about 77% of the rural people felt that Saemaul leaders accepted the position without payment in order to help the rural people live better. According to this study, the Saemaul leaders' motivation appeared sincere and honest.

A majority of the rural people (about 78% of the people in common villages and 77% in outstanding villages) admitted that Saemaul leaders accepted the leadership with a strong motivation to realize better living in their villages. Of course the motivation of Saemaul leaders alone cannot bring success to the movement. Nevertheless, the unselfish motivation and devotion of Saemaul leaders should be evaluated as an important factor in the success of the Saemaul Undong during the 1970's.

Their sincere and strong motivation was consistent with the extent of their devotion to their villages. Table 5-24 shows responses to the question: "To what extent do you and your neighbors think Saemaul leaders devote themselves to rural development?" About 46% of the 1,497 interviewees answered that the Saemaul leaders dedicated themselves entirely to village development and 37% said they worked largely for the village.

Table 5-24. Devotion of Saemaul Leaders

Unit: person (%)

Degree of Devotion	Common Villages	Outstanding Villages	Total
Devote entirely for village	259(44.4)	429(46.9)	688(46.0)
Devote largely for village	221(37.9)	339(37.1)	560(37.4)
Yes for village, or no	63(10.8)	101(11.1)	164(11.0)
Work somehow for themselves	29(5.0)	31(3.4)	60(4.0)
Work for themselves	6(1.0)	8(0.9)	14(0.9)
No response	5(0.9)	6(0.6)	11(0.7)
Total	582(100.0)	914(100.0)	1,497(100.0)

Source: Whang (1980a, 147).

If we compare the responses from rural people in common and outstanding villages, 48% of the respondents in outstanding villages thought that Saemaul leaders were fully devoted to their village's development while in common villages the percentage was 44%. This difference is statistically little significant. However, it may suggest that the devotion of Saemaul leaders is a necessary if not sufficient condition for success in the Saemaul Undong in the 1970's.

D. Morale of Saemaul Leaders

The motivational level and sense of devotion of the Saemaul leaders are closely related to their morale which is partly reflected in their level of satisfaction. In spite of the high level of motivation as well as a sense of devotion of the leaders as observed common people, the level of satisfaction of Saemaul leaders with their tasks seemed to be relatively low according to their own self-evaluation. Table 5-25 indicates that 44% of interviewed Saemaul leaders expressed comparative satisfaction with their roles and only 27% expressed a high level of satisfaction.

Table 5-25. Satisfaction of Saemaul Leaders

Unit: person (%)

Degree of Satisfaction	Common Villages	Outstanding Villages	Total
Very satisfied	7(28.0)	10(26.3)	17(27.0)
Comparatively satisfied	9(36.0)	19(50.0)	28(44.5)
Not good, not bad	7(28.0)	7(18.4)	14(22.2)
Unsatisfied	2(8.0)	2(5.3)	4(6.3)
Total	25(100.0)	38(100.0)	63(100.0)

Source: Whang (1980a, 147).

Those leaders who said they were not very satisfied or unsatisfied numbered 18 persons (28%). The implication of the table contrasts sharply with the positive observation of the people regarding leaders' motivation. In order to provide supplementary information on the satisfaction level of leaders, local government officials were asked about their opinions on the morale and working spirit of the Saemaul leaders with whom they used to work together on Saemaul projects. About 26% answered positively and 42% took a neutral position regarding Saemaul leaders' morale as shown in Table 5-26. This almost coincided with the self-perceived satisfaction level of the leaders.

It is generally known that the social and economic constraints of the rural villages in which Saemaul leaders work have put these

Table 5-26. Morale and Working Spirit of Saemaul Leaders: Opinions of Local Officials

Unit: person (%)

Level of Morale	Total
Very high	11 (3.8)
High	64 (22.2)
Neutral	121 (42.0)
Low	71 (24.7)
Very low	20 (6.9)
No response	1 (0.4)
Total	288 (100.0)

Source: Whang (1980a, 148).

leaders politically and socially in more difficult positions than the leaders of public organizations. Despite such difficulties, the level of satisfaction and morale of Saemaul leaders with respect to their work appears to be very high. This is probably because their efforts have brought about certain results that have been widely recognized both subjectively and objectively. This topic will be further discussed with regard to the social recognition of Saemaul leaders.

E. Social Recognition of Saemaul Leaders

One contributing factor to fostering rural leadership has been the intensive concern and recognition of Saemaul leaders on the part of the top political leadership.

The President's interest and concern with the Saemaul Undong are expressed at the Monthly Meeting for the National Economic Report drawn up by his economic ministers. This meeting has played an important monitoring role, especially since June of 1972. For each meeting, two outstanding Saemaul leaders of model villages of the month are invited to present their success cases to the meeting of economic ministers which is presided over by the president himself. After the session the two leaders are awarded with medals and funds and share opinions on rural problems at a luncheon meeting with the president. Regular reporting of these monthly events in the newspapers and on T.V. has greatly contributed to enhancing the social recognition of Saemaul leaders in general. In addition, it has also helped to foster rural leadership.

Recognition of the Saemaul leaders by the president and his personal interest in the movement have greatly influenced local government. Various medals, awards and prizes have been awarded to Saemaul leaders since the Citation Law was revised in 1973. This has subsequently influenced the general evaluation of the public in recognizing Saemaul leaders. It became an important turning point for the tradition-bound, conservative and government-respecting rural people to change their attitude toward Saemaul leaders.

There are many kinds of awards for individual leaders, including orders, medals, Saemaul citations, and other citations by the President, Prime Minister, Governor, County Chief, etc. Of the 63 interviewed leaders, 27 (43%) had been awarded citations while 36 (57%) have had none. If we take into consideration that many of them were incumbent leaders with less than one year's service, the percentage appears rather high. Basically this system aims at encouraging Saemaul leaders toward better performance in the Saemaul Undong.

The Government has also taken various measures to build up a conducive mood for the role performance of village leadership. For example, the Saemaul leader's certificate (I.D. card), was introduced which entitles leaders to various privileges including priority in meeting governors, priority in borrowing farming funds from banks, discounts in bus and train fares, scholarships for their children and preferential employment for their children by public organizations. Through such government efforts Saemaul leaders have been encouraged to exert self-sacrificing devotion to their jobs.

Social recognition of the Saemaul leaders has been fostered not only through the President's personal interest but also through the Saemaul training program in which Saemaul leaders were put together with both powerful elite in the society and senior government officials. Table 5-27 shows the degree of social recognition of Saemaul leaders rated by rural people.

The rural people in the 36 Saemaul villages were requested to answer the question "What is your neighbors' opinion about the position of Saemaul leader?" About 47% of them responded that "It's a very rewarding job" while 30% said "It's worth trying

Table 5-27. Social Recognition of Saemaul Leadership

Unit: person (%)

Responses	Common Villages	Outstanding Villages	Total
Very rewarding job	280(48.0)	417(45.6)	697(46.6)
Worth trying once	168(28.9)	277(30.3)	445(29.7)
Cannot tell	64(11.0)	106(11.6)	170(11.4)
Nothing so attractive	54(9.3)	94(10.3)	148(9.9)
Not worth trying	13(2.2)	17(1.9)	30(2.0)
No response	4(0.6)	3(0.3)	7(0.4)
Total	583(100.0)	914(100.0)	1,497(100.0)

Source: Whang (1980a, 150).

once." The people in common villages and outstanding villages showed little difference in responses to this question. The social recognition of leaders' position on the part of the rural people seemed rather high.

F. Personal Character Traits of Saemaul Leaders

In leadership theories, personal character is considered an important aspect worth analysing. The personal traits of Saemaul leaders are bound to have some impact on the organization and implementation of Saemaul projects as the leaders have all formerly worked in semi-primary groups with fellow farmers whose educational level is low.

For an objective analysis of the dominant personal traits of village leadership, information was collected from both evaluations by leaders of themselves and observations by the rural people. As shown in Table 5-28, about 42% of 1,497 interviewed people thought that the Saemaul leaders were sincere, 16% said they were determined and 10% said that Saemaul leaders were persuasive. According to the leaders' own judgement, sincerity (35%), responsibility (22%) and determiniation (14%) were the most noted personal traits.

There was a difference between leaders and the people as to what was the next important trait. Saemaul leaders rated patience or tenacity as the fourth important trait (13%) in performing their leadership role while rural people rated persuasion as fourth in importance (10%). This difference may be attributable, how-

Table 5-28. **Personal Character Traits of Saemaul Leaders**

Unit: person (%)

Traits	People	Leaders
Sincere	630(42.1)	22(34.9)
Determined	240(16.1)	9(14.3)
Persuasive	150(10.0)	2(3.2)
Responsible	287(19.2)	14(22.2)
Good leader	103(6.9)	3(4.8)
Tenacious, patient	54(3.6)	8(12.7)
No response	33(2.2)	5(7.9)
Total	1,497(100.0)	63(100.0)

Source: Whang (1980a, 151).

ever, to the fact that in the real process of work performance, a Saemaul leader might have conceived of his own arduous and repetitive effort to persuade the less-educated, more conservative fellow farmers as part of his personality. And similarly, rural people might have conceived on the basis of observing such efforts on the part of Saemaul leaders that persuasiveness is an essential trait of the leaders personality. In any case, it seems clear that the most important traits for successful Saemaul leadership include sincerity, responsibility, determination and the capacity to persuade others.

5. Summary

In this chapter, the socio-economic background of Saemaul leaders has been analyzed with a view to discovering what kind of persons were chosen Saemaul leaders in the Korean rural communities. The important roles performed by the leaders as well as their working relationships with village people, village chiefs or local government officials have also been analyzed in order to evaluate their relevancy to the success of Saemaul projects. In this connection, their behavioral patterns and motivational level were also analyzed.

What has been found is that the Saemaul Undong has made contributions to the identification and fostering of change agents. Saemaul leaders were found to be those who have lived in their own villages since their grandparents' generation; they are comparatively well-to-do, and are better educated than their village members; and have worked in relatively modern organizations before; their social mobility is higher than that of other village members; they have more experience with the dynamics of modernity, are more change-oriented and are highly motivated to make their villages better living communities. Among the general populace, there was found to be a growing tendency to recognize the efforts of the leaders and their achievements in society. In terms of performance, Saemaul leaders tended to carry out development projects in a democratic manner and maintain a smooth cooperative relationship with the village head. Saemaul leaders also performed roles as project planners, executors, educators and coordinatiors.

It may be concluded then that the Saemaul Undong has significantly contributed to leadership development at the village level so as to enable rural villages to build up enough momentum for self-reliant development in the future. Therefore, the development oriented role performance, particiatory attitudes and high level of motivation of the Saemaul leaders should be cultivated for further development in the rural sector.

Chapter 6

MODE OF PEOPLE'S PARTICIPATION AND ROLE OF WOMEN IN THE SAEMAUL UNDONG

Extensive participation of rural people in the rural development process is considered a key factor for its success. Hence, participation has become a major concern of social scientists, planners and practitioners. For both pragmatic and instrumental reasons, planners and policy makers advocate that greater participation on the part of rural people is necessary for integrated development in rural areas. To what extent did the rural people participate in the Saemaul Undong? What was the predominant mode of participation? What roles, in this connection, did rural women play at the village level in the implementation of Saemaul Undong, and through what organizational mechanism?

1. Extent of People's Participation

As already mentioned in Chapter 3, the number of participating rural villages in the Saemaul Undong has been approximately 35 thousand villages every year throughout the period of 1971–78, meaning that most rural villages in Korea have organized the Saemaul Undong, either large or small in scale, for their development. The number of participants in the rural Saemaul Undong alone has also increased greatly, from 72 million man-days in 1971 to 1,336 million man-days in 1978. Thus the number of participants per rural village has increased from 216 man-days to 5,274 man-days during the period of 1971-78 (Table 3-1). Considering that the rural Saemaul Undong was initially undertaken during the off-farming season, usually from December to late April, the number of participants in the rural villages seems to be quite large.

Widespread participation is evidence in terms of the people's contributions to the Saemaul Undong including labor, cash, land and other materials. According to Table 3-7, this contribution has increased more than 20 times during the period 1971-78 while the government contribution increased only about 12 times. The table also indicates that the gross amount of that investment during 1971 was two times that of the government's. As such the proportion between these two sources of investment in 1978 has increased to 33 times. Consequently, the people's contribution has become the major source of funding for the Saemaul Undong. This implies that the people's participation has become more extensive than it was earlier.

It is also interesting to note in Table 6-1 that the major part (77%) of the people's contribution during 1972 was in the form of labor but this proportion lessened through a process of cash substitution, a process which took place so rapidly that by the mid-1970's cash had become the major source of people's contribution. This fact implies that the people's commitment as well as their concrete contributions to self-help development projects grew as their confidence in the Saemaul Undong increased.

2. Factors Affecting People's Participation

The question then arises: what are factors which have fostered this extensive participation in rural development activities? Under what conditions and through what mechanisms did rural people voluntarily and positively participate in the Saemaul Undong? What is the mode of their participation? Participation

Table 6-1. People's Contribution to the Saemaul Undong

Unit: million won

Year*	Total	Cash	Labor	Materials	Land
1972	27,348	—	21,116	5,238	994
	(100.0)		(77.2)	(19.2)	(3.6)
1974	98,738	32,622	54,139	10,089	1,888
	(100.0)	(33.1)	(54.8)	(10.2)	(1.9)
1975	169,554	94,261	63,876	8,646	2,771
	(100.0)	(55.6)	(37.6)	(5.1)	(1.6)
1976	227,449	138,814	78,197	12,553	2,885
	(100.0)	(58.8)	(34.4)	(5.5)	(1.3)
1977	325,033	188,376	96,268	33,888	6,501
	(100.0)	(58.0)	(29.6)	(10.4)	(2.0)
1978	487,835	306,034	102,437	42,803	36,561
	(100.0)	(62.7)	(21.0)	(8.8)	(7.5)

*data for 1971 and 1973 are not available.
Source: Ministry of Home Affairs, *Saemaul Undong: From Its Inception until Today*, respectively 1973, 1975, 1977, and 1978.

is an action process undertaken by individuals and/or groups to reflect their own interests or to contribute their energies and resources to the institutions (and systems) which govern their lives. Participation has two different means of initiation: top-to-down and bottom-up (Dams 1980). Therefore, at the individual level, participation involves both leadership commitment from the top and people's motivation from the bottom. In the same vein, voluntary participation from the bottom and planned mobilization from the top are a source of complexity with respect to people's participation at the group level. In other words, a genuine sense of people's participation is often absent in the rural sector in most developing countries. People's participation is rather a composite phenomenon involving *individual motivation* to positively participate in the governing system, *leadership commitment* which adequately responds to the people's challenge and *government mobilization* of both human and material resources for rural development and change.

As for its role in mobilizing resources, the participation of rural people in the Saemaul Undong generally served to stimulate their already enhanced motivation which was initially evoked through regular attendance at intensive training programs. Indeed the Saemaul Training Program aims mainly at motivating rural leaders and people toward trying to achieve better lives and positive participation in community activities. And that is why a series of case studies, success stories and group discussions was organized in the training program for augmenting the future images, hopes, expectations, self-confidence and self-awareness of Saemaul leaders. It is generally agreed that the higher the people's educational level, the greater the participation of the people. So far, the rural people of Korea have been motivated by the expansion of general education, rigorous implementation of Saemaul training programs (Chapter 10) and extensive programs for public information, education and communication with respect to the Saemaul Undong. Indeed, public awareness of the Saemaul Undong has improved greatly through the mass media. The ideas and program activities of the Saemaul Undong have also been reflected in educational programs at both primary and secondary schools for better understanding of the movement.

Another important factor in promoting participation has been the firm commitment of leadership at all levels to the success of Saemaul Undong. There is no need to reiterate here the role of political leadership's commitment to the process of overall rural transformation (Chapter 4). It was found in the analysis of the Saemaul Undong during 1970–1971 that the role of village leadership is a key factor in eliciting the people's participation (Whang 1980a, 114). In short, the study found that the more able was the village leadership, the greater was the participation of the village people and *ergo* the more successful was the implementation of the Saemaul projects. In fact, this finding became the basis for intensifying the Saemaul Leadership Training Program after 1972.

According to a mailing survey of 5,372 rural farmers, their participation in the Saemaul Undong was motivated by two major forces: (a) their own village's development and honor, and (b) to make their own villages better than the neighboring one with which they were competing (Choe 1978b, 36). This finding implies that the strong sense of identity and solidarity among village members became a major motivational force for massive participation. Indeed, it has been widespread among village people that cooperation overshadowed individualism.

Extensive participation on the part of rural people in development programs such as the Saemaul Undong is realized partly through mobilization by the government. The extent of government mobilization of people and other material resources depends on the political system. Under the mobilization system of a country like Soviet Russia, the people's participation in the genuine sense tends to be minimal, while under the reconciliation system, like those found in the western countries, participation is rather encouraged. The mobilization system of Soviet politics is characterized by the following: (a) "hierarchical authority" as a source of political legitimacy, (b) loyalty in the form of "total allegiance," (c) "tactical flexibility" for decisional autonomy, (d) "unitarism" prevailing in the distribution of authority, and (e) "ideological specialization." On the contrary, "the reconciliation system is characterized by (a) pyramidal authority, (b) multiple loyalties, (c) necessity for compromise, (d) pluralism in distributing authority, and (e) ideological diffuseness" (Apter 1963, 143–145). Nevertheless, most developing countries belong to a third category, namely that of "modernizing autocracy." This system is characterized by "hierachical authority, exclusivism, strategic flexibility, unitarism, and neo-traditionalism" (Apter 1963, 147).

Therefore, in developing countries, "mass participation has been essentially a new form of mass response to elite manipulation," although "even such limited participation has a role to play in nation-building" (Pye 1965, 8–9).

In the early stage of the Saemaul Undong, the people's participation was not wholly voluntary. Rather it was partly mobilized and stimulated by the government. For the sake of analysis, one may identify three broad types of participation, namely (1) *voluntary participation*, arising from the people's own initiatives, (2) *induced participation*, which is stimulated by government or elite and incorporated with incentive systems, and (3) *forced participation*, or total mobilization by the government. Voluntary participation of a people is highly correlated with that people's level of education and training. Forced participation is achieved through the exercise of authority in a hierarchically organized society. In between these two patterns is induced participation, a mixed scanning in which psychological and material incentives are offered to the people. The pattern of people's participation in the Saemaul Undong primarily belongs to the category of induced participation. To wit, the government provided material assistance in the form of cement and steel to each rural village at the inception of the Saemaul Undong and, subsequently, the participation of rural people took the form of program responses to this inducement. The inducement may indeed be viewed as a challenge to the previously static villages. The government offer created an identity crisis, participation crisis, integration crisis, leadership crisis, and management crisis all at once for the village members. The sense of crisis was demonstrated by the fact that it took some 2–3 weeks for villagers to reach a consensus with regard to what projects should be undertaken with the donated cement and steel. This painful and protracted process of decision-making in the village served subsequently, however, to induce wider participation among the village members. Since then the village general assembly has been a major mechanism for people's participation, decision-making, and consensus building with respect to major issues related to their community lives.

It is interesting to note in light of this background that participation is defined as "a redistribution of power that enables the have-not citizens presently excluded from the political and economic processes to be deliberately included in the future. It is the strategy by which the have-nots join in determining how information is shared, goals and policies are set, tax resources are allocated, programs are operated and benefits . . . are parceled out. In short, it is the means by which they can induce significant social reforms which enables them to share in the benefit of affluent society" (Arnstein 1971, 70). Therefore, the participation of rural dwellers in the Saemaul Undong at the initial stage helped them to understand the true meaning of their participation at the decision-making stage and, later on, their voluntary commitment at the implementation stage.

In addition to the government donation of material assistance, which has in fact continued for the last ten years, a variety of social and economic incentives were provided by the government.

The principle that "the better village should receive the first support" stimulated competition between neighboring villages to achieve better performance in implementing the Saemaul projects and this in turn induced greater participation. A series of citations and especially the Presidential Awards served as incentives, both social and economic, to encourage people's participation (Chapter 4).

It goes without saying that the organizational channels provided for Saemaul leaders greatly encouraged the participation of village leadership in the decision-making processes both at the township and the county levels. Indeed, a few Saemaul leaders worked as members with the Saemaul Consultation Committee at both township and county levels. It is also interesting to note that the Saemaul leaders were given the privilege to freely meet with the county-chief or governor if they wanted to do so. These measures obviously encouraged Saemaul leaders to positively participate in the decision-making, implementation and evaluation processes of the Saemaul Undong.

3. Socio-economic Prerequisites for People's Participation

The pattern of people's participation in the Saemaul Undong, which belongs to the category of induced participation, seems to be effective in the Korean context. It was impossible to expect voluntary participation on the part of rural people in view of the initially low motivational level as well as their lack of such experience. Forced participation would have been helpful only in emergency cases and then, only for short periods of time. Under any other circumstances, of course, force is ineffective for developmental activities since it decreases people's motivation and creativity. The reason that induced participation was effective in Korea is related to certain institutional infrastructures and reforms which took place in the 1950's and 1960's before the Saemaul Undong was launched.

The essential prerequisites for the effective participation of rural people in the Saemaul Undong were as follows: (a) relatively equal access to land ownership among rural farmers through the land reform of 1950-53; (b) equal opportunities in education, offered to the people since the Liberation from the Japanese colonial rule; and (c) training in organization and leadership through the military service of rural youngsters. Indeed the sense of equal distribution of benefits among peers is an important basis for any participation. Communication skills, improved through general education, have also elicited higher participation.

A. Equity in Land Ownership

The promulgation of the Land Reform Act of 1950 provided the Korean government with the legal basis to purchase all the portion of a land owner's farm land in excess of three hectares, and distribute it to farmers who had cultivated those particular pieces of land as tenants. Previously, the latter consisted of landless farm laborers and small farmers who did not have enough land to prosper in spite of their ability and willingness to farm. According to the land reform survey of 1949, approximately 601 thousand hectares (or 29 per cent of the total farm land) was subject to redistribution by the government to small farmers and landless farm laborers. Out of this, 470 thousand hectares (79% of the target) were redistributed by government during 1949-52. As a consequence, 953 thousand households (95% of the planned 1,022 thousand households) obtained farm land during this period. The land reform was originally scheduled to be completed by 1954. However, it was not actually completed until 1964, due to the financial burden imposed on the government by the Korean War (Lee SW 1980, 331-355).

The successful implementation of the land reform brought about significant changes in the economic as well as the social aspect of rural communities. The three-hectare ceiling on land ownership per farm household helped to miniaturize farm size as shown in Table 6-2, and in so doing helped the delay of agricultural modernization in terms of productivity and mechanization. In fact, the average size of land owned per farm household in Korea has remained almost at the same level of 0.9–1.0 hectare for the last thirty years. In other words, the land reform made most Korean farmers remain primarily at the subsistence level as far as the economic benefits of farm size are concerned.

Table 6–2. Number of Farm Households by Size of Land Ownership

Unit: thousand (%)

	1965	1970	1975	1979
Total No. of Farm Households (1)	2,507	2,483	2,379	2,162
Landless Farmers (2)	—	72	94	82
Farm Household (1–2)	2,507(100)	2,411(100)	2,285(100)	2,080(100)
0–0.5 ha	901(36)	788(33)	710(31)	644(31)
0.5–1 ha	794(32)	824(34)	809(35)	764(37)
1–2 ha	643(26)	639(27)	618(27)	555(27)
2–3 ha	140(6)	123(5)	112(5)	90(4)
3 ha & over	29(1)	37(2)	36(2)	27(1)
Average Size of Land Ownership	0.9 ha	0.93 ha	0.94 ha	1.0 ha

Source: Ministry of Agriculture & Fisheries, *Nongjung Soochup* (Handbook of Agricultural Administration), 1980, pp. 62–63.

The land reform also increased the financial burden on small farmers, since they were obliged to pay 30 per cent of their average annual yield for five years thereafter as the price for the land redistributed by the government. Because the law prohibited the transfer of redistributed land for five years until these installments were paid, the farmers' livelihoods were tied to the small pieces of land. Therefore, the inflexibility of land transfer indirectly made farmers socially less mobile (Pak 1966, 93–96).

In spite of such economic restraints resulting from the land reform, the reform provided more or less equal access to production assets and, therefore, motivated farmers to work hard (Singer and Baster 1980, 3–5). The land reform also promoted egalitarianism in rural communities in terms of land ownership and thus facilitated the disappearance of class consciousness between landlords and tenants. Nevertheless, it should be noted that it took almost one generation following the land reform to effectively bring about the perceptual change on the part of farmers toward real cooperation with respect to the cooperation necessary for implementation of the Saemaul Undong. The formation of favorable attitudes of farmers toward cooperation was realized only after they began to perceive that the differences in their land ownership and living standards were insignificant and also they were all equally suffering from poverty in comparison to the prosperous urban people (Whang 1980a, 92-96). Thus, the land reform provided the social and psychological precondition necessary for cooperation among farmers and that in turn prepared the way for the rural innovation that was later ignited by the Saemaul Undong. It should be noted that the redistribution of productive assets in the rural sector by the government was inspired by the "ideology of equal opportunity" (Lee HB 1968, 51-52) and provided the psychological base for fraternity among all Korean farmers, especially those of the younger generation.

B. Massive Educationl Drive

After the Liberation from Japanese Colonial Rule in 1945, the ideology of equal opportunity became the prime mover for introducing a massive educational drive in Korean society. This began in 1948 in the form of free and compulsory education at the primary school level. Among the manifold changes manifested in the rural sector, none was more widespread or far-reaching than the education of rural youngsters. "The reason the indigenous initiative for modernization found its first thrust in the field of education in the Korean society is explained by two factors: one is the cultural tradition and the other is the patterns of the nationalist movement prior to the Liberation" (Lee HB 1968, 47). The introduction of free and compulsory elementary education was accompanied by a vast expansion of the secondary school system and, later, by a spectacular increase in higher education. The immensity of the social input into education since the Liberation is reflected in the sheer magnitude of the school population. As shown in Table 6-3, it increased from 1.5 million in 1945 to 8.0 million in 1970 when the Saemaul Undong was initiated. As a share of the total population, the school population rose from 9% to 26% during the same period.

The spread of education was expedited by the existence of *Hangul*, the indigenous alphabet invented in the middle of the fifteenth century by King Sejong. The full potential of *Hangul*

Table 6-3. Number of Enrolled Students

Unit: thousand

School	1945	1955	1965	1970	1975	1979
Elementary	1,382	2,959	4,941	5,749	5,599	5,640
Secondary	85	748	1,276	2,060	3,369	4,094
Higher	8	87	135	177	236	512
Sub-total(a)	1,475	3,794	6,352	7,986	9,204	10,256
Total Population(b)	16,000	21,500	28,700	30,900	34,700	37,600
(a)/(b) %	9	18	22.1	25.9	26.5	27.5

Source: Adopted from Ministry of Education, *Annual Report of Education*, (in respective years) and Economic Planning Board, *Statistical Yearbook*, (in respective years).

was never exploited until after the Liberation due to the social and political repression imposed during the period of colonial rule. The educational drive as such brought a great increase in the gross number of literate people as well as an increase in their percentage of the total population in the rural sector. Table 6-5 displays the remarkable change in the literacy rate among persons 5 years old and over, both throughout the whole country and in the rural sector. Specifically, out of all the persons 5 years old and over in the rural sector, 46 percent had never attended any regular educational institution at any level in 1960. However that figure dropped drastically to 26% and 20% respectively in 1970 and 1975, when the Saemaul Undong was active. The illiteracy rate, though based on inconsistent data, also suggests a significant improvement in the educational level of the rural population during the same period.

The improvement in educational level as well as the increase in the number of literate people in the rural sector have provided the motivation for rural farmers to become active participants in community decision-making. The impact of the educational drive has been so significant that it has facilitated communication between government officials and village people as well as between development field workers and rural farmers involved in Saemaul projects. Indeed, ease of communication among farmers and between farmers and government field workers and officials was a prerequisite for the efficient dissemination of rural in-

Table 6-4. Rate of School Attendance and Illiteracy

Unit: thousand

	1960	1966	1970	1975
Persons 5 years	19,672	23,710	26,261	19,540
old & over (a)	(14,066)[1]	(15,499)	(15,278)	(15,264)
Never	7,765	6,033	5,125	4,215
attending (b)	(6,452)	(4,932)	(4,003)	(3,082)
(b)/(a) %	39.5	25.4	19.5	14.3
	(45.9)	(31.8)	(26.2)	(20.2)
Illiterate (c)	4,454[2]	2,605	2,299	n.a.
	(n.a.)	(2,105)	(1,830)	
(c)/(a) %	22.6[2]	11.0	8.8	n.a.
	(n.a.)	(13.6)	(12.0)	

[1] The numbers in the parentheses indicate corresponding figures in the rural sector.
[2] Indicating the number of persons 10 years old and over in 1960. Therefore, this percentage is only an approximate figure. "Illiterate" means those who can not read and write the Korean alphabet, *Hangul*.
Source: Economic Planning Board, *Population and Housing Census Report* (for the respective years)

novations such as the introduction of high-yielding varieties of rice in Korea. Therefore, the impact of expanded education on the rural society which began in the 1950–1960's helps to explain why rural development took place so dramatically in the 1970's as demonstrated by the success of the Saemaul Undong (Whang 1980a, 199–200).

C. Training in Leadership and Organization through Military Service*

The catastrophic impact of the Korean War of 1950–53 on social institutions was immense. Life, physical and social, was never the same in both urban and rural areas. An immediate by-product of the war was widespread social disintegration reflected in the large number of wandering refugees estimated at about 5.5 million during 1951–53. The hold of the family became loosened drastically through the massive disruptions in human ecology brought on by the resettling of wartime refugees.

Another immediate impact of the war on Korean society

---

*An analogy in the rural context is made from Lee H.B. (1968, 54–60).

was the physical damage to buildings, industries, road, bridges and equipment. The value of this damage in terms of US currency was approximately $3 billion, nearly four times the value of the annual GNP of the Korean economy before the war. The combined impact of human and physical damage was reflected in a sharp reduction in production, both agricultural and industrial.

Nevertheless, the impact of the Korean War may be viewed as facilitating national modernization years later. For example, one positive aspect of the family disintegration caused by the war was the engendering of social marginals, whose newly acquired "empathy" (Lerner 1958, 47–52) would take on many different manifestations in the course of subsequent development.

The war brought millions of refugees from North Korea and also left hundreds of thousands of urban as well as rural dwellers looking for refuge in provincial towns and other rural communities. This geographical mobility forced on farmers by the war on the one hand left them with lingering psychological anxiety but on the other hand, made them positively "marginal" with respect to urban societies and other regions. The impact caused by the influx of urban refugees and the military service of rural youngsters also exposed farmers to sources of exogenous change in rural villages.

Another direct consequence of the war was the enormous expansion of the Korean armed forces. "An army without a single light tank" was transformed through sixfold expansion into an army with approximately 600 thousand men equipped with modern weapons within the space of five years. This had an important effect on "socialization at a rapid tempo of millions of young men who were mostly from the rural communities. Recruitment in the army exposed them to a sense of national and ideological identity (anti-communism and democracy) together with common symbols such as letters, numbers, signals and modern techniques in handling weapons and vehicles. All these new experiences gave them empathy—that is, interested perception of other people, other places, other ideas and techniques" (Lee HB 1968, 60).

The military service was beneficial to the social education of rural people and to some extent to the development of village leadership years later, since those who had served were experienced in efficient modern organization, in target-oriented managerial system, and in modern science and technology. This in fact promoted "social mobilization" (Deutsch 1961, 498–505) in rural communities. It was found in a recent survey that all but eleven Saemaul leaders (who were over 50 years old) had served in the army as sergeants or junior officers (Chapter 5). As most farmers had also served in the army as part of their national duty, their decision-making patterns, organizing methods, communication skills, interaction patterns, and mode of participation in project implementation under the village leadership were inevitably adopted from the military sub-culture. The basic technical training of farmers and their accessibility to modernity through military service have indeed influenced not only farmers' perception and attitude toward cooperation, work ethics, participation and rural innovations, but also indirectly contributed to investment in the basic socio-cultural infrastructure of rural villages so necessary for their take-off.

4. Role of Women in Rural Change

A. *Extent of Women's Participation*

In addition to the analysis of people's participation in general, it is valuable to look into some particular aspects of the issue of women's participation and their role in the rural development of Korea. It is generally accepted that the more modernized a country, the more important the status and role of women is in its society. To what extent did Korean women participate in the Saemaul Undong and what roles did they play in the rural development process? In view of the historical and cultural context of women's status in Korea, organizational aspects should be a prime concern in any analysis of women's participation. In Korea's past, the woman's role was perceived as strictly limited to housekeeping affairs. Women were treated rather as limited personalities and prohibited from participating in any public or social activities. Even within the family major decisions were beyond the scope of women's involvement.

Although there was an official attempt to organize village

women in the national network of women's clubs after the Liberation in 1945, its objective was limited mainly to teaching the Korean language to women over the age of 18 who had lost the opportunity to learn it due to the Japanese acculturalization policy during the colonial period 1910–1945. Nevertheless, significant female participation in rural developmental activities was realized only after the 1960's. Initially, women in the rural sector participated in village bank programs, nonformal education programs, and the agricultural extension program.

Later, however, a more dynamic reorganization of women was introduced by the Planned Parenthood Federation of Korea in connection with family planning information, education and communication activities in the form of a "mother's club" in each village. The club was organized to openly discuss family planning ideas and methods and was limited to a membership of 12 women. The qualifications for membership were the ability to read and write, affiliation with other group activities and a certain age level (between 20 and 45). Therefore, club members tended to be older, more educated, and have a higher status than average women in rural villages, and thus were more influential in village life (Kim, Ross, et al. 1972, 93–94). In 1968 approximately 17 thousand mother's clubs were organized, some of which were not so active. The specific goal of the club was to disseminate family planning ideas in the rural areas "by creating a local, voluntary organization of women which would:

(a) encourage family planning practice by example and by giving social and emotional support to acceptors;
(b) aid over-burdened family planning field workers in recruiting new acceptors and supplying contraceptives (pills and condoms);
(c) aid in the introduction of a new method (the pill) to the family planning program and help each other in recalling the dates of pill taking; and
(d) encourage participation of women in community development activities" (Chung KK 1980, 2–3).

During the 1970's there was a proliferation of many different women's organizations in villages by allowing multiple overlapping memberships. However in the mid-1970's the government tried to integrate different groups into Saemaul Women's Associations in order to eliminate unnecessary overlap and conflicts among women's organizations. Hence the mother's club which was originally organized for dissemination of the family planning program was later integrated into the Saemaul Undong framework. In this case, the pattern of women's involvement seemed to be different in the sense that all women ages 18–60 living in rural villages were obliged to be members of women's association, regardless of their own desires. Nevertheless, it should be noted that the leadership of the Saemaul Women's Association came mostly from those who actively worked with mother's clubs before its integration. Presently, each association has five types of activities. These include education, saving, family planning, environmental improvement and income increase.

As the Saemaul Undong has been active not only in the rural areas but also in cities, the number of Saemaul Women's Associations has increased from 9,472 in 1971 to 84,693 in 1980 as shown in Table 6-5. Simultaneously, the number of memberships has also increased up to 2.9 million in 1980. The number of associations in the rural sector alone increased from 35,031 in 1972 to 64,902 in 1980. Such figures indicate that not only is every natural village covered but that many rural towns have

Table 6-5. Expansion of Saemaul Women's Associations

Year	No. of Women's Association (each)	No. of Members (1,000)
Until 1970	2,572	82
1971	9,472	312
1972	28,313	1,633
1973	36,320	1,694
1974	41,672	2,090
1975	43,210	2,161
1976	45,545	2,254
1977	60,352	2,424
1978	68,194	2,552
1979	80,115	2,678
1980	84,693	2,950

Source: Ministry of Home Affairs, *Ten Year History of Saemaul Undong*, Vol. II, 1980, p. 74.

their own women's associations.

In order to promote women's participation in the Saemaul Undong, the government added the women leaders' training program in 1973 as an integral part of the Saemaul leaders' training program operated by the Saemaul Leaders Training Institute (SLTI) in Suwon since 1972. The Suwon Institute and 14 other central level institutions offer a one-week program, while provincial and local institutions provide 1–3 day training. As of June 1980, approximately 9 thousand women leaders had been trained at SLTI in Suwon, approximately 11 thousand women at other central institutions, and 13 thousand women at local institutions (Tinker & Cho 1980, 32). Subsequently, this training of women leaders has made a positive impact on promoting women's roles in introducing significant changes in rural communities in several ways. Specifically, the training has become a vehicle by which women leaders learned (a) certain skills necessary for communicating with their club members, (b) ideas for better home business, and (c) family planning. Also as a result of the formal as well as informal training, women leaders have become more confident in their role performance, more motivated to participate in the campaign for village improvement and more skillful in exercising leadership.

Aside from organization and training, another important factor which has helped to promote greater women's participation is their accessibility to the decision-making channel. Because an extensive role of women was required for the implementation of Saemaul projects at the village level, both men and women members of the village communities were obliged to participate in the village general assembly in order to discuss major issues related to community life and development. In each village, the Saemaul leadership has consisted of both male and female leaders who work closely throughout the process of Saemaul project management. Indeed, the cooperation and participation of women in the implementation of village development projects was of essential importance for their success. Moreover, it is interesting to note that the influence and contribution of women has increased as the Saemaul Undong has become more extensive and effective.

B. Actvities of Saemaul Women's Association

What roles then did rural women play in the Saemaul Undong? There have been many activities carried out by the Saemaul Women's Associations. One of the most significant activities has been (a) the monthly meeting held regularly at the village level and (b) the leaders' meeting at the township level. All important decisions are made and performances reviewed at these meetings. In some cases, education on various topics has also been provided by more experienced leaders or change agents. Otherwise the participants contribute their own ideas in both reviewing past activities and building future goals. Through those regular meetings, there has emerged a formal and informal leadership and communication network in the rural communities which has enhanced a strong sense of collective spirit (Chung KK 1980, 4–5).

At the initial stage of the Saemaul Undong rural women were more excited and enthusiastic than the men. As one writer has noted, "Rural housewives seemed to know better than their husbands the real causes of the poverty of their families: namely, the laziness and drinking habits of their husbands who used to blame their poverty on the poor policies of government and/or on the failure of their ancestors. The members of Saemaul Women's Association initiated a campaign for burning up the cards with which their husbands gambled during the off-season. The women's associations also organized a campaign for closing down the liquor stores within their villages where their husbands used to drink and thus add more hardship to their pains of poverty-stricken housekeeping. The habits of gambling and presence of drunkards in villages have thus been significantly reduced through the Saemaul Undong" (Park JH 1980, 13–14).

In addition to such constructive campaigns, there are many other positive projects which were undertaken by Saemaul Women's Associations in support of the basic ideas of the Saemaul Undong. These include:

(a) The rice savings project, a program which was organized and successfully implemented by Saemaul Women's Association in every village. The idea of the project was for each housewife to save a scoop of rice at every meal before cooking. This rice was converted into cash and deposited collectively into credit unions or agricultural cooperatives. The savings project became a source of operating funds for Saemaul Women's Association (Park JH 1980, 15; and Brandt 1977, 121–122).

(b) A mother's bank was also organized as a modified form of the rice savings project, since the original formula of the rice savings lost popularity in all but a few villages due to inconvenience in the latter stage. Each member would save a small amount of money to deposit in the bank. Additionally, a portion of the income earned by their cooperative labor was also deposited in the mother's bank. Through the mother's bank, they operated a small revolving credit union for the benefit of members. Some of the more successful villages have saved as much as three million won in this way (Tinker & Cho 1980, 37).

(c) Village co-op stores tended to become active through cooperation made by Association members. They purchase daily commodities from cities at wholesale price and sell them at a small profit to the village people, thereby earning an average monthly income ranging from ₩5,000 to ₩40,000 (or $70). There were 24,891 community stores as of 1979 all over the nation (Tinker & Cho 1980, 38).

(d) The village kitchen project was introduced by Saemaul Women's Association in order to save on cooking time especially during the busy farming season. This was done by collectively serving the village members. It also provided village women with opportunities to learn about how to improve cooking methods from a nutritional point of view. In 1979 there were about 6,000 communual kitchens operating in the rural sector. To date, most of villages have been satisfied with their operation (MOHA 1979, 79).

(e) Operation of daycare centers was another project organized by Saemaul Women's Associations. Although it was reported that approximately ten thousand daycare centers were operating in 1979 (MOHA 1979, 179), as yet there has been no analysis undertaken concerning their effectiveness. This project may be a new frontier for the Saemaul Women's Association in the future.

(f) Collection of waste and used goods such as empty bottles, papers, furniture and so forth was initiated for fund-raising purposes. Because Korean women are traditionally sensitive to saving pennies, it became a source of additional though modest savings. As such, the implications of this cooperative behavior have been rather significant in the context of rural development.

(g) The Saemaul Women's Associations have undertaken interesting development projects with the funds raised through the above projects. These include purchase of communal kitchen utensils, sponsoring of parties for elders in their villages, donation of funds for building piped water systems and community public baths, sponsoring group tours to large cities and sightseeing areas and purchasing of community properties.

C. Role of Women in Rural Change

The contributions of women to rural change is corroborated by yet another source of information, and that is the analysis of 12 success case stories written by women leaders (out of a total of 120 case studies) which have been published in the seven volumes of the Ministry of Home Affairs' Annual Report since 1973. In these stories, five points are reemphasized over and over again. They are as follows:

(a) Women played the role of initiators in the Saemaul Undong while the men followed on;

(b) The role of women leaders and cooperation of villagers were counted as prerequisites for the successful implementation of the Saemaul Undong. Also leadership attributes were described as confidence, stubbornness, unyielding strength and determination to make the villagers diligent and prosperous;

(c) Women finally overcame a most difficult cultural obstacle, paraphrased in the old proverb, "Hen's crying ruins the house;"

(d) In some cases, women's contribution made the Saemaul Undong in their villages successful without help from the men and thus no one was able to make a distinction between men's work and women's; and

(e) The prime motivation behind the women's participation was their desire to improve their environmental conditions and augment their family income (Tinker & Cho 1980, 40-42).

In brief, women in rural village played very significant roles in the process of rural development through loosely organized

associations and especially in:
- (a) facilitating communication of various innovative ideas,
- (b) adopting and initiating change in rural life,
- (c) implementing community development projects; and
- (d) immeasurably contributing toward women's equality through asserting their voices in the community affairs of formerly tradition-bound rural areas.

The contribution of women to the success of the Saemaul Undong is therefore given high credit. According to a recent interview survey of 1,497 farmers, 71 percent of them regarded the contribution of women as a positive one (Chapter 12, Table 12-24).

5. Implications of People's Participation for Rural Development

What impacts did the people's participation as such make on rural society? The extensive and positive participation of rural people in the Saemaul Undong at the village level has brought about significant changes in their rural communities, which have the following implications: (a) Participation has a "hands-on" training effect such that rural people discuss and solve their community problems together, determine their priorities, practice the dynamics of group decision-making and democracy, appreciate the value of collective action, and master the creed of self-help and diligence. Moreover, participation has helped to develop self-confidence among the farmers as well as a collective sense of power, capability and efficacy. By virtue of its immediate impact on the village environment, participation in the Saemaul Undong has enabled farmers to realize the benefits of concerted effort carried out in league with government officials. Thus, indirectly, it also lent credibility to the government.

(b) Participation is a potent force in effecting profound changes in individual behavior and attitudes via group dynamics. Through continued participation in the Saemaul Undong, the people's perceptions and attitudes have become more positive with regard to change in their physical environment, more cooperative toward government officials, more democratic toward collective decision-making, more achievement-motivated, more rational in their way of life, and more future-oriented with respect to both farming and their children (Chapter 12).

(c) Participation also helps the community to exert control and influence over its residents and institutions. Community people have, as a result, been able to mold their village into an action instrument for improving their living standard. The relationship between local officials and village people has therefore become both more harmonious and more mutually interdependent. The exploitative attitudes of bureaucrats, a holdover of the old days, have been transformed into a partners' attitude such that government officials have come to feel responsible for the successful implementation of Saemaul projects. Indeed, it has become vitually institutionalized that the promotion and transfer of local officials are tied up with achievement of the Saemaul projects (Chapter 4).

What are the lessons which can be learned from the Korean experience in the people's participation in rural development? Some of its implications are consistent with several points of the World Conference Report on Agrarian Reform and Rural Development (1979). As a basis for effective participation in the rural areas, governments should take positive measures in order to:

(a) encourage the establishment of self-reliant local organizations consisting of farmers and village people who are given positive and systematic support from governments;

(b) induce or promote active participation on the part of rural people throughout the entire process of rural development activities and projects from the stage of problem identification up to final evaluation in the project management cycle (Rondinelli 1976);

(c) mobilize support from local officials and resources to the maximum extent;

(d) mobilize energies and support of the urban social elite; and

(e) encourage extensive participation of women in rural change programs and promote their role in rural modernization.

PART III

ORGANIZATION, MANAGEMENT, AND TRAINING

Chapter 7

ORGANIZATION AND PLANNING OF THE SAEMAUL UNDONG

1. Major Tasks of the Saemaul Undong

Organization is viewed as a pattern of interaction among those who are involved in the action process for planning and implementing things to be done (Price 1968, 2; Parsons 1960, 17). Organizational character is determined by its goals and objectives, the nature of its tasks, the raw materials processed, those persons working for its goals, its social and physical environment and technologies utilized (Etzioni 1961; Thompson *et al.* 1959, 131–182 and 195–212).

The three major objectives of the Saemaul Undong are: (a) spiritual enlightenment of rural people so that they will embrace development values such as self-help, diligence, cooperation and participation; (b) fostering of village leadership and participatory organization; and (c) improvement in the physical and social environment of villages. The action agents involved in the Saemaul Undong are village leaders who play the role of change agents, village members who positively participate, local government officials, and top political leadership.

How are things organized to mobilize these action agents and get them actively involved in pursuit of these three major objectives? The major programs organized in accordance with the objectives are: (a) the nationwide campaign for spiritual enlightenment; (b) training of Saemaul leaders; and (c) planning and implementation of Saemaul projects. Spiritual enlightenment attempts to raise rural people's willingness and confidence in self-realization by promoting self-help, diligence and cooperation which provide the moral foundation for the introduction of rural innovation at the village level. The spirit of self-help makes rural people appreciate the importance of self in one's own life. It emphasizes the importance of rationality, individuality and responsibility and thereby encourages rural people to discard their fatalistic attitudes. The spirit of diligence engenders a sound "work ethic" which is necessary for social and economic development. The spirit of cooperation helps make rural people realize the importance of cooperative action in achieving those results which are in their common interest. In trying to meet commonly felt needs, cooperation is of singular importance in bringing about a synergetic and dynamic impact. In addition, it also shifts people's attitudes toward greater solidarity as well as toward national integrity. Spiritual enlightenment provides rural people with the psycho-cultural foundation for continued and voluntary social action in rural development. Ultimately by promoting self-help, cooperation and diligence and the transformation of conservative rural attitudes, the Saemaul Undong aims to upgrade the quality of rural life.

The stimulus for changing people's values and attitudes at the initial stage is provided by involving them in organizing and implementing development projects which allow them to reap the benefit of the values they have adopted. Development projects are carefully selected so as to immediately demonstrate tangible and visible results. This is because the observability of an innovation as it is perceived by members of a social system is positively related to its rate of adoption (Rogers 1971, 155–157). Accordingly, the Saemaul Undong bases its criteria for selecting development projects not upon the principle of economy but upon the principle of observability.

Leadership is one of the most important prerequisites for self-reliant rural development. Leadership development as part of the Saemaul Undong is organized for the promotion of participatory organization among the rural people and the fostering of village-based leadership (MOHA 1976, 273–281). The Saemaul Undong emphasizes the importance of fostering development agents in the rural sector for inducing, promoting and protecting developmental changes in rural communities. Saemaul leaders are identified and chosen from among villagers and offered a special training program which aims at equiping village leaders with effective leadership by making known their critical roles as change agents in rural areas.

Various types of leadership development institutions are organized for providing rural people with development agents who possess the traits and abilities expected of a good leader. The Saemaul Leaders Training Institute which opened at Suwon in 1972 is the main training institute at the central level. In addition, there are 14 other central level and 10 provincial level training institutions which provide Saemaul education and training patterned after the Suwon Institute. Furthermore, various types of informal training programs are provided at the village level. The Saemaul Leaders Training Institute plays a key role in reshaping the values and attitudes of rural people as well as social leaders and in making the social elite aware of rural problems so that they may contribute to national development through the Saemaul Undong.

The methods and subjects of the Saemaul training are quite different from those of formal education in many ways. Saemaul training attempts to motivate rural people to actively participate and to strengthen village leadership. The training is oriented not to theories and analysis but rather to practical action and empirical cases. The training places its emphasis not upon teaching but upon self-learning through analytic discussion of successful cases, group dynamics, field tours and so on. Training methods include not merely lecture style but action-oriented workshops. The Saemaul training does not emphasize sophisticated theories, instead it calls for steady and sincere practice and action. Most emphasis is given to empirical training for the mental and behavioral reform of trainees. All the trainees and trainers stay in the same dormitory during the training period. It is a rule that trainees are not supposed to communicate with the outside at all.

This training program has been offered to party leaders, members of congress, high civil servants, religious leaders, leaders of social organizations, managers of big business corporations, university professors, journalists and to other intellectual elite. It tends to make them support the ideas and strategies of the Saemaul Undong. Their active and positive involvement in the Saemaul Unding serves as a mechanism for the reinforcement of societal support for the Saemaul Undong, for social recognition of rural workers and village leaders as development agents and for building up a favorable climate toward the Saemaul Undong (Whang 1978b, 121).

Saemaul projects are action instruments for improving rural infrastructure and village economy. But the continued and vigorous implementation of Saemaul projects tends indirectly to bring about the following impact: (a) change in rural infrastructure and village economy; (b) promotion of particiatory organizations in the rural villages and fostering of community-based leadership; and (c) inculcation of developmental values and perceptions of rural people.

Participation in Saemaul projects has shown a tendency to inculcate perceptions, commitment and confidence in rural people which are conducive to self-reliant rural development. It also stimulates a sense of solidarity among the people at the village as well as at the national level. In addition, it provides rural people with the technical knowledge and capability to ma· age change-oriented projects for their own community development. At the same time it makes rural people realize the importance as well as benefits of cooperation in terms of tangible and visible results.

Saemaul projects are classified into categories of production infrastructure, income-generation, welfare and environment improvement and spiritual enlightenment. Production infrastructure projects include village environment improvement, farm road improvement, small river development, small-scale irrigation, rural electrification, fishing port improvement, small ship building, erosion control, oyster cultivation and so forth. Income generation projects include cooperative farming, off-season utilization projects, wage-distribution projects, soil preservation, support to selected villages, Saemaul factories, afforestation and so on. Welfare and environment improvement projects cover rural living environment improvement, development of isolated islands, land preservation, town environment improvement, port environment improvement, rural communication facilities, rural potable water supply facilities, mobile health clinic service, rural child care center and fishing village environment improvement. Spiritual enlightenment projects include Saemaul training, government officials' Saemaul training, study tours, publicity, scientific technology dissemination, university student service corps, nutrition improvement, rural youth activities, family planning, village library, rural credit and savings and so on.

2. Organizations in Support of the Saemaul Undong

These projects are identified and organized primarily by village people with their own initiative and sometimes with general guidance and assistance from the government. The planning of Saemaul projects at the village level involves mostly project identification by village members, simple design for project implementation, identification of the kinds and amounts of necessary inputs or resources, and the proper communication of project ideas to local officials in order to secure administrative support (Chapter 8). These activities and steps are supposed to be undertaken by village leaders, including village chiefs and Saemaul leaders, and village members in collaboration with local officials.

The Saemaul Undong as an integrated rural development scheme requires efficient planning and coordination for its success. A series of councils, from the central level down to the village, has therefore been set up to facilitate planning, implementation and coordination among ministries, and to provide diversified perspectives for well-rounded planning of Saemaul projects. The councils include, as shown Chart 7-1, the Saemaul Undong Central Consultative Council chaired by the Minister of Home Affairs and having members consisting of vice-ministers of other ministries within the central government. This council was organized for decision-making with respect to major support policies, budgetary assistance and basic guidance. At the provincial level, the Provincial Coordinating Committee was organized for co-ordination among functional departments and regional agencies in planning as well as resource allocation among various Saemaul projects. The committee is chaired by the provincial Governor and its members include the directors of the regional offices of the central agencies. At the Gun level, the county Saemaul Undong Coordinating Committee is organized for promotion and integrated guidance of Saemaul projects. The county chief chairs that committee. However, an interesting fact is that some Saemaul leaders are also included as committee members. At the Myeon level, which is the smallest unit of local administration, the Myeon Saemaul Undong Promotion Committee is responsible for making decisions with regard to specific guidance and assistance for development projects and activities in rural villages. It is chaired by the Myeon chief. Its membership includes relevant officials and government-arranged field workers as well as a few Sameual leaders. These committees at different levels of government administration are organized primarily for planning and decision-making with regard to adequate assistance, guidance and support on the part of government to Saemaul projects at the village level.

As the responsibility for planning and implementation of Saemaul projects primarily belongs to rural people themselves, the development committee has played the most important role in planning and organization of the Saemaul Undong throughout the 1970's. Although the General Assembly of village provides an important occasion for building concensus among village members, it is the Village Development Committee which is responsible for effective coordination, bargaining, concensus, planning and implementation of specific projects. This committee is chaired by Village Chief or Saemaul leader and comprises 12 other members.

Basic guidelines of planning and selecting development projects are prepared by the Central Consultative Council which is chaired by the Minister of Home Affairs. On the basis of these general guidelines which are delivered through a local administrative channel, a village project is identified and planned by the

Chart 7-1. Organizational Arrangement for the Saemaul Undong

Organization	Functions	Membership
Central Coordinating Committee	Coordination of ministries: overall policy formulation	Chaired by Minister of Home Affairs, with membership of vice-ministers of Economic Planning Board, Ministries of Education, Agriculture and Fisheries, Commerce and Industry, Construction, Health and Welfare, Communication, Culture and Information, Finance, Science and Technology and Minister without Portfolio (Economic Affairs); Office of Rural Development, Office of Forestry, Office of Supply
Provincial (or Special city) Coordinating Committee	Functional responsibility, regional coordination, and liaison	Chaired by Governor, with membership of vice-Governor of province, Superintendent of Education, provincial representative of Agricultural Cooperatives; Regional Directors of Agricultural Development Corporation, Office of Rural Development, Reserve Army; college professors, teachers in agricultural high school, directors of the Provincial Bureau of Education and Bereau of the Foresty Federation, Korean Electricity Corporation and the Communication Department
County (or city) Saemaul Undong Coordinating Committee	Integrated guidance and promotion	Chaired by major (or county chief), with membership of police chief, county agricultural cooperative, principal of agricultural high school, chief of post office, Saemaul leaders and others
Myeon Saemaul Undong Promotion Committee	Specific guidance and assistance	Chaired by chief of Eub (or Myeon) with membership of police, branch post office, agricultural cooperatives, extension service and Saemaul leaders
Village Development Committee	Planning and implementation of village development projects	Chaired by village chief (or Saemaul leader), with 10–12 members, including village opinion leaders and some elected villagers

Village Development Committee. The proposals for Saemaul projects are supposed to be approved by the General Assembly of the village people.

The selected projects are screened and reviewed by the Myeon Promotion Committee with the aim of studying feasibility, financial support and coordination. The selected projects are submitted to the County Chief who coordinates and approves the projects in consultation with the County Consultative Council. Some controversial problems are referred to the provincial Governor and solved in consultation with the Provincial Consultative Council. In this way all projects are finally aggregated and coordinated at the Central Consultative Council. The Central Consultative Council plays a key role in coordinating Saemaul projects based upon the basic guidelines and policies set up from the overall perspective of national and rural development.

The successful implementation of the Saemaul Undong also relies on other types of organizational and institutional support. Besides the Special Assistant to the President who is in charge of the Saemaul Undong, special divisions dealing with Saemaul Undong activities have been established in the Ministry of Agriculture and Fisheries, the Ministry of Commerce and Industry and the Ministry of Education.

At the central level, the Saemaul Undong Bureau operates within the Ministry of Home Affairs which is the secretariat of the Central Consultative Committee and responsible for the development of overall Saemaul Undong strategies and policies. It has four divisions dealing with the Saemaul Undong (planning, guidance, urban development and education). The Saemaul Undong Division was established within the provincial government to support and guide the activities of local governments at the county level. The Deputy County Chief and a division were instituted in every county office in order to manage services and assistance to the Saemaul Undong at the village level. Furthermore, an administrative unit exists within each township office which is responsible for planning and guiding development projects in the rural villages.

With regard to implementation of Saemaul projects, it is interesting to note that the deputy chief of local administration at each level is responsible for project implementation while the chief is responsible for project planning. In other words, the organization of Saemaul projects is characterized by a dual structure which arranges different units of action during different phases of project management, particularly when it comes to planning *vs.* implementation. In spite of its dual nature, there is no inconsistency between two sides as deputies in the local administration offices are accustomed to participating in the planning stage and, later on, taking responsibility for implementing the projects.

3. Implications of Village-Level Organization

Diffusion of innovation is subsumed in the process of rural development. Crucial elements in the diffusion of new ideas are (a) the *innovation* (b) which is *communicated* (c) through certain *channels* (d) over *time* (e) among the members of a *social system* (Rogers 1971, 18-38). Innovation and advocation are indeed the major philosophy underlying the Saemaul Undong and they take place in the form of various Saemaul projects. These project ideas are communicated through certain channels over a short period of time among members of rural communities. The innovation decision is the mental process of individuals through which steps are taken from the knowledge of an innovation to a decision either to adopt or reject it to the final confirmation of this decision.

Adoption of Saemaul projects may be viewed as a process of innovation that takes place mostly in the form of either collective decisions or authority decisions. Collective decisions are those which individuals in the social system agree upon by concensus, while authority decisions are those forced upon individuals by someone in a superordinate position of power. Since motivation as well as participation on the part of rural people in the Saemaul Undong are prerequistites for diffusion of innovation, organizational strategies are of great importance for self-reliant rural development.

In the case of Saemaul Undong, the stimulation for a new idea occurs mostly outside the rural village. Initiation of the new idea in the rural village is made through change agents, namely, Saemaul leaders or village chiefs who work in close collaboration with local officials. Because a village project is organized and planned by the Village Development Committee and approved by the General Assembly of the village, it is viewed that the decision to adopt and implement new ideas is made by the group of community members. In the Saemaul Undong, however, innovations are sometimes made outside the rural village, such as by local government officials or the top political leader, in the form of knowledge, information, persuasion and adoption.

In fact, political and government systems play important roles in stimulating rural innovation at the local level through the Saemaul Undong. Their roles are reflected in incentive measures, government support and local administration in particular, and the commitment of political leadership. So far the political and government systems call for authoritarian innovations in the rural development process rather than collective ones. At this stage Saemaul leaders play significant roles in stimulating and initiating innovations communicated from outside the rural sector. Decisions with regard to adoption or rejection of new ideas from the outside in terms of Saemaul projects are made through the close interaction between rural people and the community-based leadership. Village development projects based upon the basic guidelines communicated from the outside are organized and planned by the Village Development Committee and approved by the General Assembly of the village. In this context, Saemaul projects are viewed as innovations made through a collective decision process.

The confirmation of innovation in the Saemaul Undong is necessary for its continuance. Since the Saemaul Undong aims at building up a system for self-reliant rural development, continued adoption of innovation is of significant importance for its success. Because some Saemaul projects proposed by the government are communicated to rural villages through Saemaul leaders, it is inevitable for local administration to get involved in the Saemaul Undong. Local governments stimulate rural innovations by setting down guidelines for collective decision-making at the village level. They also integrate various kinds of development projects with respect to the required development assistance for the Saemaul projects.

The planning of the Saemaul Undong can be viewed in terms of repetitiveness, time span, scope, the subsystems involved and flexibility (Johnson, et. al. 1973-59-66). The planning of development projects at the village level is less repetitive and more short-range than planning at the central level. The Central Consultative Council pays attention to the strategic decisions while the Village Development Committee primarily focuses on the short-term budget and detailed tasks. The Saemaul Undong operates according to "management by objectives" (Humble 1970, 5-16), wherein individual managers determine what specific goals they plan to achieve and then carefully plan how these results will be accomplished. These objectives and project plans are then reviewed by their superiors and integrated into a more comprehensive framework. Beyond that, the Saemaul Undong encourages a two-way flow of information between central and local governments and rural villages. Information from the top is transmitted downward so that villagers have a meaningful context within which they can plan and organize development projects.

Chapter 8

MANAGEMENT TECHNIQUES FOR SAEMAUL PROJECTS

1. Introduction

Management techniques are defined as "instrumental devices which are used for determining goals and objectives of projects or activities and for providing effective communication and co-ordination, monitoring of performance, effective supervision and feedback within the organizational framework" (Whang 1978a, 13). Management technique is one of the critical variables which contribute to the success of rural development. Appropriate management techniques for planning as well as implementation of development projects at the village level are lacking in most developing countries in Asia. What is meant by appropriate management techniques for community-level actions? How could management techniques be improved to fit into the managerial context of integrated rural development (IRD) such as the Saemaul Undong?

An attempt is made in this chapter to clarify the concept of appropriateness and also to identify variables which determine appropriate management techniques in the rural context. It also attempts to make a critical review of management techniques which are applied, explicitly or implicitly, intentionally or habitually, in the case of the Saemaul Undong.

2. Management Techniques in the Rural Context

According to organizational theories, organizational technology (or management technique) depends on four major variables of an organization. The four middle range variables are resources, organizational goals, environment—including clients—and the internal structure of the organization (Perrow 1967, 194–208). In the same vein, it is viewed that management techniques for rural development projects at the village level largely depend on (1) the characteristics of resources to be mobilized for rural development projects, (2) the goals and purposes of integrated rural development, (3) the environmental context in which IRD projects are to be planned and implemented, and (4) the social structure in terms of the patterns of interactions among individuals involved in the management of IRD projects.

The operational concept of IRD as discussed in Chapter I would provide enormous implications on the nature and characteristics of organizational variables such as resources, goals, environment and structure, which are determinants of the pattern and nature of management techniques for development action at the community level. Rural development requires various kinds of resources including capital, technical know-how, manpower, materials, land, etc. Since manpower would be abundant but underutilized in most rural villages, rural people are identified as a major resource to be mobilized for rural development projects. In most developing countries, however, financial capital is rather limited and therefore rural manpower is viewed as a strategic resource in most Asian countries. The quality of manpower is characterized by its poor motivation and low level of education (Haque *et al*. 1975, 1–10). The source of rural manpower tends to be quite stable in most rural villages in Asia because of low geographical mobility among rural populations. The nature and characteristics of major resources provide a constraint by which choice of management technique would be determined. It is implied that management techniques for IRD projects should be: (1) simple enough to be comprehended by low-educated rural people or project managers, (2) mechanical for mobilization of people, (3) instrumental for people's participation, and (4) routine in nature for learning by repetitive actions.

The goals of IRD depend on the objectives of specific development projects. However, it is generally agreed that the objectives of IRD are the utilization of human resources and the development of the original environment of the rural people in the rural sector, rather than agricultural development. The operational objectives of IRD are identified as to:

(a) raise productivity in the rural sector, of which agriculture may be the main activity in most developing countries at their initial stage of development;

(b) ensure equitable income distribution and provide sufficient employment opportunities;

(c) establish better social, economic and physical infrastructures in the rural areas and ensure that the majority of the rural people benefit from them; and

(d) institutionalize political and administrative capabilities, including decisive participation by the rural people in decision-making and in community activities (FAO 1977, 20).

In pursuit of these objectives, various types of development projects would be organized at the community level. Development projects should be tangible, concrete and directly beneficial to the rural people, as they are supposed to be organized and implemented by the participation of the people themselves. Therefore, in spite of the vague and unspecific nature of IRD objectives, the goals of IRD projects at the community level would be identical among rural people. The goals of IRD projects are also tangible and concrete in nature. Therefore, the management techniques for planning as well as implementation of IRD projects must be those of simple, routine, and mechanistic techniques.

The environment of IRD seems to be quite complex because many layers of administration tend to be involved in planning for the package of government supports. Other societal supports are also necessary for successful implementation of IRD projects.

On the other hand the nature of subject matters to be managed is also complex in the sense that:
 (a) Successful implementation and efficient management of IRD projects require positive participation of people at the community level;
 (b) The end-results and performance of project implementation should be recognized by the people and beneficial to them; and
 (c) Coordination with various kinds of agencies, reference groups and other social forces seems to be a critical and inevitable process for the success of IRD projects (Whang 1978 b, 117–121).

The complexity of environmental context would require rather simple and stable techniques at the early stage of rural development for facilitation of easy communication among several heterogeneous actors and agencies (Perrow 1967, 121–131). In other words, methods and techniques for planning and management of IRD projects should be simple enough to allow the maximum participation of less educated or sometimes illiterate rural people who also have little access to modernity.

The social structure of community tends to be traditionally bounded. The pattern of interaction among people in the community would be stable and rather habitual. Nevertheless, when an innovative project is introduced it seems inevitable to rely on a new type of leadership. The emergence of new leadership requires a type of structure different from the conventional one. Nevertheless, because of the lack of mobility among rural people as well as the long tradition of folk culture, the social structure of the rural community is less flexible, sometimes rigid and resistant to change. In most developing countries, village members are heterogeneous in terms of land ownership, educational level, traditional sense of social status, etc.

The more heterogeneous the community members, the more rigid and less flexible the community structure (Skinner 1958). Under this structural circumstance, management techniques should be stable in the sense that mode of communications, symbol of authority, pattern of interaction, and coordination instruments would be based on the tradition and folk culture of the particular community (Thompson and Tuden 1959, 204–205).

The close interaction for necessary cooperation among heterogeneous community members may require simple techniques to facilitate mutual interaction and easy communication between and among community members, administrators and managers at different levels.

From the above discussion, it is viewed that management techniques for IRD projects should be simple enough to be understood and utilized by every individual involved in the management of IRD projects, routine in nature for learning by repetitive doing and instrumental in the mobilization of rural people to the maximum extent.

3. Specific Management Techniques Applied to Saemaul Projects

Beyond the general overview of the nature and characteristics of management techniques for rural development projects, it now seems necessary to identify specific techniques applicable to IRD projects in the context of rural villages in Asia. For the specificity as well as applicability of management techniques, Korea's experience in rural development will be reviewed from the management perspective.

Rural development projects in Korea have been organized as integral parts of the Saemaul Undong. It is a kind of social movement based on voluntary participation of rural people with a view to sharing among them developmental values such as self-help, diligence, and cooperation. It is a nationwide movement initiated by the late President Park and has been implemented with strong support from the top political leadership. Various kinds and forms of rural development projects have been organized and implemented by rural people. It is viewed that Saemaul Undong has made an enormous impact upon rural villages in Korea, including changes in individual values and attitudes, mode of village organization, economic performance and social consequences.

A question then arises as to what management system and techniques are applied to rural development projects organized within the framework of Saemaul Undong. An answer to this question requires two sets of analytical review of Saemaul projects focusing on (1) Who are really involved in various types and stages of management of rural development projects to be undertaken at the village level?, and (2) What are critical phases of the management process of rural development projects at the community level which are most relevant to the success of those projects?

In view of the socio-cultural and political context of rural development, individuals involved in the management of rural development projects differ from each other in terms of their organizational affiliations, social background, and, therefore, their professional interests. They can be grouped into two categories. The first group is those who are involved in actual management of rural development projects at the village level. In the case of Saemaul projects, village leaders and some influential village members are identified as managers at the village level. The second group is those who provide various kinds of supportive assistance for the promotion and facilitation of project management by the first group of managers. In the case of Korea, government administrators in various agencies at different levels of administration are identified again as managers who provide supportive actions. Governors of provinces, county chiefs, township chiefs, other local officials, and administrators at the central level are constantly paying special attention to Saemaul projects at the village level in order to get such projects performed successfully, as the top political leadership is highly interested in the nationwide Saemaul Undong. They are supposed to utilize appropriate management techniques to get their supportive actions and services delivered properly to the village-level Saemaul projects.

Different techniques should be applied for management of activities at different levels of administration, as the needs and purposes of job performance and the knowledge and skills of administrations are different depending on the level. Therefore, it is noted from the Korean experience that appropriate management techniques for rural development projects should be different depending on the purpose of a certain management action and the technical competence of managerial personnel.

Critical phases of project management are identified in terms of the following action steps:

(a) Project identification and definition;
(b) Project formulation, preparation, and feasibility analysis;
(c) Project design;
(d) Project appraisal;
(e) Project selection, negotiation and approval;
(f) Project activation and organization;
(g) Project implementation and operation;
(h) Project supervision, monitoring, and control;
(i) Project completion or termination;
(j) Output diffusion and transition to normal administration;
(k) Project evaluation; and
(l) Follow-up analysis and action (Rondinelli 1975; Baum 1978)).

These steps demonstrate the complexity and the comprehensiveness of project management, especially management of foreign assistance projects or development loan projects. However, the the criticalness of certain action steps should be defined in terms of their relevance and/or importance to the socio-political context and nature of the project for integrated rural development.

In case of the Saemaul Undong, there are some criteria by which critical phases of the project management could be identified. They are, for example, participation of rural people to the maximum extent, better mobilization of idle manpower in the rural sector, optimum delivery of government support and assistance to the villages, continuous interest and support from the political leadership, and the societal recognition of the developmental performance of rural communities. According to these criteria, critical phases involved in the management of Saemaul projects at the village level in Korea are identified as planning, coordination, and monitoring and evaluation. It is again noted that different management techniques are applied to different phases of the management process, although some techniques could be used consistently throughout several phases of project management. It now seems valuable to identify specific techniques for each of these critical phases in the management of Saemaul projects at the community level.

A. Management Techniques for Planning of Saemaul Projects

The planning of a Saemaul project at the village level involves mostly (1) project identification by village members, (2) simple project implementation design, (3) identification of kinds and amounts of necessary inputs or resources and (4) the proper communication of project ideas with local officials for mobilization of administrative support. These activities and steps are to be taken by Saemaul leaders and village members in collaboration with local officials. As discussed before, not all of them are well prepared for these kinds of activities in view of their educational backgrounds and experiences. However, it is noted that most village leaders served in the military as officers or sergeants. Most village members also experienced military service during or after the Korean War. The fact implies that management techniques applied in the military organization have been a common denominator among the village members, as well as village leaders, for their concerted action with respect to decision-making at the project planning stage (Whang 1980a, 132–133).

One of the important factors in defining the most appropriate techniques is the ability to allow the maximum participation of rural people in the decision-making process, which would be viewed as a precondition for the successful implementation of the particular project later on. Therefore, projects tend to be identified by rural people in terms of their felt-needs, rather than logically derived from the rigorous analysis of gaps between ideals and realities. The list of required input and resources tends to be identified by items and the amount of respective items is estimated on the basis of their previous experiences. Estimates of labor requirements and major material input are then most common procedure of planning at the village level. Saemaul projects tend to be designed in terms of a simple statement on when the project will be activated and when it should be completed. They are also defined in terms of work volumes and project location.

Project ideas clarified by village members tend to be communicated to local officials with a view to obtaining administrative support. A simple notion of cost-benefit analysis tends to be applied even implicitly by government officials at the local government level when they have to make some decisions regarding assistance and support to the project.

The level of techniques applied to identification of projects, necessary input and resources, project design as well as proposals for government support would be simple for ease of communication as well as for people's participation to the maximum extent. Nevertheless, it seems quite clear that military-oriented management techniques applied at the village-level planning stage are simple but complete in defining objectives or goals of project (why), a certain volume of substantive activities to be organized and unnecessary organization for project implementation (how). The simple statement regarding five ws and one h on a proposed project would be basic criteria for fundamental management principles as they were experienced in any action involved in military operations. Such an implicit rule of management applied at the village-level practice in project planning tends to be the unique virtue of management technique for Saemaul projects in rural villages.

B. Management Techniques for Coordination

The concept of coordination consists not only of vertical coordination but also of horizontal coordination. Vertical coordination means internal consistencies between goals and instruments of projects or between planning and implementation. Horizontal coordination means the solution of conflicts, elimination of unnecessary overlaps or narrowing of gaps between projects (Whang 1974, 987). In the case of Saemaul projects, which are mostly small-scale activities at the village level, vertical coordination is the major concern for the eradication of conflicts over resources and the elimination of unnecessary overlaps.

The problem of coordination for Saemaul projects would be relatively complex in its nature because they would involve various types of action agents, different interests and a variety of resources. The successful implementation of Saemaul projects requires effective coordination between village leaders and government officials with respect to the delivery of administrative support and government assistance. One of the important variables which determine the effectiveness of coordination is communication between the parties. In the case of Saemaul projects, a technical device for easy communication between village leaders and local government officials is simple management practice, including military briefings, planning with the use of Gantt (bar) charts, simple layouts of activities to be performed, sequential arrangement of supportive services and assistance, etc. The explicit and also simple statement about what to be done has been a mandate of techniques for better coordination between government officials and village leaders. Actions involved in the village-level coordination for people's participation and mobilization of idle manpower may be rather a matter of village leadership, because there are no serious conflicts over goals or objectives among village members once Saemaul projects are decided by the village members.

C. Management Techniques for Monitoring and Evaluation

Monitoring of project performance is defined as an action process which produces information regarding whether or not the results of project performance are likely to be as they were planned at the beginning. It also involves the facilitation and reinforcement of project performance and corrective action through proper feedback. Such data are related to resources mobilized for project implementation, time allocation and sequential arrangement and progress of work performance.

Both monitoring and evaluation of project performance are necessary as an integral part of effective implementation of projects. Although both are concerned with corrective action and problem-solving for the successful implementation of Saemaul projects, there are several aspects for which monitoring and evaluation work differently. Monitoring is concerned with the performance of specific activities or jobs comprised in a project, while evaluation is concerned with completion of the project as a whole. Therefore, indicators for monitoring project performance and their measurement are related to input and immediate output, while those for evaluation are related to performance and impacts. In temporal terms, monitoring is exercised mid-stream in the on-going project, while evaluation is at the final termination of the project cycle. In other words, monitoring is required for immediate feedback for corrective action in the mid-stream of project implementation by reviewing the mobilization of required inputs and delivery of desirable outputs. Evaluation is introduced for improvement in project planning and implementation in the next cycle of project management by reviewing the performance brought about through the accumulation of output and by further analyzing the impact of project performance upon the environment.

What are specific techniques applied to the monitoring of Saemaul projects? The monitoring techniques at the village level would be different from those at the national level because of different monitoring purposes and different levels of available skills.

The major indicators for monitoring purpose have been derived from input, process and output targets set for particular Saemaul projects. They are, for example, some indicators related to time constraints, some to key materials, manpower, etc. Theoretically, concepts such as PERT-time, PERT-cost, or PERT-manpower, which concern critical resources, would be useful.[2] However, most Saemaul projects at the village level tend to be monitored by village leaders in order to ensure the performance of certain activities which will eventually lead to completion of the project. Therefore, they are rather used to utilize Gantt chart operation by activity over a certain period of time. That is, the set of procedures starting from objective identification → activity analysis → performance measurement → analysis of gaps → attention → recommendation of corrective actions, etc.

However, monitoring at the intermediate governmental level, such as county or provincial governments, tends to be exercised by a variety of techniques and methods including Gantt chart, simple PERT technique, case study, evaluative research, field visits, or people's assessment (observatory evaluation), etc. It goes without saying that whatever techniques may be used, management techniques utilized at this level were chosen to promote people's participation in the decision-making process, as well as for efficient delivery of government support. The choice of techniques would also depend on the capabilities of officials.

The frequency of monitoring also depends on the purpose of monitoring. The monitoring by village leaders is constantly exercised and built-in over the process of project implementation. However, monitoring at the county office is exercised by field visits,

---

[2] For monitoring implications of PERT techniques, see FEC (1963).

monthly reports, or quarterly reports. For the benefit of efficient comprehension of the monitoring system for Saemaul projects, a simple chart is drawn as Chart 9-1 (Chapter 9).

4. Conclusions

There is no doubt that leadership and organization are critical factors of rural development in the Asian context. Appropriate management techniques could be a precondition to the proper exercise of rural leadership as well as conducive to organizational efficiency. Management techniques for Saemaul projects are not to be different from the techniques involved in the process of a project management at the government level, as Saemaul projects are to be managed on the basis of the principles of efficiency and effectiveness. Management of Saemaul projects requires the extensive involvement and participation of rural people and efficient coordination of multi-disciplinary factors, various kinds of resources and action instruments. It also requires use of rural folk culture and traditional values.

Therefore, the appropriateness of management techniques for rural development projects should be different from those for industrial development projects handled by government. The appropriateness should be decided in terms of major resources to be mobilized for rural development projects, objectives and goals of rural development projects, organizational structure in terms of pattern of interactions among people involved in the process of project management, and the socio-cultural context of rural communities in which rural development projects are to be undertaken. It has been stated that management techniques for rural development projects should be simple and explicit so as to easily tell all the partners or parties about how things are being organized, implemented, and evaluated, by which all the rural people can easily participate in the process of project management. Communication with all the people is the key for management efficiency in rural projects.

The Korean experience in Saemaul projects demostrates that the communication skill trained in the military and simple but complete techniques for planning, coordination and monitoring of Saemaul projects are key factors which eventually promote the efficiency of rural leadership and organizational performance. Simple PERT notions adapted to the rural context serve as an instrument for better coordination between local administrators in providing their respective services for Saemaul projects at the village level. Planning and implementation of component activities for a project by utilizing Gantt chart provide the minimum information to indicate critical activities to be planned and performed, issues of coordination, desirable means and directions, and also who are the counterparts to work with.

It goes without saying, nevertheless, that the most appropriate management techniques for the success of Saemaul projects must be those which are conducive to the exercise of rural leadership and to the motivation as well as participation of the people to the maximum extent.

Chapter 9

MONITORING AND EVALUATION OF SAEMAUL PROJECTS*

1. Introduction

The purpose of this chapter is to present an analytical description of the monitoring and evaluation system of the Saemaul Undong, with a view to identifying its strengths and weaknesses from which lessons can be drawn for improving the efficiency of Saemaul project management.

Monitoring of project performance is defined as an action process which systematically collects and analyses informations regarding project inputs and outputs and also conditions or complementary activities, which are critical to the success of the project. Monitoring is a process which alerts the project management and policy makers of the need to take corrective action to facilitate and secure the level of project performance necessary for its successful implementation. In the monitoring process, bench-mark information collected during the design or planning of the project is the basis for analysis and interpretation of implications of the progress. By its nature, monitoring is a continuous process through-

---
*The original version was published in Clayton E. and F. Petry (eds.) *Monitoring Systems for Agricultural and Rural Development Projects*, (Rome: FAO, 1981), pp.103–120.

out the project life-time. Information to be processed from the monitoring system are related not only to results, objectives and impact of the project, but also the inputs, conditions, time allocation and sequential arrangement of activities for project implementation (Chapter 8).

Both monitoring and on-going evaluation of project performance are integral parts of the effective implementation of projects. However, they differ in several aspects. Monitoring is addressed to the performance of specific activities or tasks of a project, and indicators for monitoring of project performance are concerned with inputs and immediate outputs (Onate 1977). Monitoring is carried out during the project implementation and is intended to lead to corrective action, through immediate feedback, during project implementation and operation by reviewing the mobilization of input and delivery of desirable output. The on-going evaluation also takes place during the project implementation and indicates continual analysis of project output, effects and impact. Its purpose is to provide project management and policy makers with analytical support to enable them to assess and, if necessary, adjust policies, objectives, institutional arrangement and resources affecting project implementation (FAO 1979). As a monitoring system is an integral part of the project implementation, the analysis of management context within which rural development projects are undertaken may have to precede the assessment of monitoring system.

This study is based on information collected from government documents and by interview with relevant personnels, including village leaders and local government officials at various levels.

2. Monitoring Systems of Saemaul Projects

The monitoring systems are viewed as a package of interrelated activities, gathering, analyzing and communicating information from the process of project implementation, as a means of securing a successful outcome of the projects. Hence the assessment of a monitoring system involves the following inquires:[1]

---

[1] Conceptually based on Whang (1972) and similar views were expressed in Kaul (1979) and UNAPDI, et al. (1978).

(a) Why monitoring? -- objectives of monitoring;
(b) What aspects or activities of the project are to be monitored?-- indicators for monitoring purpose;
(c) Who are responsible for gathering and analyzing information regarding the indicators? --organizational unit;
(d) How are informations collected and analyzed?--recording device, survey details, procedures, standard for analysis;
(e) To whom and when (or how often) are the processed informations supposed to be delivered?--communication, feedback, etc.

In case of Saemaul Undong, it may be necessary to inquire these questions at different levels of administration: at village, township, county, province, and central government levels (see Chart 9-1).

There are two distinctive categories of Saemaul projects which are implemented at the village level. The first category of projects are those organized and implemented by village people themselves, using their own resources including labor, finance and skills. This category of projects does not require any support or assistance from government because they are too small in scale and simple in nature. They include improvements in sewage systems, surfacing of village roads, construction of playgrounds, expansion of farm roads, construction of shops, etc. The second category includes projects which are organized and implemented by village people, but which require government support and assistance in terms of finance, technical, and engineering skills. They are relatively complex in nature and scale. They include construction of bridges longer than 20 meters, village entrance roads longer than two kilometers, medium scale irrigation projects, water supply facilities, multi-purpose village halls, etc. The most complex project is village renewal which includes landscape design, sewage, water supply, road rearrangement, complete renewal of houses and so on.

A. Monitoring System at the Village Level

Most of the village-level projects are usually implemented between mid-February and the end of May when village members become busy with farming. Therefore, the successful implementation of both kinds of projects considerably depends on their

Chart 9-1. Monitoring Systems of Saemaul Projects by Level

Element	Village Level	Township/County Level	Province & Central Level
Why Monitoring? (Purpose)	—Facilitation —Supplementary & corrective measures —Self-reinforcement	—Facilitation of delivery of material assistance —Provision of timely & proper guidance, education —Supervision of proper use of government-donated resources —Supplementary measures —Additional assistance/support	—Management support —Policy readjustment —Readaptation of overall management system —Over all on-going evaluation
What is to Be Monitored? (Indicators)	—Input —Output	—Input —Organization —Output —Progress	—Output —Performance —Impact & influence
Who Collects Information?	—Saemaul Leaders —Village Chief	—Township Chief —Deputy County Chief —County Chief with assistance officials	—Deputy Governor —Governor —Minister of Home Affairs with assistance of Bureau of Saemaul Undong
How to Collect and Analyze Informations? (Technique)	—Built in the village-level management of project	—Application of Gantt Chart to planning & monitoring —Field visits & daily report —PERT techniques —Daily	—Application of Gantt Chart to planning & monitoring —Field visits —Ad hoc case analysis & follow-up —Evaluative research
To Whom and How often is the Report? (Communication)	—For village leadership themselves —Daily & weekly	—To County Chief —To Governor —Daily/weekly —Bi-weekly/monthly —Ad hoc	—To Minister of Home Affairs & the President —Monthly, quarterly, annually —Ad hoc

efficient monitoring system. The general assembly of the village is used to make decisions regarding simple design, scale and location of projects. The village development committee is used to draw up the implementation scheme of projects in a simple form which includes time framework, financial requirements, methods as well as amount of labor contribution, etc. The village chief who is a semi-official and the Saemaul leader, who is selected from among village members, have joint responsibility for implementation of projects. Hence, both leaders are supposed to constantly monitor the performance of projects decided in the village assembly.

The major indicators for monitoring of these projects are more or less concerned with inputs; for example, cement, steel bars, sand, labor contribution, cash, other contributions in kind from the village people. Before he activates the implementation of a project at the village level, the Saemaul leader is supposed to confirm the delivery of government-donated cement and steel bars and the appropriate storage facilities of the raw materials. The Saemaul leader in collaboration with the village chief identifies and records the daily labor contribution of village members as planned in the village assembly. They also identify daily and weekly performance, in terms of output of the project, to compare with the implementation schedule. When the daily or weekly achievement has been found unsatisfactory because of insufficient participation by or contribution from village members, the Saemaul leader and or the village chief would additionally request the absent village members to provide labor or cash so as to meet the target and to share an equal burden among the community people. The village leadership is responsible for the elaboration of the detailed implementation schedule, by component activity (or job), of the project. In a project for constructing a village entrance road, for example, this includes collection of sand and pebbles from a riverside, digging the road and removing soil, surfacing of road with cement, etc. (see Form 9-2). This schedule, even in a simple form, serves as a guide for monitoring of project performance.

The purpose of monitoring by the village leadership is to find gaps between planned targets and actual progress with a view

Monitoring and Evaluation 143

Form 9-2. People's Participation by Activity

Name of Village Members	Receipt of Government-Donated Cement	Receipt of Government-Donated Steel Bars	Collection of Sand & Pebbles from River-Side	...	Digging the Road & Remove Soil Out	...	Mixing Concrete & Pavement
	(15 Jan., '79)*	(20 Jan.)	(7 Feb.)	...	(15 March)	...	(16 March)
A							
B							
C							
D							
E							
F							
G							
.							
.							
. X							
Y							
Z							

*Dates are imaginative examples.
Source: Interview with Mr. Hong, Dae-Yi, Saemaul Leader, Dae-Po 2-Ri, Dae-Wol-Myeon, Ichon-Gun, Kyung-Gi-Do.

to providing supplementary or corrective measures and, if necessary, requesting additional government support to facilitate project implementation according to the schedule. The major indicators of monitoring, at the village level, are naturally related to the detailed implementation plan which is elaborated in terms of inputs, resource, and outputs by component activites or action steps of project implementation. The village leadership used to monitor delivery of the right amount of government-donated cement and steel bars on time, the contribution of village members in terms of their voluntary service, money, or other materials, and the progress of work performance by component activity. The collection and analysis of information necessary for monitoring is built into the process of project implementation under the daily and constant supervision of the village leadership. The communication and feedback of the monitored information are again built in the process of project management by the leadership group. The village leadership does not have any obligation to report their daily or weekly performance of work to the township office. However the information necessary for monitoring at the township level are collected by frequent visits of township officials to villages, with a view to identifing actual project performance as well as providing necessary support and assistance.

B. Monitoring System at the Township Level

Almost every staff-member of the township office is assigned to one or two villages in order to make him provide general administrative services, as well as guide the management of Saemaul projects, and support and assist project operation in the village. Hence, township officials are supposed to visit their assigned villages almost every day during the period of March-April which seems to be the critical period for project implementation. The monitoring function is naturally built into this process of supporting administration. The daily progress report of projects in their assigned villages would be submitted to the Township Chief with particular reference to government-supported projects. The progress is usually measured in terms of the cumulative percentage of daily accomplishment to the planned target of projects. The purposes of monitoring of Saemual projects by the Township

Form 9-3. Daily Progress Report of Saemaul Projects

Name of Village	Planned	Yet to Start	20% in Progress	20-50%	50-80%	Completion	No. of Household-Days	No. of Man-Days
AA								
AB								
BB								
BC								
CD								
CF								
. . .								
XA								
XB								
XX								
XY								

Columns grouped under: No. of Projects (Planned, Yet to Start, 20% in Progress, 20-50%, 50-80%, Completion); Extent of Participants (No. of Household-Days, No. of Man-Days).

Source: Dae-Wol-Myeon (Township Office), Ichon-Gun.

Chief are to provide township officials with stimulus, so as to motivate and encourage village leaders and farmers to successfully implement Saemaul projects as planned and to collect basic information on the progress of project performance so as to take proper actions to facilitate project implementation. The Township Chief analyzes progress of project performance by village, as well as by project, through the use of Gantt Chart. He often visits villages to identify problems and confirm some major events in project implementation.

In other words, the major aspects to be monitored at the township level are the delivery of government-sponsored materials and their proper use, intermediate results of project implementation, level of villagers' motivation and participation, other major inputs for projects, progress of project implementation in relation to the time schedule. The basic information regarding project performance at the village level are collected by frequent field visits of officials and again analyzed through a simple format (see Form 9-3) or the use of Gantt Chart for planning and monitoring. If necessary, on the basis of progress analysis, the Township Chief utilizes his slack resource which is equivalent to 10% of the Saemaul support budget of the township.

The monitoring and supervision of Saemaul projects at the township level, are based on daily reports submitted by officials after their field visits. It has become an established principle that the success of Saemaul projects in a township is a criterion for judging the administrative capability of a Township Chief and his future promotion. Therefore, the communication and feedback of monitored information between the Township Chief and staff-members tend to be quite substantial. Also the simple format and Gantt Chart tabulation tend to help easy communication and understanding between them.

The Township Chief monitors project performance at the village level to secure their successful implementation and he also reports daily and weekly progress of project performance to the county office. The progress report of Saemaul projects, using a format similar to Form 9-3, carries statistical information including numbers of projects planned by villages, number of projects yet to start, number of projects that have achieved less than 20%,

20–50%, 50-80% of the target, number of projects completed and the extent of people's participation, measured in terms of household-days and man-days.

C. Monitoring System at the County Level

The main purposes of monitoring Saemaul projects, at the county level, are to secure the efficient delivery of government assistance to the villages, to supervise proper storage and use of government-assisted materials, to enable government to take corrective actions and to mobilize additional resources, and to provide proper and timely guidelines for project performance. The major indicators for monitoring of Saemaul projects at the county level are concerned with the deliverly of the right quantity of government-committed materials at the right time and to right place. An efficient delivery system is essential to induce positive response from the people to government-initiated rural innovations. Other aspects to be monitored are intermediate results and outcomes of project performance, the extent of popular participation and motivation, organizational capability of villages to manage Saemaul projects and also administrative capabilities of township offices in support of village development.

Hence, the most essential functions of county-level administration, in support of Saemaul projects, tend to be the planning of government assistance and monitoring of project implementation at the village level. In fact, government officials at the county level are extensively involved in the whole process of administrative support for Saemaul projects. Although the monitoring function is supposed to be exercised mostly by the County Chief (CC) and the Deputy County Chief, monitoring information is primarily supplied by Township Chiefs. Supplementary information is collected during the field visits of county government officials. More than the half of these are individually responsible for the promotion of Saemaul projects in one or two villages. Additionally, every division of the county office is responsible for promoting Saemaul projects in one township. Such an arrangement tends to stimulate county officials to closely work with township officials and village leadership. It provides support at the village level as well as a built-in monitoring system for county-level management.

The information collected by the township office is reported daily to the county office on a form similar to Form 9-3 except that it refers to a township and not a village. These daily progress reports from township offices are analyzed to identify the progress of Saemaul projects within the county as a whole.

County officials are supposed to visit the projects weekly to identify and confirm work progress. During their visits to villages, they provide guidance and suggest corrective measures; and they also identify needs for additional government support. Reports on their field visits provide the specific information for monitoring at the county level.

Information collected during the early or mid-February field visit are shown in Form 9-4 and related to the extent of people's motivation, by identifying the number of participants in morale-boosting activities (such as meetings to discuss the Saemaul spirit or village games); the extent of preparation for Saemaul projects, by identifying for example the amount of sand and gravel collected locally; the storage situation for government-donated cement and steel bars; the extent of people's awareness of Saemaul projects in the village (by randomly interviewing five village members); and whether or not the village leadership has conducted the village income survey according to the certain format instructed by the government.

Information collected during the field visits of late February to early March tend to be more extensive and is shown in Form 9-5. It is concerned with the extent of people's motivation; the delivery of raw materials; the storage system of raw materials; the progress of Saemaul projects; the maintenance of facilities constructed by SMU; and the frequency and extent of Saemaul education.

Information collected during the field visits of mid-March is concerned more with the progress of individual projects, by comparing actual performance of projects with their targets (see Form 9-6 for an example). Photographs are often taken to demonstrate the progress of project implementation. At least three times are they taken, at the beginning, during construction and at the completion.

Management techniques for planning and monitoring of Saemaul projects at the county level are relatively complex. Hence the Gantt Chart and PERT techniques are utilized, depending on the nature of projects to be monitored. The Gantt Chart approach to planning and monitoring does not require sophisticated skills on the part of officials and has, therefore, been widely applied. The approach includes objective identification, activity analysis, setting targets by activity, progress measurement of activities (comparing performance with target), analysis of gaps, atten-

Form 9-4. Field Visit Report at the Initial Stage

To: County Chief
Name of Village:
Date: (e.g. 17 February, 1980).
Reported by: (Rank and Name of Reporter)

1. Saemaul Promotion Convention in the Village
   Date:
   Place:
   No. of village members who participated:
2. Management of Input Materials:

Item	Planned	Collected	Storage Status
Cement			
Steel Bars			
Sand			
gravel			
.			
.			
.			

3. Awareness of Saemaul Project:

Name of Interviewee	Extent of Awareness (Yes or No)
A	
B	
C	
D	
E	

4. Village Income Survey;
   Yet to start _____
   Being conducted _____
   Conducted already _____

Source: Ichon-Gun (County Office), Kyung-Gi-Do.

Form 9-5. Monitoring of Progress in Saemaul Undong (Field Visit)

To: County Chief
Name of Village:
Dates: (e.g. 28 February–3 March, 1980)
Reported by: (Name and Rank)

1. Saemaul Promotion Convention
   Date:
   Place:
   Number of Participants:
2. Progress in Saemaul Projects
   A. Delivery of Raw Materials:

Item	Planned	Delivered	%
(e.g.) Cement	500 bags	500 bags	100
Steel Bars	2 tons	2 tons	100

   B. Plan for Undelivered Raw Materials: (describe date, place, amount, instrument, organization, etc.)
   C. Management of Storage:

Item	Place	Amount	Used	Method of Storage (good or bad)
A				
B				
.				
.				

   D. Progress of Government-Supporting Projects:

Project	Work Volume	Date Started*	Extent of Participation: Household Man-Day
.			
.			
.			

   * If not, indicate the planned date.
   E. Progress in Village Indigenous Projects:
      (Same as above D)
3. Maintenance of Facilities Constructed by the Saemaul Undong:
   A. (Specific information on facilities like village hall, storage, house, etc.)
   B. (Specific information on village hall)
   C. (Specific information on Saemaul Flag)
4. Saemaul Education:
   A. Village Assembly (No. of times and No. of participants)
   B. Amplified Announce System (No. of times)

Source: Ichon-Gun, Kyung-Gi-Do.

Form 9-6. Project Monitoring Report (Field Visit)

To: County Chief
Name of Village:
Date: (e.g. 15 March, 1980)
Reported by: (Name and Rank of Reporter)

1. Progress of Government-Supporting Saemaul Projects:

Project	Target	Performance	%	Remarks
.				
.				
.				

2. Progress of Village Indigenous Projects:
   (Same as the above)
3. Housing Improvement Project:

No. of Target House	No. of House Started	%	Remarks
.			
.			
.			

4. Toilet Improvement Project:
   (Same as the above)

Source: Ichon-Gun (County Office), Gyung-Gi-Do.

tion, supplementary and corrective measures or feedback, etc. However, simple PERT techniques tend to be often applied especially for implementing complex projects such as construction of a village water supply or a bridge.

How often and to whom is the monitored information reported? A summary report of Saemaul project performance is submitted daily to the CC. It contains information on the number of villages to be covered, the number of villages with completed targets, the number of projects planned and the number of projects completed by the township. In addition, the CC personally visits villages to identify problem areas or confirm progress. The daily or weekly report in the form of a statistical summary, the brief report and recommendations from field visits of his staff and his own personal visits to villages provide the basic information for monitoring purposes. On the basis of this information, the CC recommends monthly (or half-monthly) to the Governor appropriate actions. However, when a project requires special attention, because of bottlenecks or delays, he sometimes makes weekly or even daily reports to the Governor. He also makes decisions, as part of his monitoring function, regarding the use of slack resources for contingency purposes which amounts to 10% of the total resource budget for the county Saemaul projects.

D. Monitoring System at the Provincial and Central Levels

The main purposes of monitoring of Saemaul project performance at the provincial level are to facilitate and encourage county administrators to positively support village-level Saemaul Undong and if necessary, to take appropriate actions for policy readjustment regarding supportive assistance and administration. Therefore, the monitoring indicators are related to intermediate results of project implementation and time constraints affecting the schedule. Since the Deputy Governor is responsible for the implementation of Saemaul projects, he analyzes information submitted from every county office and collected from field visits by his staff members. For an in-depth analysis of particular projects, case studies are often conducted by provincial officials. The Gantt Chart technique is applied to the monitoring of the overall progress of all Saemaul projects within the jurisdictional boundary of the provincial government.

Monthly and quarterly reports in the progress of Saemaul projects are submitted to the Ministry of Home Affairs for their review and analysis. Monitoring at his level is a kind of on-going evaluation and monitoring of nationwide progress, for policy readjustment to meet changing demands and, if necessary, readaptation of the overall management system for developing rural communities. Therefore, the major indicators for monitoring at this stage tend to be concerned with the actual performance and strategies of Saemaul projects and their impact upon overall community development. They include, for example, improvements in village infrastructure and community environment, increased productivity of farming, improvement in farm-household income, attitudinal and behavioral changes of community members, level of people's participation, cooperation between government and rural people, etc. Some of the indicators are expressed in quantitative terms and others in judgmental or observatory terms. Evaluative research is sometimes commissioned to university professors as a supplementary device for monitoring or evaluation.[2] The Ministry of Home Affairs also relies on field visits of the officials to provincial and county governments or, if necessary, to villages for identification and confirmation of particular problems which may require special attention from the central government.

In this connection, it is noted that the late President expressed his interests in rural development by personally visiting villages. His frequent but ad hoc visits also serve as a mechanism for monitoring of project performance and further for making specific instructions toward policy readjustment (Chapter 4).

The review and analysis of progress of Saemaul projects, at the central level, are undertaken monthly, quarterly and annually for the central government and presidential information and action.

3. On-going Evaluation

The on-going evaluation of Saemaul projects at village, townships and county levels which follows from the monitoring activity, has several purposes. At the village level, comparison of performance enables villages to learn from each other, and stimulates competition between them. Also it introduces corrective measures for more efficient implementation of projects. Hence the on-going evaluation is not of an individual project, but of the village as a whole. It covers items similar to those monitored and is undertaken once a year (quarterly since 1980), by a team which includes county officials, township officials and a Saemaul leader from another village. This provides the latter with an opportunity to learn about strategies of project implementation from other villages[3] and encourages and motivates him to better leadership of Saemaul projects in his own village. The on-going evaluation of village-level performance is eventually fed into the central government

---

[2] For the monitoring implication of evaluation research, see Suchman (1969) and Weise (1972).

[3] For the developmental implications of people's involvement in rural project evaluation, see Emrich (1979).

to give a nationwide picture.

The on-going evaluation, at the township level, is more extensive, as it attempts to evaluate the overall performance of a township in support of Saemaul Undong at the village level. Its main purposes are to improve the administrative capabilities of the township office, to guide and support development activities in rural communities, and to expedite supportive services and actions for implementating Saemaul projects. The items evaluated at this level are as follows (weights are indicated in parenthesis):

(a) General Administrative Support of Township to the Saemaul Undong:
-Guidance on selection of Saemaul projects with consideration of feasibility (5)
-Personnel administration in support of the projects (5)
-Efficiency of clerical support (5)
-Coordination with other agencies, such as police, teachers, others. (5)

(b) Promotion of Community Mood Conducive to the Saemaul Undong:
-Frequent visits of officials to project sites (5)
-Identification with Saemaul Flag (5)
-Utilization of amplifier for public announcement and education for Saemaul Undong (5)
-Fostering of the village leadership (5)

(c) Management of Saemaul Projects:
-Delivery and storage management of raw materials (10)
-Performance and progress of project implementation (20)
-Extent of people's participation (10)

(d) Maintenance of Facilities Constructed by the Saemaul Undong:
-Repair and maintenance (10)
-Extent of utilization (10) (MOHA 1979).

The on-going evaluation of township performance was used to be undertaken by county officials once a year at the county level. However, since 1980 it is undertaken on a quarterly base with a view to emphasizing its monitoring function in order to improve administrative capacity in support of Saemaul projects during the current year.

At the county level, the on-going evaluation is undertaken annually by officials from the provincial government. Its objectives are to provide information to enable central government to assess the administrative competence of the county office and to develop or readjust policies and strategies in support of Saemaul projects for the coming year. The items examined are quite extensive and include the followings (MOHA 1979).
  (a) Performance of Major Projects Implemented with Support and Assistance of the County Office:
    -Set of Saemaul projects,
    -Special projects,
    -Housing improvement projects,
    -Small-town development projects,
    -Family planning program activities, and
    -Other priority projects recommended by the provincial government.
  (b) Evaluation of Six Villages Randomly Selected within the County:
  (c) Administrative Capabilities in Support of Saemaul Undong:
    -Timely action in support of Saemaul projects,
    -Financial administration in support of projects,
    -Personal administration in support of projects,
    -Fostering of Saemaul leadership,
    -Operation of Saemaul Consultative Council,
    -Income-boosting projects commonly owned by village members,
    -Operation of Saemaul Savings Account,
    -Utilization of Saemaul Banks in village,
    -Management of village libraries,
    -Conservation of natural environment,
    -Medical care program,
    -Priority projects recommended by county office.

The on-going evaluation of county administration is conducted by provincial officials and fed back to the central government. Its purpose is to assess the nationwide evaluation of local administration, with particular reference to development activities at the grass-root level. The evaluation is substantial in nature and extensive in its scope for the policy readjustment and system readaptation to the development process in rural communities.

As part of the on-going evaluation, the central government monitors the increase in farm household income on the average. The government compares annually the average income of farm household with that of urban wage-earner's household, with a view to measuring the extent of improvement in rural life as a consequence of the Saemaul Undong. The government also analyzes implications of the increasing numbers of TV sets, radios, bicycles, motor-scooters, refrigerators, etc. in the rural villages. The systematic monitoring of impact of the Saemaul Undong upon the standard of living in the rural sector, however, should be based on a set of social indicators concerning the quality of rural life. In the case of Korea, nevertheless, there has been no such effort made. The physical quality of life index (Morris 1979) relevant to Korean society is not available yet. It is a task to be elaborated in connection with the development of a master plan for the Saemaul Undong in the coming decade.

4. Assessment of the Monitoring System

A set of criteria should be applied for a rational assessment of the monitoring system. The criteria may include two broad categories: system's criteria and project-specific criteria.

The monitoring systems for Saemaul projects seem to be consistent with the objectives of the Saemaul Undong and fit into the institutional and administrative arrangements. The systems are well designed and facilitate project implementation. Because of the influence of the military subculture upon village leadership, upward and downward communications, from the villages to central levels seem to be efficient and effective. Although a management information system for local administration in Korea has yet to be institutionalized, the hierarchical flow monitored information is well-organized and disciplined. The monitoring systems are an integral part of the management information system, with which most local administrators used to work. Another point to be made is that the monitoring systems are built into the routine administrative procedures, particularly at the lower levels.

However, there are weaknesses to the systems. The use of generalized formats and criteria for nationwide evaluation and comparison does not promote village specific or regionally specific monitoring of project performance. The administrative cost involved in time and manpower mobilized for the extensive field visits of government officials tends to be quite high although it might be inevitable during the early stage of rural transformation. Another weakness is that a considerable portion of monitored information is judgmental sort of indicators which could hardly allow scientific decisions.

The project-specific criteria for the assessment of the monitoring system are defined as the consistency of the monitoring systems with the nature and constraints of the Saemaul Undong. The village-level monitoring system seems to promote the participation of rural people, and encourage the village leadership to participate in government decision-making, at the township as well as county levels, with regard to the planning of Saemaul projects. The participation of village leadership in the on-going evaluation of other villages enhances the efficiency of project implementation. The use of underemployed rural manpower during the slack season and the timely delivery of government support and assistance, for self-reliant development of rural communities, are operational strategies of the Saemaul Undong. The monitoring systems tend to be functional to these strategies. The monitoring systems also tend to reinforce personal motivation as well as the interests of the political elite, by rapidly feeding montiored information into the central government network. The monitoring systems would assist the social recognition of Saemaul Undong which is an important aspect of achieving its successful implementation.

Chapter 10

SAEMAUL TRAINING IN RURAL DEVELOPMENT: CONCEPTS AND APPROACH

Integrated rural development requires the deliberate efforts of both government and rural communities as well as positive support from society as a whole. Hence, rural development training should be broad enough to address not only the various types of field workers involved in rural development but also government officials, village leaders and the political as well as social elite. It should be designed to effect constructive changes in attitudes and behavior and substantial improvement in the organizational, managerial and technical competence of the persons concerned. Therefore, rural development policy makers should develop a training concept which serves as a suitable base for the elaboration and operation of specific training programs while striving to achieve effective coordination among the several programs from a total systems perspective.

Rural development training in most Asian countries is organized for training various kinds of field workers and arranged by different agencies which are concerned with different aspects of rural development. Policy makers, however, show little concern for training of community leaders whose motivation, leadership capability, technical knowledge and active participation are crucial determinants in the successful implementation of rural development policies. Most probably, moreover, except for Korea, none of the other Asian countries offer training sessions for the social and political elite of the country exclusively on rural development issues. Strategies, organization, program content and skills, and target groups of training in rural development, of course, will differ from country to country depending on development strategies as well as political and administrative constraints. Nevertheless, the two crucial training components mentioned above seem to be universally lacking in the rural development programs of other countries.

An attempt is made, in this chapter, to analyze the Korean experience with rural development training in the Saemaul Undong with a view to drawing some lessons for development of training systems in other developing countries. The conceptual clarification of Korea's rural development in terms of action implication (Chapter 2) already provided the logical basis for a discussion of who should be trained, why, and what the contents of the training should be. In this chapter, training is defined as an action program which is intended to influence the role perceptions of a certain group of people in order to modify their mode of behavior for better performance of their roles with respect to social and organizational goals. Within this context, the questions one must address are: what are the training needs for the respective groups of personnel involved in integrated rural development programs such as the Saemaul Undong? What are the strategic aspects to be taken into consideration in the design of rural development training? What is the Korean approach to such training for the Saemaul Undong? And what are the managerial implications implied in the process?

1. Training Needs for Integrated Rural Development

A. Training Needs for Community Leaders

Community leadership training has usually been introduced in West Asian countries as either an experimental project or a nationwide program. In some countries, however, this training is treated as a low prioity and therefore abandoned shortly after its installation. It is clear, therefore, that the scope and impact of the role that leaders must play in the complex process of rural development is too extensive to overlook the need for training this category of personnel. In order to build up a capability for self-reliant development in rural villages, it seems to be necessary to institutionalize village leadership training during a certain critical period. Indeed, development of community leadership based on the identification with their own villages should be a special concern of rural development policy makers.

Training needs for this category of people should be focused on how best the training contributes to the motivation, leadership capability, perspective, skills and knowledge required for performing their required roles in village development. For example, they should play a role as moderators of community opinion by encouraging people's participation in the decision-making which precedes cooperative village action. As opinion leaders they should play the role of social educators seeking to influence attitudes and behavior of the rural people with respect to various aspects of rural life. They should also be change agents and communication agents for advocating and promoting rural innovations. As the counterparts to rural field workers (such as extension workers and other community development workers) they should be able to communicate on technical matters related to the services provided by government agencies and voluntary organizations. They should be effective organizers of village cooperative action and coordinators of various types of rural development projects. They must be highly motivated to participate in the the decision-making process of local governments at the district level by all available means at their disposal in order to reflect the community's interests and make requests for specific support from the government. In this connection, they should be able to aggregate and articulate the interests, especially in terms of government support, of village people. They also must have a certain level of managerial competence in order to get community projects accomplished.

B. Training Needs for Rural Development Field Workers

Most rural development training has been concerned with training of the field worker category of personnel which includes agricultural extension workers, community development workers, health care nurses, family planning workers, teachers, etc. In fact, respective training programs arranged by specialized agencies of the government of voluntary organizations have concentrated on the development of the technical competence of field workers in their own specialized areas, for example, new seeds, irrigation, fertilizers, pesticides, livestock, rural health service, family planning, nutrition of children and other rural infrastructure. While technical knowledge and skills are the major focus of training, human relations and communication skills which are essential for working with rural people, are usually of little concern. A more important fact is that none of these training programs is really concerned with coordinating specialized field workers for the actual work of the villages. As the implementation of IRD programs requires the integration and coordination of diverse input and assistance at the rural village level, the coordination among field workers must be a primarily concern in rural development training.

It may be desirable to train this category of personnel together with a view to improving coordination skills and interpersonal communication, even after the training in their own specialized fields differently arranged by various agencies. There are, of course, several alternative forms of training possible, including seminar style briefings at field offices, or training of a corps of multipurpose field workers. But whatever form the training takes, it should be born in mind that the objective is to make field workers from different agencies fully understand their colleagues' jobs in the village in terms of the main objectives, tasks, areas, and particular client groups involved in their work. Otherwise, the field workers will not be able to initiate proper coordination. It is emphasized that any strategic restructuring of training for this category of personnel should be aimed at the improvement of their coordination capability and communication skills in addition to the improvement in their technical knowledge in the specialized areas.

C. Training Needs for Local Government Officials

As discussed before, it has been widely recognized that the role of local government at the district level in the process of rural development is of vital importance. However, training of local officials in most Asian counties tends to be incomplete in view of the extensive role they are required to play in the rural development process. Moreover, training of local officials tends to be concerned primarily with either law and order or the limited management skills required for routine administration and organization. Modern management concepts and techniques related to development projects and social structural change are scarcely ever included in their management training.

Rural development training addressed to local government officials should be aimed at improving the capability of the government for efficient delivery of support and assistance. The roles, tasks and constraints of local government in the implementation of an IRD program imply that there are many training needs for officials in this category. It is extremely important to provide them with technical knowledge about the capacity of the rural village for self-reliant development as well as an accurate estimation of rural motivation and commitment as a basis for planning government support. The knowledge and skills required for integration and coordination with respect to rural development projects should be the subject of training for local government officials (Iglesias 1976, 15–29). In addition to building managerial and technical competence, it is also desirable to institute a program to motivate officials to make their best efforts with regard to introducing attitudinal changes toward rural clients.

Local officials as managers of development projects or as development support administrators require constant development reinforcement of their management capabilities (Rondinelli 1977). In this sense, a basic management course for local government officials is the most essential part of their training for rural development. The training for local government officials, however, should go beyond the level of basic management training. Specific objectives for this type of training should include, first of all, how to improve their capacity for coordinating and integrating of the development support assistance which is provided by various agencies related to rural development at the district level. Another consideration is how to improve their capacity for delivery of rural development support and services to the community. Training objectives should also cover ways and means to encourage active participation on the part of community leadership in governmental decision-making with respect to both planning and implementation issues in rural development. Additional consideration should be given to how to enhance the credibility of the government and how to project a favorable image of government services within rural communities. This series of training needs and objectives for training of local officials will require high-level professional strategy which can only be developed through multidisciplinary efforts.

D. Training Needs for Political and Social Leaders

The Saemaul Undong as a nationwide social movement requires all kinds of societal supports in every aspect at every stage of its progress. As such, an understanding of rural development philosophy as well as specific action programs on the part of the political and social elite including congress members, cabinet ministers, party leaders, religious leaders, high-ranking officials, other sectoral elite of society is an effective booster for efficient delivery of government support to rural villages. Therefore, it is desirable to organize a training program for this category of personnel which is aimed at augmenting their understanding of (a) the real situation in rural villages, (b) the strengths as well as limitations of government policies, and (c) the specific needs of rural communities. Such training serves to promote a firm commitment on the part of the elite to rural development, so that they can play better roles in planning essential supporting policies which include legal, administrative and budgetary measures tailored to rural development needs.

It is difficult to introduce training for political and social elite within the framework of rural development training, unless revolutionary changes in the political elite and power structure take place in a country. With this in mind it is interesting to note the backgrounds and program contents of two similar but different cases involving the training of political and social elite: i.e., Saemaul training in the Republic of Korea(MOCI 1977) and the "down-to-the village" movement in China (Kuitenbrouwer 1977). What factors and conditions made these innovations workable in the two respective countries is an important inquiry for policy makers as well as students of rural development. Among the questions we may ask are: Who can make the elite within a society really cooperative with such training in view of their initial reluctance? How should the training be conducted? What legitimacy is there in introducing this type of training to the political and social elite?

2. Korean Approach to Rural Development Training

It is now worth investigating the Korean experiment as an innovative approach to training in rural development. The Saemaul training was launched in 1972 with the aim of both improving village leadership in undertaking development projects at the community level and inculcating development values such as self-help spirit, diligence and cooperation.

In 1973, Saemaul women leaders and country chiefs were included in the formal training program. As the Saemual Undong progressed, it became apparent that the social elite should also be included in the training course together with Saemaul leaders drawn from the rural villages. Therefore, starting in 1974, urban Saemaul leaders, social elite and high-ranking government officials were included in the training. This new trend was expanded in 1975 to include all social leaders (business, university, religion, labor union, mass media, etc.).

As a systematic review of the Korean case would require an extensive discussion (Whang 1975, 4–10), this chapter tries to analyze the Saemaul training program in terms of its organization, target groups (trainees), program contents and the training method with a view to identifying its uniqueness.

A. Training Institutions

There are 85 Saemaul training institutes all over the country identified by the Ministry of Home Affairs. Of these, 49 are governmental and the other 36 non-governmental. Three of them, including one public facility, were established exclusively for Saemaul training. The others provide Saemaul training in addition to their original training programs, such as inservice training for public officials and business agents (Lee M 1980, 4–6).

The Saemaul Leaders Training Institute, which opened at Suwon in 1972, is the central training institute. In addition, there are 14 other central-level and 10 provincial-level training institutions which provide training modeled after the Suwon Insitute. As a supplement, various types of training are provided at the village level on Saemaul spirit, scientific farming, agricultural machinery, health, housekeeping and family planning. In total, 158 high schools (one in each county) provide Saemaul classes for local leaders (200 persons in each school, or 31,600 in total in 1978), and a Saemaul Adult Course was established in 9,300 primary and secondary schools throughout the country (MOCI 1979, 40–41). The number of training institutes has increased since 1975, when the Saemaul Undong was extended to cover the urbanized areas of the country.

The objectives of the Saemaul Leaders Training Institute are three-fold: 1) to train a vanguard corps for the movement, 2) to support Saemaul leaders as catalysts for the Saemaul Undong, and 3) to contribute to the creation of the nationwide Saemaul spirit of diligence, self-help and cooperation. Therefore, trainees are indoctrinated to uphold three creeds which are: 1) to have a lofty ideal for modest living, 2) to keep out of debt and to be proud of thrift and saving, and 3) to prefer a life of substance to appearance. There are four educational policies for guiding training sessions: 1) training through the shared experience of trainees and staff members lodging together, 2) cultivation of the Saemaul spirit through actual practice, 3) mutual learning through group discussion and presentation of successful cases, and 4) continuous follow-up and support for the graduates (SLTC 1974).

B. Target Groups

The Saemaul training has been addressed not only to various types of field workers and governmental officials in rural development but also to community leaders and political as well as social elite.

There is no age or educational level limitation imposed on selecting the trainees, but priority is given to those who apply for taking such courses upon recommendation of either government authorities or other experts.

During the period from 1972 through 1979, the training program provided a total of 63.3 million man-sessions of instruction. Of these, 267,200 were for Saemaul leaders, 93,400 were for leaders of society, 267,200 were for national and local public officials and 62.7 million man-sessions were for agricultural trainees from different villages (MOHA 1980, 38).

The Saemaul Leaders Training Institute trained a total of 40,539 trainees between 1973 and 1979: 15,996 male Saemaul leaders, 8,156 women Saemaul leaders, 9,802 social leaders, 1,517 members from university student committees, and 5,068 staff members of agricultural and fisheries organizations (Cheong 1980, 20–21).

In accordance with the training needs of various clients, there are three main courses in the Saemaul training: 1) the course for male Saemaul leaders, 2) the course for women Saemaul leaders, and 3) the course for social leaders including officials, business managers, intellectuals and other influential members of society.

The Korean approach to rural development training is unique in terms of its mix of particpants. The main thrust of the Saemaul training is to change the values of village leaders, both men and women. It is assumed of course that indirectly this training will also effect changes in farmers' values and attitudes. Furthermore, congressmen, cabinet members, senior government officials, leading journalists, religious leaders, business managers, party leaders, university professors and other intellectual elite have participated in the training course together with the Saemaul leaders from rural villages.

Typically, village leadership consists of men and women selected from among the village members. Two leaders (a man and a woman) are elected by the villagers for training. Education and age are not requirements for the training. Once selected, these persons are sent to the Saemaul Leaders Training Institute for 1–2 weeks' training (one week for women, ten days for men, and two weeks for special training). After training, they are expected to play the role of change agents in introducing rural innovations as well as the role of manager in planning and implementing community projects.

Social leaders receive Saemaul training together with village leaders under the same conditions, and as a result, the program has had a tremendous impact in terms of making the social elite reevaluate their own roles.

Therefore, the range of clients for training has gradually been extended to include such social leaders as intellectuals, business managers, journalists and religious leaders. In this sense, the Korean approach to rural development training is unique in comparion with rural development training in other developing countries which emphasizes training of various kinds of field workers, but offers no training sessions for the social and political elite of the country exclusively on rural development issues.

C. Program Contents

The contents of training program depend on who the trainees are. As mentioned before, Saemual training offers three courses for different categories of trainees, namely, the Saemaul leaders' course, the women leaders' course, and the social leaders' course. The Saemaul leaders' course is offered to rural and ruban community leaders, agricultural cooperative staffs, model farmers, local officials assigned to supporting the Saemaul projects and others. The women leaders' course is offered to rural and urban women leaders, women members of agricultural cooperatives, women officials, leaders of women's organizations and women professors. Senior government officials, leading journalists, religious leaders, business managers, professors, labor union leaders, sometimes cabinet ministers, party leaders and other social elite participate in the social leaders' course (Lee M 1980, 7).

The training content is not fixed. Rather it is designed in accordance with the specific needs of trainees. However, there is some uniformity in terms of subject matter, discipline, successful case presentation, group discussion, mediation and other methods of training. The subjects commonly offered in every course are: the philosophy and spirit of the Saemaul Undong, the direction of the Saemaul Undong for that particular year, national security and the international situation, economic development policies, natural conservation, energy saving campaign, public ethics and morality, the presentation of successful case stories, study tours to model project villages and panel discussions.

Depending on the training needs of different clients, different subjects are offered. Rural leaders are provided with sessions on organizing the rural community, planning income boosting projects, technical know-how on the mechanization of farming, rural health and sanitation, etc. For urban leaders, classes are offered on public order and citizenship, human relations and beautification of the living environment. Women leaders attend sessions on population problems and family planning, health and nutrition, family living, simplification of family rituals, consumers' campaign and home economics. Similarly, relevant sessions are offered respectively to social leaders, business managers, college students and religious leaders (for details see Lee M 1980, 6–11)

D. Training Methods

In every Saemaul training course the following three specific features are commonly stressed (MOHA 1980, 38).

"Firstly, the presentation of the experiences of successful village Saemaul leaders (case studies) are used as an effective and persuasive means of educating other Saemaul and social leaders. For a member of the social elite, ..., the story of a poverty-stricken village man and woman who, with no formal education, finally managed . . . to extricate themselves from poverty, and is now helping other villagers to live better, gives a long-lasting impression and makes him feel that they are perhaps contributing much more to society than he is. By listening to such stories, the prominent person re-evaluates his past life style and begins sincerely to respect village Saemaul leaders and subsequently is better able to offer as much support to the village leaders as possible.

Secondly, the training emphasizes 'doing' rather than 'talking'. Every trainee lives under the same conditions, eats the same food, makes his own bed and cleans his own living quarters. . . . . No one expects or receives special treatment. A thrifty life is practiced with no alcohol, coffee or tea but only a simple diet consisting mainly of coarse grains. Through such practices, the trainees learn that "doing" in a constructive sense is much more difficult than simply talking . . .

Thirdly, self-evaluation through group discussion forces the trainee to evaluate his past life style. The evaluation focuses on what he has done in the past and what he should do in the future 1) as a person, 2) as the head of a family, 3) as the head of an office, and 4) as a leader in society. It is emphasized that he should think mainly about what he should do, not what others should do."

Usually, the training for Saemaul leaders of society requires a one week period. The training methods developed at the Saemaul Leaders Training Institute (Suwon) have become the basic model for all other training institutions. The training places its emphasis not on teaching, but on self-learning through case discussion, field work and other practical activities. All trainees are not supposed to have any contact with the outside at all throughout the entire training period. In order to understand the uniqueness of Saemaul training, it is perhaps valuable to review the daily schedule of a typical training program (Kwon 1978, 12–14).

The trainees arrive at the institute on Sunday afternoon from all over the country and register upon arrival. After registration, daily necessities such as uniforms and texts are supplied. Then the trainees are divided into groups of 18 trainees per room, and shown the dormitory where they will live during the training period. The trainees settle into their accommodations and change into uniforms.

They are then shown to classrooms and asked to fill out a questionnaire and write a brief essay on what they feel about the training. The results of the background questionnaire are then carefully analyzed and taken into consideration in formulating the training course.

After dinner, the trainees gather in the auditorium for an orientation session on what they should expect during the training period. The instructors, all of whom live with the trainees, are introduced.

Next, a film strip is shown to introduce the curriculum and daily schedule. Then the dormitory supervisor explains training life in detail. He thus prepares them to make mutual concessions for the sake of cooperative living and, as a result, trainees are able to step into "training through living together". Finally, the trainees join in singing wholesome and joyful songs under a music instructor's direction. The day ends with a roll call at 22:00. This roll call checks that everything is in order at the end of the first busy day.

For the remainder of the training program of one to two weeks, the daily schedule is very tight. Saemaul songs wake the trainees at 5:00 every morning and shortly thereafter they assemble outside. After a brief morning roll call, they jog around the lake in front of the institute and then undertake physical exercises.

Following their return to the dormitory, they wash and clean up until breakfast at 07:00. At 08:00 all the trainees gather in the auditorium, where they meditate and sing the Saemaul songs together. Then a volunteer from among the trainees presents his or her experiences on the Saemaul programs of their village. Morning classes start at 09:00 and last four hours.

The trainees are allowed one and a half hours for lunch and relaxation. This is followed by afternoon classes ending at 18:10.

After dinner, the trainees meet again to participate in group discussions for three hours until 22:00. This is immediately followed by a brief evening roll call. The trainees retire at 22:30, unless further discussion is required.

The above description demonstrates the consistent pattern of Saemaul training, from the assessment of training needs upon trainees' arrival at the Institute, to the constant monitoring of training effects, to the final evaluation. Before their departure, trainees are supposed to fill in a questionnaire which is concerned with two main items: (a) what the Saemaul Undong is and (b) what it changed in their way of thinking, if anything. In addition, the records of group discussion are analyzed to assess the effects of training.

In addition to these activities, there are four kinds of follow-up activities sponsored by the training program. The first one is communication through letters and publications. The second activity consists of trainers visiting trainees within the rural areas. The third one is a one-day session at the county level which is convened by the Institute in order to encourage trainees to keep up their role performance and to provide them with a counseling service relevant to the actual problems they encounter. Fourthly their attendance at the alumni meeting serves as a mechanism for reinforcing their cooperative ties as well as their commitment to the Saemaul Undong.

3. Managerial Implications of the Saemaul Training

What lessons may be drawn from the Korean experience in the management of the Saemaul training? The roles that are expected of the personnel involved in rural development are very complicated as well as closely interrelated if a meaningful contribution to rural development is to be made. Therefore, rural development training requires a strategic consideration of the ways and means available for realization of training objectives in terms of the mixture of clientele groups, sequential order of training courses, institutional arrangements, and integration and coordination of various types of training program in rural development.*

A. Strategic Mixture of Clients in Training Setting

Because personnel involved in IRD program should not work in isolation but think in the same terms and work together, a proper mixture of target groups in a particular training setting may be desirable to generate various positive impacts, visible and invisible, short-term and long-term, upon the participants. For example, if a district level training program is organized both for technical field workers representing different agencies and organizations and for community leaders of rural villages, it will facilitate communication and coordination between community leaders and field workers as well as between different field workers themselves. It will also encourage them to share a common conceptual framework which will be necessary to provide relevant services and assistance to rural villages. It will be an opportunity for them to make a collective commitment to achievement of certain rural development projects. It could be also expected that community leaders understand some issues in coordination with neighboring villages. The participation of cabinet ministers, party leaders, and other social elite together with village leaders in a training program will be an opportunity for political and social elite to understand the real picture of rural situation and needs. It also serves as a mechanism for social recognition of community leaders as development agents. The "down-to-the-village" move-

---
*Primarily rely on Whang (1978b, 126–128)

ment may be effective through direct and physical contact with rural farmers and the actual rural village environment, if politically acceptable. It is emphasized that the four broad categories of personnel are closely interrelated and mutually reinforcing in the process of rural development. Therefore, an attempt should be made possibly through training, to develop certain ties and common conceptual frameworks for all of them to work together from the total perspective of rural village development.

B. Sequential Order of Training Courses

It is indicated that the rural development process cannot be a short-term transformation but a transformation of the total society which takes the period of a generation. A short-term training course may not meet the training needs of a particular group of personnel because of the role complexity in the process of rural development. The changing nature of problems in rural communities after a certain period of rural change may require different ways to play the same or different roles. Therefore, it seems to be necessary to organize a series of training courses for a particular category of personnel involved in rural development. The sequential order of a series of training courses should be arranged in view of training needs of individuals in a particular situation. It is contended that the sequential order should be consistent with the whole idea of client-centered training rather than simple continuation or routinization of a training program for its program survival.

It also may be necessary to repeatedly provide the same individuals with the same or similar training courses within a certain time interval for continuous reinforcement of knowledge and attitudes required for the performance of their roles. The issue of reinforcement seems especially acute in the case of training of political and social elite. It should be also remembered that the pattern of mixture of client groups can be changed throughout the training series to facilitate dynamic interaction between client groups for better simulation to the real context of rural development action. In other words, a particular person must be arranged through deliberate planning to be trained together with a certain category of personnel in the first occasion and with another kind of personnel in the subsequent training program and so on.

C. Institutional Arrangements

In connection with a series of different training courses for individuals involved in the rural development process, it may be desirable to consider the spatial arrangement of training courses in terms of central level training, district level training, field training, mobile or changing location training. Community leaders and field workers may not require field training since they have been working most of their lives at the field level. However, training program organized by district training centers or subsequent programs organized by central training institutes may be desirable for community dealers and field workers for broadening and modernizing their perspectives. Mobile training may be necessary for systematic follow-up at the field level after the training at the central or local level. For the political and social elite, a form of field training may be more desirable to develop a sense of identity with rural people and for better understanding of rural problems and needs.

Another strategic consideration is related to the nature of the hosting institute for training in terms of sources of finance, resource persons, and institutional image. Broadly speaking, government agencies, universities, voluntary organizations, or other forms of independent institutes can do this training. The arrangement of hosting institutes will be based on the training objectives, clients, training methods, and other environmental constraints of a particular training program. It is also related to the feasibility of training in a given contextual and temporal framework.

Rural development training can be formally or informally organized in various forms including a physically identifiable formal training setting, formally arranged self-learning situation, formal arrangement of practical contact with problem areas or learning environment, informally disguised training, on-the-job training in the field, or formal and informal brain-storming sessions. The specification of training methods will be decided most probably after consideration of strategic aspects of rural development training as discussed before. Given the emphasis on relevant role performance, however, serious consideration should be given to extensive role practice and role modelling for all categories of personnel.

D. Coordination of Training Program

The complexity of rural development programs requires positive involvement of several categories of personnel. Therefore it also requires different forms of training programs organized and hosted by different agencies and institutes which pursue different organizational objectives with different sources of authority. Such diversity of training would naturally require effective coordination for their better functional integration with rural development policies and programs and for efficient as well as effective operation of training programs. The need for coordination seems to be more acute in view of the nature of multi-purpose training programs ranging from hardware technical and management training to software behavioral and attitudinal change. The strategic consideration of institutional aspects, spatial arrangement and temporal sequences, sometimes necessary overlapping contents, and training methods would call for major efforts for coordination.

The issue is related to who is responsible for coordination of all kinds of rural development training programs organized by different agencies and organizations at various levels. In some countries, a Ministry or Department of Rural Development has the responsibility. In some other countries, the function is performed by a Ministry of Home Affairs which also deals with local governments, or by a Ministry or Department of Personnel. Nevertheless, none of these seems to thoroughly perform the necessary coordination function, probably because of the lack of a clear definition of their scope and authority for coordination. Unless some ministry or department has authority and power to initiate coordination of rural development training, there will not be available any activity for, or planning of, coordination. An answer to this may be that someone who is responsible for overall rural development policies must initiate the coordination in connection with the implementation of development program.

4. Conclusions

Rural development should be achieved through the initiative of rural communities, positive participation and commitment of rural villagers, and their patient effort over a critical period of time. The government should provide a series of deliberately planned efforts to *support* rural development activities and projects which are initiated, organized, and implemented by rural people. Government support should cover stimulation and inducement of desired rural changes through technical, financial, organizational and institutional assistance and services. In other words, it is contended that rural development strategies should be bottom-up, grass-root, community-based and need-motivated, rather than government-initiated top-down service!

Rural development following these strategies is identified as a complex process taking place as an integral part of total systems change in the country. Therefore the administrative implications of integrated rural development suggest to make a deliberate effort for training of various categories of personnel involved in important aspects of rural change. Policy makers in charge of rural development used to be concerned with training of personnel in the public sector working for rural development. The impact of training government officials alone, however, tends to be limited unless rural people are really motivated and committed to the improvement of rural life. Rural reorganization is essential for the positive participation of people in the decision-making. Of importance is the community-based leadership which works closely with rural people and government officials. The role of government officials in support of rural development will also be inefficient without the real understanding of, and consistent support for, rural development projects on the part of the political and social elite. Rural development training has so far been offered mostly to extension workers, community development workers and other technical field workers. The needs for training of community leaders such as heads of farmers' associations, women's club leaders and other cooperative leaders have not been seriously and systematically assessed by policy makers. Ways and means to influence the perceptions and attitudes of various types of political and social elite tend to be viewed as a matter beyond the scope of their management and outside of their business area.

Therefore, it is contended in this chapter that rural development training should be offered to all categories of personnel involved in the rural development process from the total integrated perspective, not only training for personnel in the government sector but also those in voluntary organizations including community leaders, rural villagers, and the political, social, bureaucratic and intellectual elite. The *big-push, all-out* training in rural development will generate meaningful impact in accordance with the government support for rural development.

The training needs for respective categories of personnel are identified by making inference of their roles from the administrative implications of the Saemaul Undong. Specific training needs in a given country would have to be defined through careful role analysis for all four categories of personnel. A strategic mixture of clients is suggested for the simulation of training environment to the real picture of their role in rural communities. The integration and coordination of different training programs could be facilitated on the basis of specific training needs identified through integrated systems analysis of the roles of individuals concerned. Sequential order and spatial consideration of training should also be strategic concerns in the design of the whole package of rural development training.

For the successful implementation of rural development programs such as the Saemaul Undong, the training program should be operated not only for managerial and technical learning, but also geared to social education, mobilization of political and societal support and cultural change in rural communities. Although training is not an almighty tool, it can be a powerful instrument to stimulate and activate rural development if it is properly organized. An integrated package of training programs for personnel involved in rural development, if they are deliberately prepared on the basis of overall training strategies, will contribute to the improvement of government capacity for rural development action and also to formation of vision and capabilities of community people for their self-reliant development.

PART IV

IMPACT AND RESULTS

Chapter 11

IMPACT ON NATIONAL ECONOMY AND RURAL EMPLOYMENT

A series of investment projects for physical and social infrastructures was undertaken by the Saemaul Undong in the rural sector. The Saemaul Undong, organized as nationwide social movement, ignited people's zeal for better rural life from the beginning. Through a massive drive for their self-help effort and voluntary participation in Saemaul projects, rural people mobilized their resources and energy as much as possible. An attempt is made in this chapter to analyze the extent to which such an effort stimulated development and change in the national as well as rural economy with special focus on rural employment.

1. Impact on National Economy

The extent to which the Saemaul Undong has contributed to the national economy could be analyzed in terms of income redistribution, increase in private savings, regional development, capital formation, export promotion and technical improvement. The statistical data for this analysis were collected not only from the accumulated files of government documents and records but also from existing studies and other sources of data.

A. Income Redistribution

The Korean economy recorded an approximately 9% annual average growth rate during the period 1962–1979 which was largely attributed to rapid industrial development during the First and the Second Five-Year Plan periods. However, this rapid economic growth based on industrial development brought about an increase in the gap between farm household income and urban laborer's household income. As a result of rapid industrial growth in the 1960's the ratio of the average farm household income to the average urban laborer's household income had rapidly decreased to levels of 60% in 1967, 62% in 1968, 65% in 1969, and 67% in 1970. Since the inception of the Saemaul Undong, however, the gap between farm household income and urban laborer's household income has tended to become narrower. As shown in Table 11-1, the ratio of the average farm household income to the average urban laborer's household income has rapidly increased to the level of 79% in 1971, 83% in 1972, and 87% in 1973. Consequently, the average farm household income during the period 1974–1977 has been equal to or more than the average urban laborer's household income, although the farm household income was slightly lower during 1978–1979.

At the initial stage of the Saemaul Undong (1971–73), it was mainly concerned with the improvement of the rural environment so that the ratio of the average farm household income to the average urban laborer household income remained at 83% though improved. During 1974–76, however, the Saemaul Undong tended to emphasize income-boosting projects as a result of which this ratio had increased to 102% in favor of rural income. Since 1974 the emphasis has been placed upon income-generating projects such as cooperative farming projects, intervillage joint projects, production infrastructure projects and fishing village income-generation projects in order to increase farm income. Moreover, to increase non-farm income emphasis has also been placed upon construction of Saemaul factories, wage-earning projects and off-season utilization projects. A variety of projects as such might have improved farm household income.

Table 11-1. Rural and Urban Household Income, 1970-78

Year	Urban Laborer's Household Income (A)	Farm Household Income (B)	B/A (%)
1970	381,240	255,804	67
1971	451,920	356,382	79
1972	517,440	429,394	83
1973	550,200	480,711	87
1974	644,520	674,451	104
1975	859,320	872,933	102
1976	1,151,760	1,156,254	100
1977	1,405,080	1,432,809	102
1978	1,916,280	1,884,194	98
1979	2,629,596	2,227,483	85

Source: Economic Planning Board, *Handbook of Korean Economy*, 1980, pp. 221-222.

Nevertheless, scientific evidence is lacking in proving the extent to which the Saemaul Undong alone has contributed to the increase in farm household income. The higher rice price policy which was adopted in 1969 and was in effect throughout the 1970's (Moon 1980, 126-133) was undoubtedly a major factor contributing to the increase in farm income. Therefore, it should be noted that the Saemaul Undong has partly contributed to this increase in farm income.

B. *Private Savings*

One of the economic achievements of the Saemaul Undong is the cultivation of the rural people's will to increase private savings. Since the Saemaul Undong has emphasized the spirit of diligence and thrift and savings for the increase in income, the increase in the private savings in the rural sector may be attributed to the cultivation of the habits of thrift and savings as evidenced through the nationwide savings campaign.

Before the establishment of a Saemaul Fund in each village, rural farmers used to utilize mutual savings clubs or lay cash aside because of the lack of modern banking institutions in the rural areas. The amount of cash installations made through Saemaul Fund was 2.7 billion won in 1971 and 406 billion won in 1979. It has increased by 150 times over the 10 year period. As shown in Table 11-2, the increasing rate of Saemaul Fund savings

Table 11-2. Private Savings and Saemaul Funds

Unit: billion won

Year	Total Private Savings (A)	Saemaul Funds Installation (B)	Savings in Agriculture & Fisheries Co-operatives (C)	Percentage (%) B/A	C/A
1971	327.9 (100.0)	2.7 (100.0)	18.0 (100.0)	0.8	5.5
1972	489.5 (149.3)	3.5 (129.6)	15.3 (85.0)	0.7	3.1
1973	1,014.7 (309.5)	12.7 (470.4)	35.9 (199.4)	1.3	3.5
1974	1,336.0 (407.7)	16.1 (596.3)	56.0 (311.1)	1.2	4.2
1975	1,430.9 (436.4)	23.5 (870.4)	77.7 (431.7)	1.6	5.4
1976	2,244.4 (684.5)	45.7 (1,692.6)	113.9 (632.8)	2.0	5.1
1977	3,323.8 (1,013.7)	120.4 (4,459.3)	185.5 (1,030.6)	3.6	5.6
1978	4,563.1 (1,391.6)	246.9 (9,144.4)	232.9 (1,293.9)	5.4	5.1
1979	5,623.7 (1,715.1)	406.0 (15,037.0)	229.1 (1,272.8)	7.2	4.1

Numbers in parenthese indicate index
Sources: A) Economic Planning Board, *Handbook of Korean Economy*, 1980, pp. 33-34.
B) Ministry of Home Affairs, *Ten Year History of the Saemaul Undong*, Vol. II, 1980, p. 71.
C) *Ibid.*, p. 72.

tended to be higher than that of private savings. Although the cash installations cannot be compared with savings, this suggests that the Saemaul Undong rapidly absorbed money to spare in the rural sector into the semi-modern banking facilities and cultivated the habits of thrift and savings promoted by the nationwide savings campaign.

The ratio of savings made through Saemaul Funds to total private savings was merely 1% during 1971 but grew to 7% in 1979. Although the ratio seems to be still meager, it could be interpreted that the Saemaul Undong tends, in part, to make a positive contribution to the increase in private savings.

C. Balanced Regional Development

Balanced regional development is also an economic achievement of the Saemaul Undong. This could be discussed in terms of the increase in income, rural infrastructure and increasing non-farm income made available through Saemaul factories.

The Saemaul Undong partly contributed to balanced regional development between urban and rural sectors by accomplishing Saemaul projects such as roof improvement, housing improvement, sanitary water supply, rural electrification and rural communication facilities. The establishment of Saemaul factories in rural areas provided rural people with sources of non-farm income. Since 1973, Saemaul factories have been invited to set up in rural and fishing areas in order to absorb idle labor into the non-farm sector. Its impact on capital formation as well as employment creation in the rural areas will be discussed in Section 3.

The Saemaul Undong contributed to balanced regional development through its selective-sequential approach to each village at different development levels. Since 1974 the Saemaul Undong has adopted a step-by-step approach for advancing each village to a higher level. According to this strategy, all the villages in the country were classified into three categories: underdeveloped, developing and developed villages. Table 11-3 shows the minimum requirements for reclassification of village status and Table 11-4 shows thirty three specific activities to be evaluated for village promotion. All the villages in the country are assessed annually for their reclassification and promotion on the basis of these criteria.

According to Table 11-5, during 1972, 2,307 villages (7%) out of 34,665 villages in the country belonged to the category of developed village, 13,943 villages (40%) were developing villages and 18,415 villages (53%) were underdeveloped. It was found that, through the Saemaul Undong, the number of developed and developing villages increased while the number of underdeveloped villages decreased during the period 1972–1977. At the end of 1977, underdeveloped villages no longer existed, while developed villages comprised 67% and developing villages 33% of the national total. Furthermore, the portion of developing villages decreased to a level of 3% in 1979. This suggests that the number

Table 11-3. Requirements for Village Reclassification

Project	Promotion from Underdeveloped Village to Developing Village	Promotion from Developing Village to Developed Village
Village Road	Completion of Main Road	Completion of Main and Feeder Roads
Farm Road	Feeder Farm Road into the Village	Main Farm Road to the Village
Bridges	Small Bridges (10m or more)	Small Bridges (20m or more)
River Control	Small Streams passing through the Village	Small Rivers near the Village
Community Facilities	Village Hall, Storehouse, Workshop, etc.: more than one	Village Hall, Storehouse, Workshop, etc.: more than two
Roof Improvement	50% of All Houses	80% of All Houses
Saemaul Fund	Over 300,000 Won	Over 500,000 Won
Savings in Saemaul Fund per Household	Over 10,000 Won	Over 20,000 Won
Annual Income per Household	Over 700,000 Won	Over 900,000 Won

Source: Ministry of Home Affairs, *Ten Year History of the Saemaul Undong*, Vol. II, 1980, pp. 23–24.

of poor villages in the rural sector decreased partly due to the promotion of Saemaul Undong, although this is hardly based on scientific evidence.

D. Export Promotion and Technical Improvement

The Saemaul Undong has also in part contributed to export promotion through the establishment and utilization of Saemaul factories. As shown in Table 11-6, the amount of exports made through Saemaul factories increased during the period 1973–1977. From 1973 to 1977, $477 million worth of goods produced by Saemaul factories were exported which comprised about 2% of the total amount of exports of the country during the same period. Although the percentage seems to be relatively small, the rural economy made a positive contribution to the national economy by performing a strategic role in economic and social development. The rural economy had been viewed as a burden to the national economy in the process of industrial development before

Table 11-4. Project List for Village Reclassification, 1976

A. Production Infrastructure Projects (12 projects)
   Farm Road Construction
   Small Bridge Construction
   Small River Control
   Irrigation Facilities
   Cooperative Production Facilities
   Cooperative Warehouse
   Farmland Extension
   Erosion Control
   Pier and Port Facilities
   Intervillage Cooperation
   Rural Electrification
   Rural Communication Facilities

B. Income-Generation Projects (6 projects)
   Cooperative Rice Farming
   Increased Barley Production
   Increased Production of Organic Fertilizer
   Cooperative Income-Generating Activities
   Oyster Cultivation
   Sideline Income-Generation Activities

C. Welfare and Environment Improvement Projects (7 projects)
   Improvement of Village Roads
   Drainage Control
   Roof Improvement
   Living Environment Improvement
   Piped Water Facilities
   Village Wells
   Village Hall

D. Spiritual Enlightenment Projects (6 projects)
   Village Development Committee
   Self-Defense Activities
   Women's Club Activities
   Village Fund
   Village Credit Union
   Village Cleaning

Source: Shin, Yun-Pyo, *Jiyeog Gaebal Ron* (Regional Development Theories) Seoul, Beob Jeong Sa 1977, p. 87.

the Saemaul Undong was organized.

The Saemaul Undong also contributed to the promotion of technical improvement in the rural sector. In 1975, the Saemaul

Table 11-5. Reclassification of Villages

Unit: village (%)

Year	Total	Underdeveloped Village	Developing Village	Developed Village
1972	34,665(100)	18,415(53)	13,943(40)	2,307(7)
1973	34,665(100)	10,656(31)	19,763(57)	4,246(12)
1974	34,665(100)	6,165(18)	21,500(62)	7,000(20)
1975	35,031(100)	4,046(11)	20,936(60)	10,049(29)
1976	35,031(100)	302(1)	19,049(54)	15,680(45)
1977	35,031(100)	–	11,709(33)	23,322(67)
1978	34,815(100)	–	6,114(18)	28,701(82)
1979	34,871(100)	–	976(3)	33,893(97)

Source: Ministry of Home Affairs, *Ten Year History of the Saemaul Undong*, Vol. II, 1980, p. 22.

Table 11-6. Contribution of Saemaul Factories to Export

Unit: million dollars

Year	Total Exports (A)	Exports of Saemaul Factory Products (B)	B/A (%)
1973	3,225	23.5	0.7
1974	4,460	57.0	1.3
1975	5,081	87.1	1.7
1976	7,715	182.1	2.4
1977*	10,046	125.8	2.8
Total	24,998	475.5	1.9

*Only the first half of the year is included.
Source: Ministry of Home Affairs, *Saemaul Undong: From Its Inception Until Today* 1978, p. 186.

Technical Service Corps was organized under the sponsorship of the Ministry of Science and Technology with participation by scientists in various fields such as agriculture, food processing, Saemaul factories, engineering, health, etc. The Saemaul Technical Service Corps provided necessary technical support required for village Saemaul projects, scientific farming, fishing and marketing, and technical know-how for credit unions, farmers' groups, etc.

It is also noteworthy that technical learning classes or vocational training activities were organized by the Saemaul Undong to improve the technical skills of village people for the improvement of agricultural productivity. About 606 thousand rural youngsters and village people have had the chances to have access to these opportunities for substantial training and about 24 million rural people in gross terms had training in farming during the winter seasons throughout the 1970's (MOHA 1980, 63–64).

2. Impact on Village Economy

The Saemaul Undong has also made a significant contribution to the village economy. It is accepted that the Saemaul Undong as an integrated rural development made a positive contribution to the increase of gross village income, change in the village production pattern, improvement in village infrastructures, and social development at the village level.

The analysis should deal with the extent to which the Saemaul Undong has contributed to: (a) the increase in gross village income and the diversification of village income sources, (b) farm mechanization, product mix of agricultural crops and pattern of land utilization, and (c) social development investment at the village level and the improvement in the standard of living of farmers.

The statistical data regarding these aspects of village economy were collected from a field survey of 36 sample villages in which village chiefs and Saemaul leaders were interviewed according to the interview schedule (Whang 1980a, 249–254).

A. Increase in Village Income

It was found that the more successful the Saemaul Undong at the village level, the more rapidly the village economy grows in view of the increase in farm household income, diversification of income sources and increased opportunities for non-farm income.

Firstly, the Saemaul Undong contributed to the growth of the village economy in view of the average farm household income. As shown in Table 11-7, the average farm household income in those villages winning the Presidential Award for their outstanding performance in the Saemaul Undong was 1.3 million won during 1976 and 2.1 million won during 1978 while that of other villages was 1.1 million and 1.8 million won respectively. During the period 1976–1978, the rate of increase in farm household income in the outstanding villages was 61% while that of the common villages was 54%. This suggests that the Saemaul Undong has made significant contributions to the increase in farm household income, although there is little statistical evidence for such an interpretation.

Table 11-7. Average Farm Household Income in 36 Sample Villages

Unit: thousand won

Contents	1976 Out-standing Village	1976 Common Village	1978 Out-standing Village	1978 Common Village
(1) Agricultural Income (C + F)	1,105	886	1,823	1,388
Agricultural Crop Gross Receipts (A)	1,197	878	1,796	1,291
Management Expenditure (B)	171	108	252	149
Agricultural Crop Income (C = A−B)	1,026	770	1,544	1,142
Grains	898	652	1,179	844
Vegetables	151	147	351	219
Special Crops	22	14	38	12
Fruits	48	15	92	136
Vinyl-house Crops	–	–	22	28
Other Crops	–	–	6	–
Monopoly Crops	46	7	56	25
By-products	32	43	52	27
Livestock Gross Receipts (D)	95	133	329	291
Management Expenditure (E)	16	17	50	45
Livestock Income (F = D–E)	79	116	279	246
(2) Off-farm Income	186	251	258	363
Forestry	23	53	13	29
Fisheries	–	–	–	–
Construction	16	16	46	60
Mining	12	3	0.6	–
Manufacture	25	63	68	106
Wholesale & Retail Trade	8	6	13	13
Transportation	2	5	3	40
Public Administration	100	144	84	87
Service	–	2	3	24
Income Transfer	–3	12	28	64
Total Income (1 + 2)	1,291	1,137	2,081	1,751

Source: Whang (1980a) 171.

Table 11-8. Composition of Farm Household Income
(36 Sample Villages) Unit: %

	1976 Outstanding Villages	1976 Common Villages	1978 Outstanding Villages	1978 Common Villages
Total Income (1) + (2)	100.0	100.0	100.0	100.0
(1) Agricultural Income (A + B)	85.6	77.9	87.6	79.3
Crop Income (A):	79.4	67.9	74.2	65.2
Grains	69.6	57.3	56.7	48.2
Vegetables	11.7	12.9	16.9	12.5
Special Crops	1.7	1.2	1.8	0.7
Fruits	3.7	1.3	4.4	7.8
Vinyl-House Crops	–	–	1.1	1.6
Other Crops	–	–	0.3	–
Monopoly Crops	3.6	0.6	2.7	1.4
By-products	2.5	3.8	2.5	1.5
Livestock Income (B)	6.1	10.2	13.4	14.1
(2) Off-farm Income	14.4	22.1	12.4	20.7

Source: Whang (1980a, 172).

Secondly, the Saemaul Undong has also contributed to the village economy through the diversification of income sources. Table 11-8 shows that the ratio of non-farm income to the average farm household income in the outstanding villages was 14% in 1976 and 12% in 1978 while that of common villages was 22% and 21% in the same years. It is interesting to note that the ratio of non-farm income to the average farm household income in the outstanding villages was lower than that of common villages. This is partly attributed to the high-price policy and the diffusion of high-yielding varieties of rice. It is also implied that the Saemaul Undong has been more concerned with agricultural productivity rather than non-farm income sources.

Table 11-8 also indicates that the major sources of farm household income were diversified and changed during the period 1976–1978. In the outstanding villages during 1976, 70% of farm household income originated from grain products; 14% from non-farm sources, 12% from vegetables and 6% from livestock farming. During 1978, however, grains income was 57%, vegetable income 17%, livestock income 13% and non-farm income became 12%. Therefore, the contribution of vegetable and livestock income increased while that of grains and non-farm income decreased. In common villages, non-farm income became the second major source of farm household income during the same period. The contribution of non-farm income was 21% in 1978 while that of grain income decreased to the level of 48% during the same period. This suggests that outstanding villages chose vegetables and livestock for sources of the increase in farm household income while common villages with less arable land chose non-farm income as a second major income source through working in Saemaul factories and neighboring industrial parks.

Table 11-9 shows the rate of increase by major sources of farm household income during the period 1976–1978. The rate of increase in grain income in outstanding villages was 31% while that of common villages was 29%. But the rate of increase in vegetable income in outstanding villages was 133% while that of common villages was only 49%. Furthermore, the rate of increase in livestock income in outstanding villages was 253%

Table 11-9. Rate of Increase in Income by Source, 1976-78
(36 Sample Villages)

Unit: %

	Outstanding Villages	Common Villages	Total
Total Income	54.0	61.2	58.7
(1) Agricultural Income	56.7	65.0	62.5
Crop Income	48.4	50.0	49.8
Grains	29.4	31.3	30.7
Vegetables	49.0	132.5	102.0
Special Crops	−14.3	72.7	47.4
Fruits	806.7	91.7	202.9
Vinyl-House Crops	–	–	–
Other Crops	–	–	–
Monopoly Crops	257.1	21.7	41.9
By-products	−37.2	62.5	19.4
Livestock Income	112.1	253.2	190.2
(2) Non-Farm Income	44.6	38.7	42.1

Source: Whang (1980a, 174).

while that of common villages was 112%. This implies that the more successfully the villages respond to the Saemaul Undong, the more rapidly the village economy grows and the average farm household income increases.

B. Change in Agricultural Production Mix

The Saemaul Undong has introduced changes in the pattern of agricultural production and technology in terms of the extent of farm mechanization, product mix of agricultural crops and pattern of land utilization.

Firstly, the Saemaul Undong promoted farm mechanization through the dissemination of agricultural machinery and technical training for the operation of agricultural machinery. As shown in Table 11-10, the amount of agricultural machinery disseminated in the rural sector rapidly increased during the period 1970-1979. On the average, 1.4 power tillers, 1.1 moist & dusters, 1.6 power threshers and 1.6 pumps were owned by every 100 farm households during 1970. But during 1975, 5.5 power tillers, 2.6 mist & dusters, 5.0 power thresher and 2.8 pumps were utilized by every 100 households in the rural sector. Furthermore, 11.3 power tillers, 10.9 mist & dusters, 8.6 power threshers and 8.8 pumps were distributed during 1978. It is especially remarkable that large-scale agricultural machinery such as seeders and binders were introduced into the rural sector during 1978. As shown in Table

Table 11-10. Agricultural Mechnization in 36 Sample Villages

Unit: each per 100 households

Kind of Machine	1970 Outstanding Villages	1970 Common Villages	1975 Outstanding Villages	1975 Common Villages	1979 Outstanding Villages	1979 Common Villages
Power Tiller	1.7	1.1	5.9	4.8	12.8	8.9
Moist & Duster	0.8	1.5	2.0	3.5	11.3	10.2
Power Thresher	1.1	2.4	3.3	7.5	8.0	9.4
Pump	2.3	0.6	3.4	2.0	12.4	3.3
Seeder	-	-	-	-	-	0.2
Binder	-	-	-	-	0.3	-

Source: Whang (1980a, 175).

Table 11-11. Composition of Farm Household by Income Source (36 sample villages)

Unit: % (household)

	1970 Out-standing Villages	1970 Common Villages	1970 Total	1975 Out-standing Villages	1975 Common Villages	1975 Total	1978 Out-standing Villages	1978 Common Villages	1978 Total
Total	100.0 (830)	100.0 (638)	100.0 (1,468)	100.0 (804)	100.0 (630)	100.0 (1,434)	100.0 (846)	100.0 (621)	100.0 (1,467)
Grains	74.0	55.3	65.8	69.5	47.9	60.0	64.9	51.0	59.8
Grains + Livestock	0.7	0.2	0.5	1.5	0.2	0.9	1.3	0.6	1.0
Grains + Sericulture	6.3	23.2	13.6	6.8	27.0	15.7	6.3	15.8	10.4
Grains + Vegetables	8.8	4.2	6.9	8.5	4.9	6.9	10.5	4.2	6.6
Grains + Fruits	5.3	12.1	8.2	6.5	14.4	10.0	6.7	21.3	13.1
Grains + Special Crops	1.0	3.4	2.0	1.0	3.3	2.0	2.4	4.3	3.2
Grains + Other Crops	3.8	1.6	3.0	6.2	2.3	4.5	7.9	2.8	5.9

Source: Whang (1980a, 176).

11-10, farm mechanization became so extensive as to be about 8 times the level of early 1970.

Secondly, the Saemaul Undong also had an impact on the product mix of agricultural crops allowing maximization of resource utilization. As shown in Table 11-11, the percentage of farm household income primarily derived from grain production which was 66% during 1970 became about 60% during 1975 and 1978. This percentage in outstanding villages which was 74% during 1970 became 69% during 1975 and 65% during 1978. But this percentage in common villages which was 55% during 1970 became 48% during 1975 and 51% during 1978. This suggests that the number of farm households primarily depending on grains income decreased through the differentiation of the village economy. Therefore, it is remarkable that the degree to which the farm household income was dependent upon income from livestock, fruit and special crops increased as the Saemaul Undong progressed.

Thirdly, the Saemaul Undong has introduced change in the pattern of land utilization. As shown in Table 11-12, in 1976 about 79% of the arable land was allocated for the cultivation of food grains while about 62% of arable land was so allocated in 1978. On the other hand, the portion of arable land allocated for non-grain crops such as vegetables, fruit and special crops underwent a relative increase. The cultivation of these non-grain crops was introduced for the diversification of household income sources. Therefore, the Saemaul Undong gave an impetus to the change toward commercial farming in Korean agriculture.

C. Standard of Livng in Rural Villages

Although there are a variety of indicators for social development, the analysis should deal with the extent to which the Saemaul Undong has contributed to the improvement of the educational level and the diffusion of facilities for cultural life.

Despite the rapid migration of rural people with a high educational level into the urban sector in the 1960's due to urbanization and industrialization, the general level of education in the rural sector has greatly increased during the 1970's (Chapter 6). The educational level of householders in rural villages has

**Table 11-12. Pattern of Land Utilization of Average Household
(36 Sample Villages)**

Unit: 10 acres (%)

		1976		1978	
		Outstanding Villages	Common Villages	Outstanding Villages	Common Villages
Grain Crops	Rice	5.9 (35.6)	3.8 (34.9)	5.2 (35.8)	3.4 (29.8)
	Wheat & Barley	5.1 (30.7)	3.7 (33.9)	0.9 (6.2)	3.1 (27.2)
	Beans	1.4 (8.4)	0.2 (1.8)	1.4 (9.7)	0.7 (6.1)
	Potatoes	—	0.2 (1.8)	0.6 (4.1)	0.1 (0.9)
	Miscellaneous Grains	0.3 (1.8)	0.7 (6.4)	0.4 (2.8)	0.3 (2.6)
	Sub Total	12.7 (76.5)	8.2 (75.2)	8.5 (58.6)	7.6 (66.7)
Vegetables		1.8 (10.8)	1.6 (14.7)	3.8 (26.2)	2.4 (21.1)
Special Crops		0.7 (4.2)	0.6 (5.5)	0.9 (6.2)	0.6 (5.3)
Fruits		0.7 (4.2)	0.1 (0.9)	0.3 (2.1)	0.3 (2.6)
Monopoly Crops		0.5 (3.0)	0.1 (0.9)	0.8 (5.5)	0.3 (2.6)
Other Cash Crops		—	—	0.1 (0.7)	0.1 (0.9)
Others		0.2 (1.3)	0.1 (0.8)	0.1 (0.7)	0.1 (0.8)
Total		16.6(100.0)	10.9(100.0)	14.5(100.0)	11.4(100.0)

Source: Whang (1980a, 178).

rapidly increased during the last decade. The percentage of householders who received more than six years of formal education was 32% in 1979 (Whang 1980a, 180) while it was 12% in 1969 (Lee MG 1973, 205).

In addition, the school attendance ratio of the population in the rural sector which was 59.0% in 1970 became 71.5% in 1975 while that of the urban sector which was 56.4% in 1970 became 57.5% in 1975. But it is remarkable that the percentage of students enrolled at the college and university level in the rural sector was lower than that of the urban sector. As shown in Table 11-13, the school attendance ratio of the population aged 18-24 years which was 4.4% in 1970 became 4.1% in 1975 while that of the urban sector which was 14.8% in 1970 became 17.3% in 1975.

Table 11-13. School Attendance Ratio

Unit: %

Ages	1970 Whole Country	1970 Urban	1970 Rural	1975 Whole Country	1975 Urban	1975 Rural
6–11	87.9	87.2	88.2	89.5	88.5	90.3
12–17	59.2	65.1	54.1	67.7	71.4	64.3
18–24	9.8	14.8	4.4	12.6	17.3	4.1
Total	57.9	56.4	59.0	58.8	57.5	71.5

Source: Economic Planning Board, *Population and Housing Census Report*, (in respective years).

The extent of household electronic appliances purchased at the village level has rapidly increased aided by the increase in farm household income and rural electrification. As shown in Table 11-14, for example, the number of TV sets purchased in the rural sector in 1979 increased by about 4 times the 1975 level. As shown in Table 11-15, the extent of household electronic appliance ownership in households in outstanding villages was more than that of common village households. It is interesting to note that farmers in outstanding villages prefered tape recorders to audio sets while those in common villages prefered audio sets to tape recorders. This indirectly suggests that rural people in

Table 11-14. Electronic Appliances of Rural Households

Unit: %

	1970[1]	1975[2]	1979[3]
TV Sets	0.8	15.7	63.6
Electric Fan	–	17.5	47.8
Audio Sets	3.5	7.0	11.8
Refrigerator	0.4	1.3	5.7

Source: 1) Economic Planning Board, *Population and Housing Census Report*, 1970.
2) Economic Planning Board, *Population and Housing Census Report*, 1975 (5% Sampling Survey).
3) Whang (1980a, 182),

Table 11-15. Domestic Electronic Appliances Adopted by 36 Sample Villages

Unit: %

	Outstanding Villages	Common Villages	Total
TV Sets	61.4	65.0	63.6
Electric Iron	45.5	53.5	50.4
Electric Fan	43.9	50.2	47.8
Electric Rice Cooker	45.8	47.2	46.6
Tape Recorder	11.3	14.7	13.4
Audio Sets	12.2	11.5	11.8
Refrigerator	4.8	6.2	5.7
Auto-bicycles	3.6	4.9	4.4

Source: Whang (1980a, 182).

outstanding villages tend to have a propensity for realistic consumption while rural people in common villages tend to have a propensity for conspicuous consumption.

3. Rural Employment Strategies Underlined in the Saemaul Undong*

A. Extent of Rural Employment

To what extent did the Saemaul Undong contribute particularly to rural employment? There has been no systematic and comprehensive analysis of its impact on the pattern and level of employment in the rural sector. Nevertheless, its positive impact

* This part was presented in *Journal of East and West Studies*, X, 2 (1981, 23–41).

can be viewed through a variety of indicators. Regardless of the financial rewards for their labor contribution, the number of man-days contributed by the participation of rural people in the Saemaul Undong seems to be remarkable, especially if it is considered that most Saemaul projects were undertaken during the off-farm season (from December to April). As already shown in Table 3-1, the people's labor contribution has been steadily increasing since 1971. As Saemaul projects produce community goods in most cases, their labor contribution was not motivated by wage earnings but by the convenience of community life and development. Therefore, their labor participation on a voluntary basis cannot be viewed as employment to be counted in terms of income earning.

Another indicator in an analysis of employment impact is the changing rate of unemployment in the rural sector. As shown in Table 11-16, since the inception of the Saemaul Undong, the unemployment rate in the rural sector has decreased rapidly from 1.6% in 1970 to 0.8% in 1979, more than the rate of the whole country which decreased from 4.5% to 3.8% during the same period. Although there is no scientific evidence regarding any direct relationship between the Saemaul Undong in the rural areas and this decrease in unemployment rates, no doubt the Saemaul Undong has been organized along the line with labor-absorbing projects. The Saemaul Undong has indeed served as an employment-oriented development strategy to absorb increasing numbers in the labor force and to mitigate the level of unemployed or underemployed population in the rural areas.

B. Strategies for Generation of Employment Opportunities

What approaches were applied in the Saemaul Undong to increase rural employment in Korea? There are three major concepts (or variables) involved in additional employment in the rural sector. These are: (a) employment opportunities—the supply side; (b) people's motivation to work—the demand side; and (c) work arrangement—market conditioning.

A conventional approach to providing employment opportunities in Korea was to mobilize rural farmers or laborers for labor-intensive public work projects such as irrigation, dam construction,

Table 11-16. Economically Active Population

Unit: thousand person

Year	Whole Country Eco. Act. Population (A)	Unemployment (B)	B/A (%)	Rural Sector Eco. Act. Population (C)	Unemployment (D)	D/C (%)
1970	10,199	454	4.5	5,198	83	1.6
1971	10,542	476	4.5	5,094	75	1.5
1972	11,058	499	4.5	5,408	73	1.3
1973	11,600	461	4.0	5,682	57	1.0
1974	12,080	494	4.1	5,773	68	1.2
1975	12,340	510	4.1	5,673	71	1.3
1976	13,061	505	3.9	5,914	58	1.0
1977	13,440	511	3.8	4,709	61	1.1
1978	13,932	442	3.2	5,585	48	0.9
1979	14,206	542	3.8	5,402	46	0.8

Source: Economic Planning Board, *Annual Report on Economically Active Population Survey*, 1979.

reforestation during the off-farm season to utilize the food aid under the PL480 Title II in the 1960's as a wage inducement. However, in the Saemaul Undong, employment opportunities were provided primarily in two ways: one made within the agricultural sector and the other being through the expansion of off-farm employment opportunities. The accelerated growth of agriculture might be an important condition for a high employment policy and the high employment policy became, in turn, an important condition for continued rapid growth of Korean agriculture.

In the agricultural sector, both land and labor productivity have increased rapidly during the 1970's mainly due to the introduction of high-yielding varieties, increased fertilizer and chemical inputs, and other technological developments. The interesting point is that even in spite of the technological progress, the level of the agricultural labor force has remained almost the same throughout the 1970's. From this, it can be inferred that agricultural development in Korea has so far been labor-absorptive rather than labor-saving in nature.

The Saemaul Undong, indeed, works to encourage farmers to

cultivate special cash crops to increase their income. It is stimulated by the government's technical assistance. The so-called "income-boosting projects" belong to this category which was emphasized by the Saemaul Undong particularly during the 1973–76 period. These included sericulture, mushroom cultivation, livestock farming, tea, hops, chinese herbs, fruit, oysters and other special crops which tended to absorb the idle labor force and improve labor productivity.

The Saemaul Undong was also active in organizing wage-earning projects which were linked to the improvement of the rural infrastructure in the agricultural sector and village environment. These included public works, small river rearrangement, road reconstruction, farm road construction, irrigation, new land development, sewage projects, reforestation and so forth. Table 11-17 indicates that, during the period 1974–79, the Saemaul Undong conducted 52.4 thousand wage-earning projects with the financial support of the Government. Through the implementation of such projects approximately 69.2 million man-days of rural employment were additionally made so as to provide a source of wage income within the rural and agricultural sector especially during the off-farm season.

Table 11-17 Saemaul Wage-earning Projects, 1974–79

	1974	1975	1976	1977	1978	1979	Total
Gov't Support (in billion won)	15.1	24.0	19.6	13.2	15.1	34.2	121.2
No. of Households Benefited (in thousand)	446	446	446	462	462	483	–
No. of Persons Employed (in million man-days)	15.5	15.9	13.1	7.4	6.1	11.2	69.2
No. of Projects (in thousand)	9.7	11.3	9.6	4.6	4.9	12.4	52.4
Wage Income Earned per Household (in thousand)	26.5	33.8	27.5	17.7	17.3	41.2	–

Source: Ministry of Home Affairs, *Ten Year History of the Saemaul Undong* Vol. II (1980), p. 42.

The second source of employment opportunities was the increase in Saemaul factories since 1973 as an integral part of the Saemaul

Undong. According to the statistics, so far approximately 680 Saemaul factories are actively working in rural areas, while 57 factories are located in urban areas. About 760 factories were established during the period 1973-77, of which about 240 factories have been closed (KRIPDC 1980). This implies that there are risks involved in locating factories in rural areas which might be related to some difficulties of accessibility to a quality labor force, adequate market, and transportation facilities, raw materials and lack of other infrastructure. In spite of such difficulties the Saemaul Undong established substantial number of Saemaul factories. The Saemaul factories, indeed, provided a considerable number of employment opportunities, as shown in Table 11-20, by enlarging the non-agricultural sector in rural areas. The number of employees working in Saemaul factories has grown due to the annual increase in construction of Saemaul factories which has provided approximately 318 thousand

Table 11-18 Impact of Saemaul Factories

Year	Capital Investment (in million won)	No. of Employees (in thousand)	Wage Earnings (in million won)
1973	2,167	19.1	956
1974	3,955	22.6	3,570
1975	3,320	33.6	7,717
1976	7,200	48.9	16,329
1977	3,625	60.6	27,837
1978	4,674	67.5	42,895
1979	6,978	68.0	64,232

Source: Ministry of Home Affairs, *Ten Year History of the Saemaul Undong*, Vol, II (1980), pp. 41-42.

employment opportunities over the whole period 1973-79. The rural people's wage income has grown by the amout of 164 billion won throughout the same period by being employed in Saemaul factories.

Although an increasing number of Saemaul factories have been constructed, the impact on employment seems to be still limited. By 1979, 5.9% of the total labor force in rural areas was employed by Saemaul factories which have definitely contributed to rural employment as they are foot-loose industries. Off-farm employment opportunities are related to industries located in local industrial centers which could be accessible to rural people through daily commuting, if transportation is available. However, the transportation and communication network between rural and urban areas are somewhat limited. Therefore, the off-farm employment opportunities in Korean rural areas are further limited. As shown in Table 11-19, although the ratio of off-farm income has gradually increased over time, it is not so significant as in Japan and Taiwan where the majority of rural income depends on off-farm employment (75% in Japan in 1978, and 48% in Taiwan in 1978). The average share of off-farm income for the Korean farms was only 28% in 1978 and 31% in 1979. It should be pointed out in this connection that the portion of wage and salary income of the off-farm income in Korea tends to be smaller by as much as 53% of it as indicated in Table 11-20. In other words, although off-farm income in Korea has increased, it has not relied on the expansion of employment opportunities in the non-farm sector.

Therefore, the employment opportunities in rural areas have increased through the stimulation of the Saemaul Undong mostly

Table 11–19 Average Farm Household Income by Source

Unit: thousand won: (%)

Year	Farm Income (A)	Off-farm Income (B)	Total Farm Household Income (C)	Share of Farm Income A/C (%)
1964	104	22	126	82.5
1966	101	29	130	77.7
1968	137	42	179	76.5
1970	194	62	256	75.8
1971	292	64	356	82.0
1972	353	76	429	82.3
1973	390	91	481	81.1
1974	542	132	674	80.4
1975	715	158	873	81.9
1976	921	235	1,156	79.7
1977	1,036	397	1,433	72.3
1978	1,356	528	1,884	72.0
1979	1,531	696	2,227	68.8

Source: Mninistry of Agriculture and Fisheries. 1980

Table 11-20 Structure of Off-Farm Income

Unit: %

Year	Total Off-Farm	Wages & Salaries	Others*
1965	100	40.1	59.9
1970	100	48.0	52.0
1975	100	55.0	45.0
1976	100	50.2	49.8
1977	100	47.8	52.2
1978	100	50.3	49.7
1979	100	53.6	46.4

*Including property income, income transfer, etc.
Source: Whang, I.J., *Rural Development Startegies to Cope with Rapidly Growing Industries in Korea* (National Council of Economy & Sciences, Seoul, 1980), p. 213.

within the agricultural sector. In other words, the Saemaul Undong stressed a strategy for labor-absorption within the agricultural sector with a secondary stress on the increasing role of Saemaul projects for off-farm employment.

C. Strategies for Motivating Rural People

Most developing countries tend to be concerned with the supply side of employment opportunities as the major thrust to alleviate rural unemployment and poverty. However, it seems too presumptive in many cases, unless the rural people are readily motivated to work harder and to improve their rural life. As indicated earlier, spiritual enlightenment was organized as a major integral part of the rural development strategy. It emphasized the inculcation of values and attitudes toward self-help, cooperation and diligence, which indeed was an attempt to reconstruct the work ethic of rural as well as urban people in Korea.

In pursuit of this spiritual change, three major activities are worth noting in this chapter. First, in selection of development projects at the village level the priority was given to physical infrastructure in the initial period of the Saemaul Undong. They included improvement in the village environment such as the village entrance roads, farm roads, village halls, sanitary water supply, village laundry place, etc. The benefit of such projects completed by the villagers' cooperative and self-help efforts could then be immediately identifiable because they were visible and tangible in nature. Therefore, the participation of rural people in the implementation of these projects tended to reinforce their cooperative attitudes, a self-help spirit and motivation especially in the early stage of such a movement.

Second, village leadership was of critical importance for initiating and reinforcing this spiritual enlightenment. Therefore, leadership training was a strategic component of the Saemaul Undong to motivate rural people and maintain the motivational level of farmers for village development activities as well as for their better life. The Saemaul Leaders Training Program was organized under government sponsorship with a view to fostering village leadership as well as inculcating work ethics, namely self-help, diligence and cooperation (Chapter 10).

Third, the people's motivation could be further reinforced by the dominant social norms if they are favorable to the Saemaul Undong. Therefore, a remarkable program was broadly undertaken for information-education-communication (IEC) activities which made a far-reaching change in the attitudes of the general public and created a favorable social mood. As mentioned before, the wider participation of the societal elite from every sector provided the effective IEC of the Saemaul Undong and, thus, the rural people were embraced psychologically within the action framework of the Saemaul Undong. Social recognition of the Saemaul Undong and the developmental role of Saemaul leaders as change agents was further emphasized by the top political leadership (Chapter 4), further in the form of a variety of awards, incentives and privileges endowed in connection with the Saemaul Undong.

D. Linking Opportunities and Motivation

Rural employment could not take place in a vacuum. Especially, the creation of opportunities and the process of motivating people tend to be based on different sources in the rural sector. Therefore, there is no such guarantee for the automatic link between job opportunities and motivated people to the actualization of an increase in rural employment. In a pure economic sense, the link between supply and demand could be established at a certain price level (or wage level) through the market mechanism. However, the market for rural employment could not be a free, competitive, and complete one where the price mechanism works efficiently.

The Saemaul Undong, in this respect, appears to be quite unique in its nature. As it attempted to undertake social and community infrastructure projects which produce public goods, wages could not play a determinant role in linking motivation to employment opportunities. Instead, indirect rewards and compensation including social recognition or their own awareness of the benefit of such projects would be an effective reward system in the case of the Saemaul Undong. As pointed out earlier, the increase in additional income by undertaking income-boosting projects served as an important mechanism for the increase in employment at the individual or household level since those projects produced private goods as an income source.

Another important mechanism for linking people's motivation with employment opportunities was the leadership role in village organization. It is interesting, in this connection, to note that village leadership was successfully exercised by Saemaul leaders in close collaboration with the village chief. Saemaul leaders tended to initiate and organize village development projects sometimes with the guidance of local officials, which was in a sense itself conducive to the creation of work opportunities in the village context. They also motivated village people to participate in the decision-making process either through Village Development Committee or the Village General Assembly, through which the rural people most likely made a commitment to their active participation in the implementation of those projects. Saemaul leaders tended to play a critical role in motivating villagers to work harder through the campaign of the Saemaul Spirit. In other words, they play partly an educator's role and also an advocator's role in introducing technological innovation into their agricultural enterprising. Lastly, they also play a manager's role in planning, designing and implementing Saemaul projects at the community level (Chapter 5).

In brief, the leadership and organizational strategies underlined by the Saemaul Undong played a unique role in linking employment opportunities supplied and the people's motivation to work in the rural context of Korea.

4. Summary and Conclusions

The Saemaul Undong has contributed to the development of the national economy as a whole through a series of investment projects for rural development. The Saemaul Undong contributed partly to the abolishment of income differentials between the urban and rural sectors by increasing farm household income. It also contributed to the cultivation of the habits of thrift and savings as well as an increase in private savings. The Saemaul Undong also made a positive contribution to balanced regional development between urban and rural sectors as well as among rural villages. In addition, the Saemaul Undong provided rural people with opportunities for employment through Saemaul factories to increase their non-farm income. Furthermore, it partly contributed to export promotion through Saemaul factories although the level of this contribution is low.

The rural economy tended to be treated as a burden on the national economy in the process of industrial development before the Saemaul Undong was organized. It now can be stated from the above analysis that the Saemaul Undong activated the rural economy as a strategic part of the national economy to perform a significant role in economic and social development. Hence, the Saemaul Undong has provided the government with a rationale for the generous allocation of resources in favor of rural development.

In this respect, special attention should be paid to the rural employment strategies underlined in the Saemaul Undong. Some lessons drawn from the Korean approach are as follows:

First, the strategies adopted by the Saemaul Undong to increase rural employment seem to be quite systemic and comprehensive in the sense that they attempted to influence: (a) the supply aspect by creating employment opportunities; (b) the demand aspect by motivating rural people to self-help, diligence and cooperation; and (c) intervening mechanisms to link supply and demand.

Second, employment opportunities tended to be created within the agricultural sector with a view to improving the labor-absorbing capacity of agriculture in the early stage of rural development. However, at a later stage, it tended to encourage the creation of off-farm employment opportunities. It seems to be a logical and solid approach to introduce differentiation of emphasis by stage, especially in the long run.

Third, even for the creation of off-farm employment, so far the Korean approach has emphasized rather foot-loose industries in rural areas, namely Saemaul factories, although their construction and introduction into rural areas has depended considerably upon government support. It also seems to be wise, however, to encourage local industrial centers with a view to providing off-farm employment opportunities for commuting rural people because this approach can only be possible when socio-economic pressure for any increase in rural income is mounting, people's motivation and technical skills becoming higher, and the transportation and communication network between rural areas and industrial zones becoming more efficient.

Fourth, the motivation of rural people, reconstruction of the work ethic, and formation of a societal mood in favor of rural employment and hardwork have been organized by the major activities of the Saemaul Undong. This aspect used to be neglected in many developing countries. The approach also seemed to be a nationwide mobilization of instruments available in every sector of the society including special training, nationwide IEC activities and strategic selection of village development projects.

Fifth, the appropriate reward system seemed to be of essential importance in the arrangement of actual employment and participation in the working situation. It did not necessarily rely on the market principle in the rural context. Another important consideration, in this connection, is the organizational approach by which village leadership can play a most critical role in the actualization of rural employment. It also should be born in mind that the organization and leadership role should be elaborated within the socio-cultural context of the particular rural community.

The Saemaul Undong is an employment-oriented strategy for rural development in Korea. During the last decade, the increase in rural employment was primarily absorbed within the agricultural sector. Beside the strategic elements analyzed above, there are some significant socio-economic conditions which supported such an approach (Chapter 13).

The first factor is the basic infrastructure for rural and agricultural development which was already in place partly due to Korea's rapid economic growth in the 1960's prior to the inception of the Saemaul Undong. Thus, the Saemaul Undong could work its multiplier effects on economic growth as well as on income distribution.

The second factor is technological innovation in agriculture which helped to improve agricultural productivity. The dissemination of high-yielding varieties of rice, increased inputs of fertilizer and chemicals, and other new technology augmented the material base for the Saemaul Undong.

The third factor is positive government support and efficient local administration. The high rice price policy not only provided farmers with incentives to produce more rice but also directly enhanced the level of farm household income.

The fourth factor is the structure of food demand in the 1970's which was conducive to agricultural growth and development under the Saemaul Undong. An increased amount of rice production promoted by the Saemaul Undong was easily consumed by an increasing demand for it. Now the per capita consumption of food grains is gradually decreasing while demand for animal protein food tends to increase. Under these circumstances, the Saemaul Undong may have to adjust to the changing pattern of food consumption (Kada 1980, 30).

However, the strategies underlined in the Saemaul Undong can not continue because of changing socio-economic conditions. As economic development raises the wage level of both industrial and agricultural workers there emerges a strong pressure for farm mechanization. The increase in per capita income tends to bring about a change in the pattern of food demand toward more consumption of livestock products, vegetables, and fruit and less cereals. The need for diversification of farm products as such may require a different use of the labor force. Therefore, it seems to be difficult to continue the same strategies for rural employment by absorbing labor within the agricultural sector on the basis of labor-intensive farming. The future frontiers of rural employment in Korea will be an increase in off-farm employment in local industries through daily commuting.

Chapter 12

IMPACT ON VALUES AND PERCEPTIONS OF RURAL FARMERS

1. Introduction

The Saemaul Undong was introduced for planned social change in Korean rural communities to promote rural development and modernization. Rural development can be identified in terms of changes in the individuals in the rural villages, the community structure and organizations, and the rural environment (Whang 1978, 115–117). Changes at the individual level are identified in terms of their internalized values and perceptions. Those at the organizational level are identified in terms of changes in the pattern of interactions among the rural people and in the village leadership. A most significant change in rural environment is related to the rural economies. In this chapter, however, the values and perceptions of the rural people are analyzed with a view to partly evaluating the extent to which the Saemaul Undong has contributed to rural development in Korea.

Since Weber's classic study (1959) on the development of capitalism, the importance of human factors such as the values and perceptions of people in economic development has been widely recognized. From it's very inception, accordingly, the Saemaul Undong in Korea has tried to inculcate developmental values and perceptions in the rural people. As a matter of fact, spiritual enlightenment for the inculcation of developmental values such as self-help, diligence and cooperation was adopted as part of the goals and programs of the rural Saemaul Undong. Beyond that, it has also played a strategic role in promoting the movement. An analysis of the influence of the Saemaul Undong on the values and perception of the people is necessary for understanding the process of motivating rural people as well as inducing their participation in rural development activities. The content and degree of changes in the values and perceptions of rural people will provide critical information for adjusting the basic strategies and policy directions of rural development in accordance with the possible changes in rural areas in the future. To what extent did the Saemaul Undong have an impact on the values and attitudes of people?

The major hypothesis discussed in this chapter is that ever since the Saemaul Undong was launched in 1970, changes in values and perceptions of rural people have become developmental and their attitudinal pattern has become more modernized.

The measurement of changes in values and attitude should not aim at finding the individual preferences or internal psychological conditions of an individual as is usually done by social psychologists (Macklin 1969, 85–146). It rather should aim at discovering action potentials (Kim KD 1966, 226–228). Therefore, values are defined as concepts that pursue purpose and become the criteria for selection of particular courses of action (Kluckhohn 1951, 388–433). In other words, an attempt was made in this chapter to find out what values have been newly inculcated or reinforced by the Saemaul Undong and what implications these new values will have in the future course of rural modernization. Therefore in this chapter, the role of values is viewed as a prerequisite for social change and development (Kim KD 1967, 179–200).

However, there still remains room in which cultural sanctions, institutional mechanisms and other situational factors may intervene in the process of causal links between individual values and anticipated actions. In other words, situational facilitating factors (Kim IC 1971, 174–182) as well as other environmental variables

(Kunkel 1965, 257-277) that may provoke specific motivations or action patterns should be taken into account in any reasonable interpretation of value implications.

Furthermore, values and attitudinal patterns are not considered one-dimensional but rather multi-dimensional attitudinal constructs (Kim KD 1971). Since this study aims mainly at examining the predictability of particular actions in terms of values, items which are internally consistent, universalistic, highly abstractive, and which also serve as indirect referents of actions are defined as values. On the other hand, other items which are considered to be under direct and concrete influence of situational factors and which are closely related to concrete actions are defined as attitudes. In other words, changes in the values and perception of rural people in this study are grouped into two categories: development-oriented values and general attitudinal patterns.

In this chapter, the development values of people are analyzed in terms of their change-orientation, future-orientation, achievement motivation and rationality. Their attitudes are discussed in terms of attitudes toward a particular behavior and socio-cultural structure of a village, perception of agriculture, cooperative attitude and solidarity with neighbors, ability to communicate and views on the role of women and young people.

As changes in these values and attitudes differ depending on the degree and speed of development in each village, a comparative analysis is made in this chapter. Villages were grouped by two standards: (1) whether they won the presidential award (outstanding villages) or not (common villages), and 2) whether they were developing villages or developed villages as classified by the government (MOHA 1980). The difference in these two standards is that the former criterion depends on the speed of village development while the latter is based on the degree of development. A presidential award does not indicate an absolute degree of development because it is awarded depending on results and achievement of a particular village in a certain period of time. However, the classification of villages into the categories of developing and developed villages depends on the annual evaluation of a particular village's status according to ten specific items. A developing village can be a winner of the presidential prize for its outstanding performance in Saemaul projects within a short period of time. However, whether it belongs to the category of developing or developed villages is judged on the basis of the absolute requirements in terms of development level. Therefore, it is very meaningful to apply both standards to any analysis of the implications of changes in the values and perceptions of rural people.

The data for the systematic analysis were collected through interviews with 1,497 heads of farm households as they are the primary participating units in the Saemaul Undong at the village level. The respondents are those who have lived in the 36 sample villages selected by a stratified sampling method (Appendix One). To secure higher reliability of the interview data, a mailing questionnaire was applied to 288 government officials at both the county and township levels who serve the 36 villages (Chapter 5) and therefore have frequent contact with the persons sampled.

2. Value-Orientations of Rural People

A. Change-Orientation

Rural development requires changes in internalized values of individual members of a rural community. In an analysis, not only the content of changes but also change procedures themselves must be considered. Change-orientation refers to the criteria by which an individual tends to accept new ideas, technological innovations or new living modes in a social system (Inkeles 1974, 15–35). It means the internalized criteria by which an individual chooses a certain course of action in favor of changes in his environment, and either infuses changes into his environment or adapts himself to the environmental changes around him (Whang 1970, 22).

To study change-orientation in rural people, this study questioned people on whether they "feel a necessity for development of new varieties of rice" and on their acceptability of a new variety, if it is developed. As shown in Table 12-1, 70% of the total rural people answered that development of new varieties should continue while only 7% said they did not feel any necessity or there was no need to develop new varieties. Therefore, it may be concluded that change-orientation toward technological innovation in agriculture is very high.

There was no conspicuous difference in regard to the necessity for new variety development between outstanding and common villages and between developed and developing villages, as shown in Table 12-1. This may indicate that change-orientation, as far as new varieties are concerned, has been highly inculcated since the development of new varieties was widely advertised for their dissemination from the very beginning of the rural Saemaul Undong. Another finding in this table is that although people in outstanding villages were apt to adopt a new variety, they showed little positive response in the survey because of the severe damage they have suffered in recent years from insects and blight. It is impossible to make an accurate interpretation with this information alone as this is not a longitudinal study but rather a comparative study on a time spot. However, it seems to be clear that village people become strongly oriented to change and innovation in farming technology.

Table 12-1. Necessity of New Variety Development: Outstanding vs. Common Villages

Unit: person (%)

Responses	Common Villages	Outstanding Villages	Total
Should develop continuously	400 (68.6)	640 (70.0)	1,040 (69.5)
May have to develop	144 (24.7)	201 (22.0)	345 (23.0)
Almost no need to do	29 (5.0)	54 (5.9)	83 (5.5)
No need at all	7 (1.2)	13 (1.4)	20 (1.3)
No response	3 (0.5)	6 (0.7)	9 (0.6)
Total	583(100.0)	914(100.0)	1,497(100.0)

Source: Whang (1980a, 71).

The second question regarding their willingness to accept new varieties appears to be more action-related since it referred to more realistic and concrete cases, while the first question on the necessity of new varieties was more abstract in nature. People's responses to the second question were comparatively more cautious than they were to the first question. Only 3% of them took the most positive position—that is, "Will cultivate new varieties," while 31% took a slightly positive position by replying that they would try after observing the results of cultivation by agricultural experiemental stations. Twenty seven percent took a conservative position by saying that they would plant new varieties only after looking at the result of other farmers' trial cultivation. In view of the serious damage to new varieties in 1978 from which the farmers suffered, their reply to that particular question might be biased, since this study was conducted in 1979. The change-orientation not only includes innovation-orientation with which people anticipate the better results of a new approach but also includes the psychological cost of risk-taking (Kim HJ 1979, 57–74). Considering the fact that most of the surveyed people were petty farmers with only around one hectare of land, the psychological cost of risk-taking could have strongly affected their attitude toward the cultivation of new varieties.

Table 12-2. Willingness to Try New Varieties

Unit: person (%)

Responses	Developed Villages	Developing Villages	Total
Will cultivate new varieties	96 (25.8)	357 (31.7)	453 (30.3)
Will do so after government experimentation	116 (31.2)	350 (31.1)	466 (31.1)
Will do so after other farmers' trial	111 (29.8)	296 (26.3)	407 (27.2)
Will do so after 3–4 years, if good	38 (10.2)	92 (8.2)	130 (8.7)
Not at all	6 (1.6)	20 (1.8)	26 (1.7)
No response	5 (1.3)	10 (0.9)	15 (1.0)
Total	372 (100.0)	1,125 (100.0)	1,497 (100.0)

Source: Whang (1980a, 73).

There was no significant difference in their willingness to cultivate new varieties between outstanding and common villages. Nevertheless a difference was found, as shown in Table 12-2, between developed and developing villages. People in developed villages were far more positive toward the cultivation of new varieties than those in developing villages.

It is necessary to remind the reader here that change-orientation includes the psychological cost of risk taking. The failure of farmers in outstanding villages to demonstrate conspicuous innovation-orientation might have come from their bitter experience with bad crops in 1978 and subsequent judgment that their economic and psychological costs were higher than the value of innovation.

Despite the widely recognized achievements of the rural Saemaul Undong it is generally admitted that its success largely depends on trial and error especially when it is pushed forcibly by government. This may explain why farmers in rapidly developing outstanding villages exhibit a tendency to withdraw from their change-orientation.

On the other hand, farmers in more developed villages regardless of their development speed might find themselves at a certain level of wealth by virtue of which they can overcome psychological costs to a considerable extent. As forcible and drastic changes may bring about undesirable side-effects instead of cultivating change-orientation and an innovative attitude among the people, the farmers' actual ability to pay for the opportunity cost of risk-taking and the felt-needs for better results have probably become conditions for both formation and retainment of change-orientation. From the analysis of people's interview, rural people seemed to be oriented to change and innovation, especially in developed villages.

Supplementary information regarding people's value orientation is provided by the observation of government officials which indicates that the rural farmers were more positive toward changes as shown in Table 12-3. The question was put to local officials: "What is the attitude of the rural people toward adopting new ideas in daily life?" Thirty one percent (or ninty) of the 288 government officials said most people had become positive toward innovation as compared to the initial stage of the Saemaul Undong, while 39% (or 111 officials) viewed that many of them had become somewhat positive to change. In other words, about 70% of the officials said that farmers seemed to be more innovative and change-oriented as a result of the Saemaul Undong. This view is consistent with the results of the interview with the rural people. These indices show that the Saemaul Undong has brought about changes in values and perceptions of rural people with respect to change-orientation and innovation.

Table 12-3. Views of Government Officials on the People's Attitudes toward Change

Unit: person (%)

Attitude Judgment	Persons
Most are positive	90 (31.3)
Some are positive	111 (38.5)
Half and half	56 (19.4)
Some are negative	29 (10.1)
Most are negative	2 (0.7)
Total	288(100.0)

Source: Whang (1980a, 74).

B. Future-Orientation

Future-orientation is a time-dimensional criteria by which a person's behavior is regulated and planned into the unknown future (Whang 1970a, 22). One pursues values of the future according to this criteria, and his goal-orientation or expectation becomesn important criterion in selecting a certain direction and thus displaying a certain pattern of behavior.

Some remarkable efforts have been made for conceptualization of time-orientation toward past, present and future in terms of human values (Lee HB 1968, 15-40; Kluckhohn 1951; Inkeles 1974). It is believed that a modern personality is characterized by a dominant future-orientation as opposed to a past-orientation. In a study of Korean farmers' attitudes (Keim 1972, 65-100), future-orientation could be defined as their ability to welcome and project into the future without clinging to either the past, for fear of the unknown future, or to the present for opportunistic reasons. Future-orientation was defined as the zeal of people for the future (Rogers 1969, 51-56) as demonstrated by their desire to educate their children and encourage them to engage in prestigious jobs. In order to identify the time-orientation of rural farmers, in this chapter their responses to two questions in the interview were analyzed: (a) uses of a substantial amount of additional income, and b) the degree of their future concern.

According to Table 12-4, to the first question "For what will you spend your money if you receive some?" 18% of people answered "For the care of their parents and improving their ancestors' graves" which implicitly indicates past-orientation. On the other hand 26% were present-oriented in view of their answer that they would use the money to make their daily life more convenient. About 56% said they would use the money "Either for their children's education or for the purchase of farming equipment," which suggests that they have future-orientation. This implies that rural people have become considerably future-oriented.

Table 12-4. Use of Money

Unit: person (%)

Responses	Developing Villages	Developed Villages	Total	Common Villages	Outstanding Villages
For parent's & ancestor's graves	71 (19.1)	194 (17.2)	265 (17.7)	112 (19.2)	153 (16.7)
For coveniences of life	124 (33.3)	258 (22.9)	382 (25.5)	141 (24.2)	241 (26.4)
For children or for farm equipment	171 (46.0)	660 (58.7)	831 (55.5)	321 (55.1)	510 (55.8)
No response	6 (1.6)	13 (1.2)	19 (1.3)	9 (1.5)	10 (1.1)
Total	372 (100.0)	1,125 (100.0)	1,497 (100.0)	583 (100.0)	914 (100.0)

Source: Whang (1980a, 76).

Table 12-4 shows the different responses given by farmers in developing versus developed villages and in common versus outstanding villages with regard to the first question. People in developed and outstanding villages appear to be more future-oriented than those in developing and common villages since 17% of the people in the former group is past-oriented while 19% in the latter group has such value. This confirms the hypothesis that villagers in more developed areas tend to be more futuristic. There is no significant difference between common and outstanding villages in both future- and present-orientations. However, the difference between developing and developed villages seems to be significant. Fifty nine percent of the people in developed villages are future-oriented while only 46% in the developing villages are future-oriented. In other words, there is no significant difference in future and present-orientations between common and outstanding villages, while there is notable difference between developed and developing villages.

It is interesting to note, in this connection that despite the successful results of the Saemaul Undong in decreasing past-oriented attitudes among farmers, it might have contributed even more to the formation of present-oriented values among them because most Saemaul projects have aimed at immediate results and performance. This may explain why the people in outstanding villages were less future-oriented although they had achieved rapid development.

The response of rural people to the second question shows that people in developed villages are more future-oriented than those in developing villages. According to the frequency of "Thinking about their lives 5–10 years later" shown in Table 12-5, sixty three precent of the rural people think of it very often or frequently. The percentage of people who think about the future very frequenty was much higher in developed villages reaching 65% as compared to 56% in developing villages. There may be a controversy on the reliability of measuring one's future-orientation level in terms of frequency of thinking about one's future life. However, the study had to employ an interview method because of the limitations of social science studies at the present time.

It is very difficult to tell whether or not the Saemaul Undong has really inculcated a future-orientation in village people or whether people in developed villages were more future-oriented from the very beginning. In order to collect supplementary data on the value impact of the Saemaul Undong, the opinions of government officials are also analyzed.

About 83% of the 288 government officials thought that rural people had become more positive about their future as compared to the earlier period of the Saemaul Undong. This interpretation is based on their answers to the question, "What do you think of the attitudes of the farmers in planning for their future as compared to an earlier stage of the Saemaul Undong?" As shown in Table 12-6, 112 officials (or 39%) of the total 288 answered that most of the rural people used to make plans for their future life while 126 officials (or 44%) answered "a considerable number" of them did so. It is hard to tell how accurate this judgement is. Nevertheless, developmental values and future-orientation among

Table 12-5. How Often People Think about the Future

Unit: person (%)

Responses	Developing Villages	Developed Villages	Total
Very often	91 (24.5)	365 (32.4)	456 (30.5)
Often	118 (31.7)	363 (32.3)	481 (32.1)
Sometimes	90 (24.2)	258 (22.9)	348 (23.2)
Not so often	46 (12.4)	113 (10.0)	159 (10.6)
Almost none	22 (5.9)	25 (2.2)	47 (3.1)
No response	5 (1.3)	1 (0.1)	6 (0.4)
Total	372 (100.0)	1,125 (100.0)	1,497 (100.0)

Source: Whang (1980a, 78).

Table 12-6. Future Planning of Rural People Observed by Government Officials

Unit: person (%)

Responses	Persons
Most farmers think & plan for future	112 (38.9)
A considerable number of them do so	128 (44.4)
Approximately do and half don't	30 (10.4)
Many farmers do not	14 (4.9)
Most farmers never do	4 (1.4)
Total	288 (100.0)

Source: Whang (1980a, 78).

rural people have been reinforced by the Saemaul Undong, the process of "social mobilization" (Deutsch 1961, 493–514), generation change, improved education, and the influence of mass media.

C. Achievement Motivation

Achievement motivation means a person's desire to do better for his own internal satisfaction not for the sake of social recognition or prestige.

According to various comparative analyses between countries or societies, the achievement motivation of people is regarded as a prerequisite for rapid development and change in a country. Characteristically, it influences economic development in the next generation rather than the immediate one. (McClelland

1961, 36).

But in this study the concept of achievement motivation was mainly used to analyze the process of formation of entrepreneurship in the development of capitalism, rather than for an assessment of pre-modern society or peasants (Sutcliffe 1974, 238–246). In a survey of Latin American peasants which proved the importance of achievement motivation among farmers for the modernization of rural communities, motivation is defined as a social value by which an individual wants to become better in the future (Rogers 1969, 242–272).

In this study, the level of achievement motivation among rural people was indirectly measured by asking people's views about their own life 5 to 10 years in the future. The question appears simple but it is simply designed to reflect the hopes and desires of the people sampled. According to Table 12-7, forty percent of the rural people sampled thought that they "Will be much better off than now," while only 15% viewed that they "Will be almost the same as now or worse." This confirms the hypothesis that rural people have a very high desire or achievement motivation for further advancement in the future.

As seen in Table 12-7, there was no significant difference between developed and developing villages on this matter. This may reflect the pessimistic attitudes of the farmers at that time although the question was dealing with the future. The farmers were complaining about the liberalization of agricultural product importation by the government while they were themselves suffering from bad crops due to serious pest problems and blight in 1978. Worse than that was the fact that the grain purchase price set by the government increased only 13.2% and 14.3% in 1977 and 1978 respectively, the lowest increase since 1973. Thus, the widespread dissatisfaction among farmers at the time of the survey might have influenced their reaction to the question even though they were highly motivated up until 1977.

A complementary analysis was attempted to find changes in achievement motivation among the rural people throughout the 1970's from the point of view of government officials. It is assumed that the higher their achievement motivation, the greater would be their desire and effort to solve their problems spontaneously.

Table 12-7. Prospect of Farmers' Future Life

Unit: person (%)

Responses	Developing Villages	Developed Villages	Total
Much better off	138(37.1)	466(41.4)	604(40.4)
Getting a little better	171(46.0)	497(44.2)	668(44.6)
Almost no change	50(13.4)	115(10.2)	165(11.0)
Getting a little worse	6(1.6)	35(3.1)	41(2.7)
Getting worse	3(0.8)	10(0.9)	13(0.9)
No response	4(1.1)	2(0.2)	6(0.4)
Total	372(100.0)	1,125(100.0)	1,497(100.0)

Source: Whang (1980a, 80).

A total of 288 government officials were asked to answer the question "How much do you think the motivational level of rural people has changed in terms of solving their own problems as compared to what it was at the initial stage of the Saemaul Undong?" As shown in Table 12-8, 37% (or 105 officials) of the 288 respondents answered that their motivation was "increasing greatly" while 38% (or 110 officials) said it was "increasing slightly." This means that about 75% of the officials took a positive position on this issue by answering that the achievement motivation of the rural people was greater than it was at the early stage of the Saemaul Undong.

The above analyses indicate that the achievement motivation of rural people is considerably higher as a result of the Saemaul Undong. It is impossible to measure the extent to which the Sae-

Table 12-8. Achievement Motivation of Rural People Observed by Government Officials

Unit: person (%)

Responses	Persons
Increasing greatly	105(36.5)
Increasing slightly	110(38.2)
Same as before	19(6.6)
Decreasing	44(15.3)
Decreasing greatly	9(3.1)
No response	1(0.0)
Total	288(100.0)

Source: Whang (1980a, 81).

maul Undong has contributed to value change among the rural people. Nontheless, as the Saemaul Undong has worked for the establishment of "well-to-do villages", it seems obvious that it has stimulated rural people's achievement motivation.

D. *Planning and Rationality*

Planning is an action process in which various alternative courses are evaulated and from among them the best way is chosen for the realization of one's goals and objectives. Planning used to be based on the perception that the future could be controlled and managed by a deliberate effort of humans in planning the process by which they could mold their lives. In a broader sense, planning implies a self-confidence with which one can understand his situation and control those future matters which are the objects of that planning. Hence, this is related to the concept of efficiency. Efficiency depends on the ability to control one's environmental elements and pursue his own goals. Thus, planning involves predicting the future, recognition, creativity, data processing and efficiency.

In order to measure the planning-mindness among rural people, a question was asked regarding their plans and estimates for the expenses of cultivation and income. According to Table 12-9, 25% of the 1,497 persons answered that they make plans "very concretely" while 49% said they set up "rough plans". This response implies that although their planning may in reality be very primitive, at least one may say that a majority (70%) of the rural

Table 12-9. Planning for Farming

Unit: peron (%)

Responses	Developing Villages	Developed Villages	Total
Make very concrete plans	282(25.1)	94(25.3)	376(25.1)
Make rough plans	549(48.8)	181(48.7)	730(48.8)
Follow instant decisions	248(22.0)	66(17.7)	314(21.0)
Make no plan	31(2.8)	10(2.7)	41(2.7)
No response	15(1.3)	21(5.6)	36(2.4)
Total	1,125(100.0)	372(100.0)	1,497(100.0)

Source: Whang (1980a, 83).

people displayed a positive attitude toward planning.

As shown in Table 12-10, the percentage dropped much lower when the rural people were asked whether they annually calculate cost and income after the harvest. About 20% of rural people said that they write down all expenditures and compare the total with income later, while 42% of them said that they estimate the total cost and income after the harvest. In any case, consideration of cost and income may indicate that they gave a positive attitude toward economic rationality. The results show that 62% of the Koreans sampled espouse rationality in their rural life and farming.

Table 12-10. **Estimating Cost and Income of Farming**

Unit: person (%)

Responses	Developing Villages	Developed Villages	Total
Usually write down all the expenses	217(19.3)	83(22.3)	300(20.0)
Estimate roughly after harvest	491(43.6)	135(36.3)	626(41.8)
Make at least some estimation of the balance	325(28.9)	102(27.4)	427(28.5)
Do not estimate at all	74(6.6)	31(8.3)	105(7.0)
No response	18(1.6)	21(5.7)	39(2.6)
Total	1,125(100.0)	372(100.0)	1,497(100.0)

Source: Whang (1980a. 83).

It seems noteworthy here that their response to the planning and accounting question falls far behind their response to the questions regarding change-orientation, future-orientation and achievement motivation. However, it should be remembered here that future planning requires not only the ability to perceive one's own future but also certain technical elements such as data processing ability. Of the sample interviewed, only 30% were educated at a middle school level or over, while about 69% were educated at only an elementary school level. Moreover, about 24% had no education at all. This means that even if the rural people espoused highly development-oriented values, they may have lacked the skills and methodology to make rational planning. Nevertheless it should be remembered that rural people are planning-oriented as they are future-oriented, based on the responses of local government officials in Table 12-6.

E. Summary

An important hypothesis of this chapter is that the Saemaul Undong has brought about profound changes in the values and perception of rural people. To verify this, extensive interview surveys were conducted among rural people with respect to change-orientation, future-orientation, achievement motivation and planning. In addition, a supplementary study was also conducted through a mailing questionnaire addressed to local officials who had been in direct contact with the people. The results of two studies showed that rural people were positive and development-oriented. In other words, their values and perceptions were found to be highly change-oriented, future-oriented and motivated. In planning, however, they displayed a relatively less modernized score compared to their scores on the other three items. This seems quite natural in view of the high technical ability required for planning in spite of the low educational level of rural people.

According to the opinions of government officials, the Saemaul Undong has induced change in the internalized values and perception of rural people toward a more development-oriented, and modernized outlook.

Comparisons between the developed and developing as well as outstanding and common villages lead to the conclusion that with regard to change-orientation and future-orientation of rural people, the difference between developed and developing villages was rather remarkable if compared to the difference between outstanding and common villages. This may have been because outstanding villages which were not necessarily well developed might have felt a heavy psychological burden due to their risk-taking, while developed villages might have somehow achieved the economic capacity to cope with those risks and thus the people were more change-oriented. As for achievement motivation and planning there were no significant differences between the villages sampled.

3. Attitudinal Pattern of the Rural People

Attitudinal patterns among rural people could be identified with reference to specific stituations and concrete reality. An attempt is made here to analyze their views on agriculture, cooperation and solidarity, participation in village projects, communication with the government, attitudes toward women and children and their perception of government officials.

A. Views on Agriculture

Two questions were asked regarding the respondents' attitude toward farming: (a) whether or not rural people think that technical improvement is necessary for agriculture and (b) whether or not they wish to give up farming in order to get other jobs. Table 12-11 shows that 712 persons (or 48%) out of total 1,149 said that a "Considerable level of technical improvement is needed in the farming sector", and 551 persons (37%) said "A little improvement is needed". These figures may indicate that some of them tend to perceive agriculture as a profession and feel proud of their vocation as farmers.

Table 12-11. Necessity of Technical Improvement

Unit: person (%)

Responses	Common Villages	Outstanding Villages	Total
Considerable improvement needed	266(45.6)	446(48.8)	712(47.6)
A little improvement needed	194(33.3)	357(39.1)	551(36.8)
Possible without much improvement	83(14.2)	87(9.5)	170(11.4)
No need at all	36(6.2)	17(1.9)	53(3.5)
No response	4(0.7)	7(0.7)	11(0.7)
Total	583(100.0)	914(100.0)	1,497(100.0)

Source: Whang (1980a, 87).

On the other hand, only 53% of the interviewed people said that they had no intention to change their vocation and about 45% expressed their desire to quit agriculture, as shown in Table 12-12. This supports the interpretation that even if the rural people have pride and a favorable perception of agriculture, other situational variables tend to force them to quit agriculture. Of course a propensity to social mobility is itself considered part of modernity, but the former interpretation seems to be a more important consideration in view of the recent socio-economic development of rural villages.

Table 12–12. Desire to Change Vocation

Unit: person (%)

Responses	Common Villages	Outstanding Villages	Total
Not wish to change vocation	320(54.9)	473(51.8)	793(53.0)
Yes if possible	204(35.0)	347(38.0)	551(36.8)
Wish to change by any means	34(5.8)	80(8.8)	114(7.6)
No response	25(4.3)	14(1.4)	39(2.6)
Total	583(100.0)	914(100.0)	1,497(100.0)

Source: Whang (1980a, 87.)

As for professionalism in agriculture, people in outstanding and developed villages showed a more positive response than those in developing and common villages as shown in Table 12-13 and 12-14. The difference in attitude was more conspicuous between common and outstanding villages. On the other hand regarding the second question, people in outstanding and developed villages displayed a stronger desire to change vocation as shown in Table 12-12 and 12-14.

This phenomenon does not arise from the level of development

Table 12–13. Necessity of Technical Improvement: Developing vs. Developed Villages

Unit: person (%)

Responses	Developing Villages	Developed Villages	Total
Considerable improvement needed	172(46.2)	540(48.0)	712(47.6)
A little improvement needed	113(30.4)	438(38.9)	551(36.8)
Possible without enough improvement	65(17.5)	105(9.3)	170(11.4)
No need at all	19(5.1)	34(3.0)	53(3.5)
No response	3(0.8)	8(0.8)	11(0.7)
Total	372(100.0)	1,125(100.0)	1,497(100.0)

Source: Whang (1980a, 88).

Table 12-14. **Desire to Change Vocation: Developing vs. Developed Villages**

Unit: person (%)

Responses	Developing Villages	Developed Villages	Total
Not wish to change	217(58.3)	576(51.2)	793(53.0)
Yes if possible	113(30.4)	438(38.9)	551(36.8)
Wish to change by any means	21(5.6)	93(8.3)	114(7.6)
No response	21(5.6)	18(1.6)	39(2.6)
Total	372(100.0)	1,125(100.0)	1,497(100.0)

Source: Whang (1980a, 88).

or speed of development in villages but rather from other intervening situational factors. A thorough analysis of those situational variables would require further study. Nevertheless, it may be assumed that the recent changes in government policies, such as lowering the rate of increase in the government purchase price of rice and liberalization of agricultural imports may have had strong impact. Another factor might be related to people's dissatisfaction about the lack of education opportunities for their children in the rural areas. And in fact, demand for such facilities is increasing due to the increase in farm income and their traditionally strong zeal for education. This may be why those in well-to-do or financially improved villages show more positive responses in this regard.

B. Cooperation and Solidarity of the Rural People

Historically, rural Korean villages have been characterized by the extended family system which is based on Confucian ethics and by an agrarian society which primarily depends on rice cultivation due to geographical and climatic conditions. Under these circumstances, rural Korean villages have developed quite naturally into the primary community units of rural Korea, bound together through both kinship and territorial boundaries. However, despite this strong sense of community perception, it is generally understood that Korean villages lacked a coherent set of cooperative attitudes before the Saemaul Undong was introduced. The three major targets of the spiritual revolution through the Saemaul Undong stimulated the promotion of cooperative attitudes. Therefore, the movement has carried out cooperation-emphasizing projects over the past 10 years, enhancing considerably the cooperation and solidarity of rural people over the past decade.

In order to sound out their sense of solidarity, two questions were asked of a sample of rural people. In the case of selling land, what is the primary condition that they consider—price or neighborhood? And what do they usually think of the neighborhood relationship in their village?

According to Table 12-15 which analyzed the result of the question "To whom would you sell your land if you leave your village?" 28% (or 420 persons) out of total 1,497 said they "would sell to neighbors even if it were at a lower price." About 13% (or 193 people) said that they would sell to outsiders if a better price was offered. Beyond these findings, however, a reliable analysis is impossible here since 54% of the respondents were undecided.

Table 12–15. To Whom to Sell Land When Moving Out: Common vs. Outstanding Villages

Unit: person (%)

Responses	Common Villages	Outstanding Villages	Total
To neighbors even at lower price	209(35.8)	211(23.1)	420(28.1)
Not decided yet	278(47.7)	533(58.3)	811(54.2)
To outsiders if better price	64(11.0)	129(14.1)	193(12.9)
No response	32(5.5)	41(4.5)	73(4.8)
Total	583(100.0)	914(100.0)	1,497(100.0)

Source: Whang (1980a, 89).

As a back up to the survey on cooperative attitudes and solidarity among rural people, the opinions of government officials were analyzed. Responses to the question "How do you think the cooperative attitudes and solidarity of the rural people have changed compared to the initial period of the Saemaul Undong?" are shown in Table 12-16.

About 20% gave the positive response that "Their cooperative attitudes were much more intensified than before". But 45% appeared more passive in this respect by saying that such attitudes have increased a little. It can be concluded, however, that the cooperative attitudes and solidarity of the rural people have been reinforced by the Saemaul Undong, as compared to what they were earlier during the initial stages of the Saemaul Undong.

The analysis of answers to other questions which were raised to measure cooperative attitudes also indicates that their neighborhood relationship has been improved over time after the Saemaul Undong was launched. Table 12-17 shows that 35% (or 524 persons) out of the total sample of 1,497 thought that the relationships among villagers had improved considerably while 36% (or 512) said that the relationships had improved only a little. This suggests that the cooperative attitudes of the people have been enhanced as a result of the Saemaul Undong.

Table 12-16. **Cooperative Attitudes of Rural People: Opinions of Government Officials**

Unit: person (%)

Responses	Persons
Intensified much more than before	57(19.8)
More intensified	129(44.8)
Little change in cooperative attitudes	35(12.2)
Tends to be less	60(20.8)
Disappeared considerably	7(2.4)
Total	288(100.0)

Source: Whan (1980a, 90).

To clarify the implication of Table 12-15 concerning cooperative attitudes and solidarity, a comparative analysis was made between developed and developing villages as shown in Table 12-18. A conspicuous difference in the level of solidarity was found between the people of developed and developing villages. People in outstanding villages were found to be more mindful of land price than those in common villages according to Table 12-15. About 36% of the people in common villages said they would sell their land to neighbors even at lower price while only 23% gave the same answer in the case of outstanding villages. This supports the interpretation that the faster a village's economic development is, the worse neighborhood relationships become.

Both the rural people themselves and the government officials who assist them in support of the Saemaul projects indicated that cooperative attitudes and solidarity among people have grown

Table 12-17. Relationship between Rural People: Common vs. Outstanding Villages

Unit: person(%)

Responses	Common Villages	Outstanding Villages	Total
Improved very much	198(34.0)	326(35.7)	524(35.0)
Improved a little	195(33.4)	307(33.6)	502(33.5)
No improvement	132(22.6)	143(15.6)	275(18.4)
Worsened a little	43(7.4)	121(13.2)	164(11.0)
Worsened very much	13(2.2)	14(1.5)	27(1.8)
No response	2(0.3)	3(0.4)	5(0.3)
Total	583(100.0)	914(100.0)	1,497(100.0)

Source: Whang (1980a, 91).

Table 12-18. To Whom to Sell Land When Moving Out: Developing vs. Developed Villages

Unit: person (%)

Responses	Developing Villages	Developed Villages	Total
To neighbors even at lower price	114(30.6)	306(27.2)	420(28.1)
Not decided yet	185(49.7)	626(55.6)	811(54.2)
To outsiders if at better price	48(12.9)	145(12.9)	193(12.9)
No response	25(6.8)	48(4.3)	73(4.8)
Total	372(100.0)	1,125(100.0)	1,497(100.0)

Source: Whang (1980a, 92).

stronger over time. Economic development tends to incline people toward economic rationality, income and monetary value. Consequently, cooperative attitudes and solidarity among people are apt to be distorted by economic factors such as price and income. Thus people in outstanding villages where economic development takes place more rapidly were found to consider economic rationality more important as a criterion for cooperation than those in common villages.

C. *Cooperative Attitudes toward Neighboring Villages*

Cooperative attitudes and solidarity with neighbors was found to be a fundamental binding force for the Saemaul Undong at the village level. As the Saemaul projects become more extensive and complex in nature, planning as well as implementation of such projects covering wider areas will require stronger cooperation among neighboring villages than before. This in turn requires a broadening of special perception on the part of the rural people from an "our village" concept to "our area" one. In other words, their cooperative attitudes and solidarity must eventually be broadened to admit other villages.

Two questions were asked in order to gauge the attitudes of the people toward villagers of neighboring villages. The first question was "Do you think people of your neighboring village would welcome you or not if you participate in their village meeting?" This was designed to find out the extent to which a villager would welcome people from other villages to participate in his village meeting. The second question was "Do you think a project will be successful if you and the people of the neighboring village work together?"

Answers to the first question are analyzed in Table 12-19. If the 1,497 people, 241 people (or 16%) gave a positive answer of "Will be very much welcomed," while 473 persons (or 32%) answered by saying "May be welcomed a little." On the other hand 52% of them showed a negative response either saying "They will pay no attention," or "They will dislike it." This implies that the

Table 12-19. **Response of Neighboring Village People If You Participate in That Village Meeting**

Unit: person (%)

Responses	Common Villages	Outstanding Villages	Total
I will be welcomed very positively	106(18.2)	135(14.8)	241(16.1)
May be welcomed a little	189(32.4)	284(31.1)	473(31.6)
They pay no attention	189(32.4)	260(28.4)	449(30.0)
They dislike it a little	84(14.4)	185(20.2)	269(18.0)
They dislike it very much	11(1.9)	44(4.8)	55(3.7)
No response	4(0.7)	6(0.7)	10(0.6)
Total	583(100.0)	914(100.0)	1,497(100.0)

Source: Whang (1980a, 93).

Saemaul Undong was successful in contributing to chance cooperation and solidarity strictly within a village, but failed in enhancing intervillage cooperation.

Table 12-20 shows the results of the second question regarding the possibility of success in inter-village joint projects. According to their responses inter-village joint projects were expected to be "very successful" by 21% of the respondents. A total of 478 persons (or 32%) of rural people said such projects would be "good'.' The response then was more or less positive. And yet it is notable that 28% of the people were sure that such projects would be "difficult" which was even higher in proportion than those who said they "cannot tell" (18%). Despite the fact that solidarity within a village is strong, this failure in terms of cooperation with other villages may be the result of Saemaul Undong strategy which calls for competition between villages. Of course, it is true that traditionally, villages or groups have displayed this same exclusiveness toward other villages but it cannot be denied that the Saemaul Undong has indeed encouraged this attitude ever further.

Table 12-20. Views on Intervillage Joint Projects

Unit: person (%)

Responses	Common Villages	Outstanding Villages	Total
Will be very successful	125(21.4)	184(20.1)	309(20.6)
Will be good	204(35.0)	274(30.0)	478(31.9)
Cannot tell	116(19.9)	165(18.1)	281(18.8)
Will be a little bit difficult	118(20.2)	236(25.8)	354(23.6)
Will be very difficult	18(3.1)	53(5.8)	71(4.7)
No response	2(0.4)	2(0.2)	4(0.3)
Total	583(100.0)	914(100.0)	1,497(100.0)

Source: Whang (1980a, 94).

With regard to inter-village collaborative projects, government officials were even more skeptical than the rural people. According to Table 12-21, only 13% of the officials said that people will be "Much more positive than they would be in a village level project" to the question "What do you think of the participation and cooperation of the rural people in the inter-village joint projects which have been organized since 1976 as compared to their inter-village projects?" About 20% (or 58 officials) gave at least a positive response of "A little bit more positive". On the other hand, a majority (66%) of them answered with a pessimistic response. This also implies that projects have mainly been done at the village level, while restricting the cooperative attitudes of people toward neighboring villages.

Table 12-21. People's Attitude toward Inter-village joint Projects: Opinions of Government Officials

Unit: person (%)

Responses	Person
Much more positive than in village project	39(13.5)
A little bit positive than in village	58(20.1)
Almost the same level of participation	62(21.5)
More passive than in village project	106(36.8)
Much more passive than in village project	22(7.6)
I don't know	1(0.3)
Total	288(100.0)

Source: Whang (1980a, 95).

This attitude will be of little help in the successful implementation of intervillage collaborative projects which will be one of the main thrusts of the Saemaul Undong in the 1980's. The government has pushed forward inter-village projects since 1976 for which more than two villages were brought together to cooperate. The ultimate goal of this type of project is to realize a balanced and harmonious development of rural communities and the whole region in social, economic and cultural fields and to narrow the income gap between the rural and urban areas. So far the Saemaul Undong has achieved environmental improvement and spiritual enlightenment to a considerable extent. The next step to be taken will be expansion of both its scope of activities and the regional unit which it covers. This is why inter-village projects are encouraged to enable people in a few villages to plan together and work together to realize their common goals and interests. As the village economy develops, the principle of "economy of scale" becomes increasingly applicable in the case of inter-village joint projects. The cooperative attitude of people beyond their own villages is a prerequisite for the success of these kinds of projects.

D. Communication Skill with Government Agencies

The communication between rural people and government officials is a basis for the dissemination of government initiated innovation. The extent of rural communication serves as a gauge of the mutual relationship. An attempt was made to measure the extent to which rural people can better communicate with government officials with regard to their views and opinions on village development. A question was asked of the people interviewed: "To what extent do you think recommendations made by the village meeting are accepted by the Gun or Myeon office?" Table 12-22 shows that 58% (or 873) out of 1,497 people said they were "Very well" or "Well" received by the government offices. Only 26% responded negatively.

Table 12-22. Acceptance of Villagers' Recommendations by Local Officials

Unit: person (%)

Responses	Developing Villages	Developed Villages	Total
Very well accepted	112(30.1)	249(22.1)	361(24.1)
Well accepted	88(23.7)	424(37.7)	512(34.2)
Not so well, not so bad	47(12.6)	176(15.6)	223(14.9)
Not well accepted	70(18.8)	180(16.0)	250(16.7)
Almost no acceptance	51(13.7)	90(8.0)	141(9.4)
No response	4(1.1)	6(0.6)	10(0.7)
Total	372(100.0)	1,125(100.0)	1,497(100.0)

Source: Whang (1980a, 96).

People in developed villages were found to be better in their ability to communicate with government agencies than those in developing villages. However, little difference was found between the people in common and outstanding villages.

E. Attitudes toward Government Officials

The traditional relationship between government officials and the people in Korea was characterized by a "bureaucratistic" subculture (Riggs 1964) in which officials were superior to peasants. In Korea the elitist ruling attitudes of the officials toward the public orginated, in spite of poor administrative services, in the Yi Dynasty and were further intensified during the period of Japanese colonial rule. Consequently, people used to be reluctant to visit the government office to request assistance. They preferred rather to follow passively the orders from the government.

However, the Saemaul Undong has brought about a change in this relationship. Due to the devoted efforts of local officials, mutual cooperation and credibility on both sides has been revitalized and accordingly, government service and guidance functions have been reinforced. In rural development projects, the relationship between the rural people and the local government officials is a very important factor (Whang 1978, 118-121). Local government officials play an important role in establishing a channel which links the central government with the rural people.

To examine the extent to which the Saemaul Undong has influenced the attitudes of the rural people toward government officials, a question was asked of the people regarding their perception of the attitudinal change of local officials over the period: "To what extent do you think the attitude of local officials toward people has changed from what it was 7 or 8 years ago when the Saemaul Undong started." Positive responses came from the majority (83%) of those 1,497 persons interviewed as shown in Table 12-23. People in outstanding villages made more positive responses than those in common villages.

Perhaps surprisingly, government officials answered that rural people's attitudes toward officials were even more friendly and democratic than the rural respondents said they were. As shown in Table 12-24, 52% (or 149 officials) of the 288 officials answered that "the rural people appeared to perceive officials as being substantially more accessible than before" in view of their manner toward officials. Forty one percent (or 119 officials) of the 288 answered that "rural people tended to perceive officials as more easily accessible than they were before" as reflected in their manner. The remainder of the officials answered that the people perceived officials as still difficult to contact.

Table 12-23. Attitudes of Local Officials to People

Unit: person (%)

Responses	Common Villages	Outstanding Villages	Total
Became much more cordial than before	272(46.7)	440(48.1)	712(47.6)
Became a little bit more cordial	182(31.2)	342(37.4)	524(35.0)
Same as before	100(17.2)	91(10.0)	191(12.8)
Became a little bit unfriendly	22(3.8)	29(3.2)	51(3.4)
Became very unfriendly	3(0.5)	3(0.3)	6(0.4)
No response	4(0.6)	9(0.1)	13(0.8)
Total	583(100.0)	914(100.0)	1,497(100.0)

Source: Whang (1980a, 98).

Table 12-24. People's Manner Against Officials: Officials' View

Unit: person (%)

Responses	Person
Became substantially more accessible	149(51.7)
Became more easily accessible	119(41.3)
Still somewhat difficult to access	15(5.2)
Still very difficult to access	5(1.7)
Total	288(100.0)

Source: Whang (1980a. 98).

This change in mutual perceptions has come about as a result of frequent dialogues between the people and local officials and positive support from the government through direct contact brought about through the Saemaul Undong. As a result, the Saemaul Undong tends to form a foundation for grass-root democracy from the local level by improving the relationship between the people and the government and eradicating bureaucratism. In most developing countries, remnants from colonialism and the bureaucratistic system tend to hinder rural innovation. Hence, it may be argued that the Saemaul Undong has built up momentum for self-reliant rural development by contributing to the improvement in government-people relationships.

F. Attitudes toward Women and Children

The importance of the role of women in integrated community development is widely accepted. As a matter of fact, the Saemaul Undong adopted this principle as an important strategy in order to induce the active participation of women and to organize women's role in rural change. As discussed in Chapter 6, women's role in the Saemaul Undong has been quite extensive. Therefore, an attempt is made below to find out what changes and influences have been brought about in the social status and recognition of women as a result of their active participation in rural development. As such the following question was raised to the village people during the interview survey: "To what extent do you think the Saemaul Women's Association was helpful in the implementation of the Saemaul Undong?".

It is noted that 71% of the people gave positive answers, that is, that the Saemaul Women's Association was helpful. In a comparison between villages, people in developed villages were more positive on this issue than those in developing villages. But there was little difference between common and outstanding villages. From this data, it may be stated that even if women have contributed much to the economic development of Korean society, it will take time for them to secure the corresponding social status to which they are entitled(Whang 1980, 99).

G. Summary

Despite the fact that a majority of rural people agreed that there is a need for technical improvement in agriculture, 45% of them wished to change their vocations to the non-farm sector. Despite their pride about agriculture itself, the actual conditions of rural society both economically and socially seem to have forced them to consider leaving their farm villages. Their desire to abandon farming appeared stronger in the developed and outstanding villages respectively than in developing and common villages. The rigorous implementation of the Saemaul Undong has strengthened a cooperative attitude toward neighbors within their villages through Saemaul projects. However, it has also been found that those in more successful villages, such as outstanding villages, were less cooperative toward their neighbors than in common villages. Particularly where economic interests were involved, people tended to pursue economic gain at the expense of traditionally cooperative attitudes.

As for cooperative attitudes toward neighboring villages in terms of conducting inter-village projects, those in outstanding villages tend to lag, indicating that there are some strategic shortcomings in the Saemaul Undong in this respect. It seems essential to expand the scope of project areas beyond a single village to include inter-village regional projects in view of the need for economy of scale and improved health, sanitation and welfare. Therefore, the promotion of cooperative attitudes toward neighboring villages should be a new frontier of spiritual enlightenment in the 1980's. The level of communication and the mutual relationships between the rural people and government agencies were also improved by the Saemaul Undong. Their relationships were reflected in their changes of attitude and perception towards government officials. In view of the perceptions of the rural people themselves as well as the officials' observation on the basis of their own experience, the relationship between the people and the officials has become more cooperative, democratic and friendly than before. Previously the relations were rather stiff, unequal and deterministic.

There is not enough academic evidence that these changes have resulted solely from the implementation of the Saemaul Undong. However, it is obvious that the Saemaul Undong and its projects have at least partly influenced and reinforced these changes in the people's values and perception.

PART V

SUMMARY AND POLICY IMPLICATIONS

Chapter 13

FACTORS OF THE SUCCESS AND THEIR TRANSFERABILITY

To what extent is the Saemaul Undong transferable to other developing countries for rural development? This question begs two sub-questions: (a) To what extent did the Saemaul Undong contribute to rural as well as national development in Korea? and (b) What are the factors and conditions which have been helpful to the success of the Saemaul Undong? An attempt is made in this chapter to summarize what was discussed in the previous chapters by replying to these two questions with a view to estimating the extent of transferability of the Saemaul Undong to other developing countries.

1. Performance and Impact of the Saemaul Undong

The first inquiry is related to the analysis of various impacts of the Saemaul Undong upon rural change and development in Korea during the 1970's. The analysis should deal with the extent to which Saemaul Undong has contributed to capital formation in the rural sector in the form of physical infrastructures, the improvement in rural employment and economy, changes in values and attitudes of rural people, the fostering of change agents, the promotion of participatory organization, and broadly the rural development and the nation-building process in Korea. The evaluation of the Saemaul Undong has been so far attempted by several other studies. They all conclude that the Saemaul Undong has made positive contributions to self-reliant rural development in Korea. The impact of the Saemaul Undong may be elaborated in terms of the following findings:

A. Performance of Saemual Projects

Saemaul Undong has been widely expanded in terms of numbers of participating villages, mobilized manpower, and the amount of the total investment in the Saemaul projects. During 1978 alone, thirty six thousand villages which means most rural villages in fact are involved in the Saemaul Undong, for which 634 billion won was mobilized both from rural people and the government. In addition, 271 million man-days of labor were voluntarily contributed (Table 3-1).

During the period 1971-78, about 2,000 billion won was invested in Saemaul projects, out of which 28% was supported by the government and 72% was contributed by the village people (Table 3-6). Because of the increasing level of people's motivation to rural development, the portion of government financing of Saemaul projects tends to be falling. The amount of government contribution has increased about 12 times over the period 1971-78. In the meantime, the people's contributions increased more than 20 times, including their voluntary work, money, small pieces of land and other materials (Chapter 3). Thus, the government investment in Saemaul projects has induced a greater mobilization of labor and funds as well as the voluntary participation of the village people in rural development. In other words, the initial contribution of government has had a snow-ball effect so as to bring about an accelerated mobilization of rural resources through self-help effort. During the early stage of the Saemaul Undong, the investment in physical infrastructure was emphasized. However, the changing pattern of fund allocation shows that since 1975 the emphasis was shifted to projects aimed at increasing rural incomes and, more recently, the emphasis on rural housing projects has also increased.

As a result, significant changes have taken place in various aspects of rural communities such as farm roads, small-scale bridges, agricultural production facilities, including nursery farms, agricultural mechanization, marketing and transportation, cooperative farming, rural housing and rural electrification.

B. Impact on Farmers' Value System

The continued implementation of the Saemaul Undong over the past ten years has brought about significant changes in rural communities at the individual as well as the organizational levels. It is found that a considerable part of farmers was considered change-oriented so that they tend to be more positive toward rural innovations and new varieties of rice. Their change orientation seemed to be more intensified after the Saemaul Undong was initiated. It is also confirmed that a large number of farmers are future-oriented in their value system and tend to be more futuristic in these days than in the early stage of the Saemaul Undong. The farmers' achievement motivation seems to be very high so as to be confident of improvements in their future life. They demonstrate their willingness to make vigorous efforts for its realization. Their motivational level tends to be higher than in the early 1970's. Solidarity and cooperation between farmers also tend to be more intensified along with the successful implementation of the Saemaul Undong.

The changes in values and perceptions of individual farmers as such seem to be a significant phenomenon in rural communities from the development point of view.

C. Impact on Organizational Behavior

Organizational changes are reflected both in village leadership and in the participatory behavior of village people. In other words, the Saemaul Undong has contributed to fostering of community-based village leadership which can efficiently play the role of development agent in the rural transformation process. As the average incumbency of Saemaul leaders was 4 years over the past ten years, there are currently at least 3–4 leaders, latent as well as manifested, in every village.

It is interesting to note that in view of their social background, Saemaul leaders are more educated, enjoy more income and have relatively richer land assets than the average farmer in their villages. More than half of the leaders enjoy annual incomes well above the national average farm household income, that is, more than 2 million won during 1978. Their social mobility seems to be relatively higher than the average farmer in terms of their experience in non-agricultural jobs, although their present jobs involve them predominantly in farming. It seems to be ironical that the geographical mobility of leaders seems to be less than farmers. A majority of village leaders live in the same village as their grandparents' generation, while the geographical mobility is rather higher in case of the farmers. (Table 13-1) The longevity of their stay might be one of the conditions for becoming a leader as their credibility among farmers and their personal motivation seem to be correlated with the length of stay.

Table 13-1. Social Background of Village Leaders

Unit: %

Background	Saemaul Leaders (N = 63)	Farmers (N = 1,497)
Age (40–49)	48	32
Education (Secondary)	68	27
Income (₩2 million and over)	52	28
Previous Occupation (non-farm)	34	19
Village Affiliation (from grandparents)	75	53

Source. Readopted from Chapters 5 and 12.

The Saemaul leaders played a significant role in organizing and implementing the Saemaul Undong at the village level as initiators, promoters, coordinators, educators, advocators or implementors of Saemaul projects. The Saemaul Undong eventually contributed to the identification and fostering of village leadership which will be the source of self-reliant development in rural communities.

The Saemaul Undong also promoted a participatory pattern of interaction between village members with respect to decision-making, planning and implementation of Saemaul projects.

Their positive participation in the decision-making process at the village level led them to close cooperation in the implementation of projects. The people's participation in decision-making has been further extended to the governmental decision-making at the township, county and provincial levels with respect to Saemaul projects. It is also noteworthy that the Saemaul Undong has contributed to the development of "grass-root" democracy in Korean society.

D. Impact on the Village Economy

The more successful the Saemaul Undong at the village level, the more rapidly the village economy grows in terms of farm household income. The average farm household income in the outstanding villages winning the Presidential Award was much greater than that of common villages. The cropping system in the outstanding villages tends to be more diversified in view of land use patterns for cultivation of food grains *vs.* other cash crops.

Nevertheless, it is interesting to note that the ratio of non-farm income to farm household income in the outstanding villages was lower than that of common villages during the period under study. It is implied that the Saemaul Undong has been more concerned with agricultural productivity rather than non-farm income sources. In fact, during the period 1971–78, the income-increasing projects have been boosted by the high rice price policy and also by the technological breakthrough in the form of the diffusion of high-yielding varieties of rice. However, there is no doubt that the emphasis on the role of Saemaul Undong in the increase in opportunities for non-farm income will be a new frontier of Saemaul projects in the future.

In view of the extent of farm mechanization, the product mix of agricultural crops and the pattern of land utilization, the Saemaul Undong has also introduced change in the structure of agricultural technology in rural villages. Over the period 1970–78, farm mechanization is now 8 times more extensive than in the early 1970's.

E. Impact on the National Economy

It is true that the Saemaul Undong has been an instrument

for the ignition of people's will for rural development from its beginning. Through their self-help effort and voluntarily organizing of Saemaul projects, rural people have mobilized their resources and energy to the maximum extent possible for increase in their income.

The gap between farm household income and urban laborer's household income has decreased since the inception of Saemaul Undong. The Saemaul Undong has also contributed to the increase in private savings. Regional development during the period is partly stimulated by the Saemaul Undong in view of an improvement in rural incomes, rural infrastructure and off-farm income made available through Saemaul factories.

One of the economic achievements of the Saemaul Undong is the promotion of capital formation and the increase in employment opportunities in the rural sector. It is also remarkable that technical learning classes as part of vocational training activities were organized by the Saemaul Undong with a view to improving agricultural productivity as well as improving villagers' employment opportunities in the industrial sector.

The Saemaul Undong has, indeed, made the rural economy an integral part of the national economy and enabled it to perform its strategic role in the process of economic and social development. This contrasts to the situation before the Saemaul Undong was initiated, when the rural economy was viewed as a burden on the national economy in its process of industrial development.

2. Factors Contributing to the Success of Saemaul Undong

What then are the factors and conditions which are conducive to the success of the Saemaul Undong? They can be grouped into three broad categories: (a) organizing strategies of the Saemaul Undong, (b) dynamics of political and government systems, and (c) social and cultural conditions of rural communities in Korea.

A. Organizing Strategies of the Saemaul Undong

It is noteworthy that the Saemaul Undong was organized without an academic research base or theoretical reference. The strategies and program content of the Saemaul Undong have been adapted to fit Korean society and culture through the continued process of trial and error. Some successful implementation rather provided a realistic base for the nationwide application of the Saemaul Undong.

(1) *Village as a Unit of Community Action*

The rural village was chosen as a strategic unit of community action in the Saemaul Undong in Korea. It has the unit primarily responsible for planning, organizing and implementing various kinds of Saemaul projects and activities during the 1970's. Hence, the rural village became the focus for coordination and management of all types of government support and assistance. The rural village was identified as a basic unit of rural action in Korea because it was viewed as conducive to the pursuance of traditionally common interests, physically close interaction and cooperative action among villagers.

As rural development involves far-reaching change in values and perceptions of village people, it cannot be achieved solely through pursuing calculated economic rationality. Therefore, the Korean approach was based rather on managerial criteria in terms of conduciveness to the perceptual identity, the sense of common interests, the active participation and cooperation among community people, and the exercise of community-based leadership.

The identification of the rural village as the unit for community action in the initial stage of rural development in Korea seemed appropriate. However, in the later stage, when the village economy has grown and has more and stronger linkages to the external systems through arrangements of marketing, communication and transportation, and also when the community people recognize the desirability of certain visible and invisible changes, it might be possible to expand the unit of rural community up to a more economically viable size such as the township or county.

(2) Integrated Objectives of Rural Development

One of the major objectives of the Saemaul Undong is to change farmers' values and perceptions toward developmental values such as self-help, diligence, and cooperation. Another objective is to introduce changes in community organization toward the more active participation of rural villagers and the fostering of community-based leadership. The third objective is to improve rural infrastructures and the village economy by undertaking Saemaul projects. These three objectives are indeed integrated into the total package of the Saemaul Undong system.

In most developing countries, the strategies for integrated rural development tend to be concerned little with internalized values and attitudes of rural people as an integral part of integrated rural development. They seldom attempt to introduce change in farmers' perceptions and attitudes toward their rural life, organization and environment. They rather perceive the lack of people's motivation and pessimistic attitude of farmers as given constraints. Organizational behavior of villages such as the dependency syndrome, the lack of cooperation, and the poor leadership tend to be viewed as a given subculture of village communities (Haque et al. 5-11). Most developing countries tend to be concerned with a wide range of development projects without making a serious attempt to introduce changes in people and organization.

In this respect, it should be noted that the three major objectives of the Saemaul Undong aiming at individual, organizational, and environmental changes of rural village are well integrated into the overall strategies of rural development in Korea.

(3) Strategic Choice of Development Projects

The Saemaul Undong is also characterized by a variety of development projects planned and implemented at the village level. It should be noted that the priority at the village level was given to physical infrastructures in the initial period of the Saemaul Undong. The benefits of such projects completed by their cooperative and self-help efforts could then be immediately identifiable because they were visible and tangible. Therefore, the implementation of these projects tended to reinforce cooperative attitudes, a self-help spirit and motivation. Thus, the selection of physical infrastructure projects is viewed as strategic in the Korean context, especially at the early stage of its rural development.

However, at the latter stage, especially since 1975, the emphasis has been placed more on income-boosting projects. This is because the small-scale projects for physical infrastructures had been most completed and rural people were becoming more interested in cooperating to improve their incomes and economic pay-offs. In view of the changing circumstances of rural communities, the future investments should be concerned more with large-scale physical infrastructures which require cooperation between several villages for more efficient production and marketing and also for the improvement in the quality of life in the rural sector. They may include, for example, farm mechanization projects, marketing arrangements, and regionally based welfare centers.

The selection of development projects should be realistic enough to meet the basic and felt needs of rural people so as to motivate their cooperation, self-help and participation.

(4) Saemaul Leadership Training for Resource Mobilization

Rural people, community-based leadership and government supports are identified as three major resources which have been mobilized to the fullest extent throughout the Saemaul Undong during the 1970's. The wise utilization of people's zeal and energy through their maximum participation could be realized through a proper mode of organization in rural villages. This may require village leadership which in fact consisted of both Saemaul leaders (men and women) selected from village members. They play a development role as change agents introducing rural innovations and also managers' role in planning and implementing community projects. Their leadership role is performed in collaboration with the village chief who is a semi-official person appointed from village members by the township office. The incorporation of women leaders in the village leadership made possible the utilization of their talents for community action programs within the given socio-structural and cultural context.

For the optimum and coordinated use of these resources, leadership training was emphasized as a major part of Saemaul Undong. The Korean approach to rural development training is unique in view of its objectives, participant mix, curricula, training methods and eventual impact. The main thrust of Saemaul training was value change of village leaders, men and women, assuming that they will eventually introduce changes in farmers' values and attitudes. The mixture of participants provided different sectoral elite with a common conceptual framework of the Saemaul

Undong by which the nationwide mobilization of resources could be realized. It also induced the participants to make a *collective* commitment to the achievement of rural Saemaul projects. The training program has also facilitated the mutual communication and coordination between different policies and programs. Of utmost importance is that the training course enabled political and urban elites to understand in real terms the rural situation and its development needs.

The training methodology also deserves special attention. The program is conducted in a "closed oven" situation. The program enhanced their motivational level, self-confidence about their role performance and leadership capability of village leaders and also provided them with new perspectives, world outlook and communication skills for persuading rural people. Besides, the training course serves as a mechanism not only for the social support to and recognition of farmers and village leaders but also social control over local administration in support of rural development.

B. Dynamics of Political and Government Systems

Political and government systems also played important roles in stimulating rural development at the local level. Their roles are reflected in the incentive measures, government support and local administration in particular, and in the political leadership commitment.

(1) Positive Political and Societal Support

As rural development implies profound changes in major aspects of rural villages, top leadership commitment to the Saemaul Undong is of essential importance to its success. The strong commitment of the top political leadership, sometimes in the form of Presidential pressure on local government (Brandt 1977), has been reflected in the favorable allocation of resources to the rural sector and the necessary changes in legal as well as administrative frameworks. As discussed in Chapter 4 (Table 4-1), besides political and international affairs, one of the most frequently raised categories of issues and themes in the New Year's Press Conferences of the late President Park was related to rural and agricultural development. On the average, the President spent about 9% of his total speech time for projecting the future image of rural society, discussing government policies and support for rural development, and the roles of farmers and village leaders.

The President also expressed his great concern about rural development by personally visiting rural villages. His frequent field visits also served as a mechanism for identificaton of problems and for providing opportunities to make specific instructions and guidelines for program design as well as for monitoring program performance. The mobilization of societal support for the Saemaul Undong reinforces the values and ideas of rural development. It seemed to be worthwhile to get the ruling elite, including party leaders and urban intellectuals, to understand the ideas and changes implied in the Saemaul Undong. One way of doing this is to have them participate in the training course with Saemaul leaders and to become actively involved in the movement. Their participation in the training tends to be conducive to a favorable allocation of resources and to the mobilization of adequate support for rural development.

(2) Catalytic Role of Government

Government provided deliberately planned and consistent support for rural development over a period of time from its beginning until the stage of its strategic withdrawal. Periodic evaluation of the capacity of particular villages for self-reliant development was also included within the package of government support.

The functions of the local government which were the maintenance of law and order now became reoriented toward rural development. Local governments tend to be easily accessible to the community people. While encouraging village leaders to positively participate in the process of governmental policy-making, they become more concerned with the community needs and try to efficiently deliver their best services to rural people.

In delivery of their services, the coordination and integration of various kinds of development projects with respect to required development inputs at the village level are promoted primarily by county-level local officials. The package of government support also tends to fit into the total scheme of village development activities so as to provide supplementary inputs.

Another element conducive to the developmental role of local government in the Saemaul Undong is the improvement in the mutual relationship between government officials and community people. The mutual discord between the two sides in the past created a lack of government credibility. A perceptual change toward interdependence as well as an attitudinal change toward cooperation and collaboration between officials and people is one of the critical indicators of improvement in the local support system. In this connection, it is noted that the evaluation of local officials on the basis of the success of Saemaul projects which they supported is almost institutionalized, assuming that the community's performance is correlated with local officials' service.

The utmost importance of local government support to the rural community is related to the managerial capability of local government in delivery of required services and assistance. A remarkable point is the discipline of local government officials in the process of their service delivery. The timely and accurate delivery of materials and services to villages according to the planned schedule is an indicator of outstanding performance and commitment of the local administrator which, in turn, contribute to the credibility of government. The strong commitment of local government is also reflected in arrangements for special assignment of local officials, by which each staff member is assigned to take responsibility for efficient support for, and monitoring of, the implementation of Saemaul projects at the village level.

(3) Incentives and Supporting Policies

A variety of incentives were provided both for villages and individual farmers. They include, for example, the government donation of materials such as 335 bags of cement and steel bars to each village. The donation, indeed, induced positive responses from village people, in the form of their active participation in decision-making with regard to what to do with the cement and also their positive cooperation to achieve the results. It also imposed a series of challenges to village people in terms of identity crisis, leadership capability, and managerial competence. Awards and citations given to outstanding village leaders and farmers also served as a good incentive system to make village people commit their best efforts.

The government provided different packages of support and

assistance to villages depending on their level of development. The principle of "the better village the first support" became an effective stimulator of people's motivation to better achievement in Saemaul projects. The competitive mood between neighboring villagers contributed substantially to the success of the Saemaul Undong at the early stage, even though the psychology of excess competition tended to be an obstacle to the implementation of inter-village Saemaul projects which have been recently encouraged as a new thrust of Saemaul Undong.

The high rice price policy has boosted farmers' income substantially, while the policy is currently being criticized because the accumulation of financial deficit generated through the government purchase of rice at a higher price than its sales price tends to create an inflationary pressure. The high rice price policy, nevertheless, encouraged farmers to work harder and to participate in rural development activities in the form of the Saemaul Undong (Ban *et al.* 1980, 145–253).

The heavy investment of government in research and development of High-Yielding Varieties (HYV) and their nationwide dissemination eventually made Korea self-sufficient in rice. The dissemination of new rice seeds and the intensification of the Saemaul Undong seemed to be a mutually reinforcing process of change in rural villages.

C. Social Transformation in Rural Communities

Another set of reasons for the success of the Saemaul Undong is related to some significant social changes which have taken place in Korea since the liberation of the country from Japanese rule after World War II. They include changes generated and affected by a series of major events: land reform, a massive educational drive, the Korean War of 1950–53 and industrial development in the 1960's.

(1) The Successful Implementation of Land Reform

The successful implementation of the land reform during 1949–53 had made significant impact on rural communities. It is the economists' criticism that the three hectare ceiling of land ownership by a farm household had eventually miniaturized the farm size (Table 6-2) and thus most Korean farmers remain primarily small farmers at the subsistence level. In spite of such economic restraints resulting from the land reform, farmers have more or less equal access to the production assets and are motivated to work harder. The land reform promoted egalitarianism in rural communities in terms of land ownership and the disappearance of class consciousness between landlords and tenants of the past. Nevertheless, it took almost one generation following the land reform to effectively bring about the perceptual change of farmers toward real cooperation in respect to the implementation of the Saemaul Undong. The land reform indeed provided the social and psychological precondition for cooperation among farmers in promoting rural innovations, as the redistribution of productive assets provided the psychological base for equal partnership of all the farmers.

(2) Massive Education Drive

The education of rural youngsters was a most widespread and far-reaching change manifested in the rural sector since 1945. The introduction of free and compulsory elementary education was accompanied by vast expansion of the secondary school system and, further, by a spectacular increase in higher education. The immensity of the social input in education had brought about a significant improvement in the educational level as well as a dramatic increase in the number of literate people in the rural sector. The impact of the educational drive has been so significant in terms of the motivation of farmers to participate in community decision-making and the improvement of communication between government officials and village people. Indeed, the easy communication between farmers and government field workers was a prerequisite for the efficient dissemination of rural innovations such as the introduction of high-yielding varieties and modern farm technologies. Therefore, the cumulative impact of education on the rural society during the 1950–60's explains itself why rural development took place so dramatically in the 1970's as demonstrated by the success of the Saemaul Undong.

(3) The War-Time Catastrophe and Military Influence

The Korean War of 1950–53 had brought serious damage to Korean society and the economy. One related aspect of the family disintegration caused by the war was the engendering of social marginals. The geographical mobility forced on farmers by the war had left them with psychological anxiety and uncertainty. The external influence made by the influx of urban refugees and the military service of rural youngsters also provided farmers with exogenous change in rural villages.

The enormous expansion of the Korean armed forces was a natural consequence of the Korean war. It had an important effect on socialization at a rapid tempo of millions of young men who were mostly from the rural communities. Through the military service they were exposed to a sense of national and ideological identity. The military service had implications of social education in terms of organizational training, behavioral change and leadership development. They had opportunities to have experiences in efficient modern organization, in a target-oriented managerial system and in modern science and technology. As most farmers in fact served in the army as part of their national duty, their decision-making patterns, organizing methods, communication skills, interaction patterns, and mode of participation in project implementation under the village leadership tend to be adopted from the military sub-culture. The basic technical training and the access to modernity during their military service indeed influenced farmers' perception and attitude toward cooperation, work ethic and participatory behavior.

(4) Industrial Development in the 1960's

The successful implementation of the First and Second Five-Year Economic Development Plans (1962–71) facilitated the rapid economic growth and accelerated the industrialization process in Korea. The average annual growth of GNP during the period of 1962–71 was approximately 9.5%. The average annual growth rate of the mining and industry sector during the same period was approximately 20% while that of the agriculture and fishery sector was approximately 4%. As a result, the extent industrialization had gradually increased as indicated by its share of GNP which expanded from 16.4% in 1962 to 22.4% in 1971 (EPB 1980, 3–4).

In accordance with the rapid economic growth, the central government budget had rapidly increased. By the "trickle down" effect of the rapid growth of the industrial sector, a certain amount of the government energy accumulated during the 1960's could be generously reallocated in favor of the rural sector during the 1970's. The heavy investment of government in research and development for technological innovation during the late 1960's and early 1970's made possible the development of the high-yielding varieties of rice, such as the Yushin and Milyang varieties of rice as derived from IR667. This innovation in rice varieties contributed to a perceptual change of farmers with respect to the extension service of the government and thus enhanced the credibility of the government.

The high rice price policy was also introduced from 1968 as an incentive to encourage farmers to produce more rice. Although there is no evidence of the extent to which the high price policy contributed to the stimulation of the production of more rice, the policy indeed motivated them to participate in the government-introduced rural innovations, particularly in Saemaul projects. The Green Revolution in Korea and the government drive for self-sufficiency in rice was possible because of the development of high-yielding varieties of rice and the consistent policy of raising the rice price.

It goes without saying that the donation of cement and steel to all the villages for the ignition of the Saemaul Undong at the beginning was possible in the 1970's because government resources had become relatively affluent. In other words, the rapid industralization in the 1960's made the government generous and/or capable of making a favorable allocation of budgetary resources to the rural sector. As already shown in Table 3-5, the amount of government assistance to the Saemaul Undong from both the central and local governments has increased more rapidly than the development expense out of the generous government sector budget of the central government. The latter was spent for the promotion of economic development in general.

It seems interesting, in this connection, to note that the continued and increasingly active participation of people in the Saemaul Undong has been promoted by an indigenous fanaticism rooted in traditional rural folk, namely, *Shin-ba-lam* (godly wind)*. It is a kind of self-propelling exciting mood in which rural people

---
* For the anthropological interpretation, see Kim HH (1978, 321–330).

tend to become happy and excited about the results of their efforts and more enthused about working hard in the field. Once the *Shin-ba-lam* has been created in the village or in the people's mind, people tend to be more enthusiastic about what they achieve. The *Shin-ba-lam* was indeed ignited and further intensified by a series of Saemaul-promoting factors, which include the strong commitment of the top political leadership, positive support from the local governments, the innovation of new rice seeds, the government purchase of rice at a higher price than the market price, and so on. Some of these factors were able to be effective only after the accumulation of governmental energy following rapid industrialization.

3. Extent of Transferability

From the above discussion, it is clear that the Saemaul Undong, as the Korean version of integrated rural development, has contributed considerably to rural development during the 1970's. An *integrated* process of significant changes in values and attitudes of individual farmers, community organizations, the rural infrastructures and village economies provided a firm basis for self-reliant development in the rural sector. It is in this sense that the extent of transferability of the Saemaul Undong as a rural development model seems to be a subject of academic inquiry.

It is also clear that there are various factors and conditions which were conducive to the success of the Saemaul Undong. They include strategic aspects of the Saemaul Undong itself, government policies and supporting mechanism, and socio-cultural conditions provided by the preceding social change.

Indeed, the implications and lessons drawn from the experience of the Saemaul Undong in Korea seem to be enormous from both academic and practical points of view. No doubt some of the above-mentioned conditions and factors would be applicable to or available in some other countries, while others may not. Some technical aspects of lessons from the Saemaul Undong, for example, managerial techniques, monitoring and management information systems, would be transferable with little adaptation. The Saemaul training program could also be adaptable to conditions in other developing countries. The approach, methodology and subject matter of Saemaul Training could be applied to the training of village leaders as well as rural development field workers.

However, some other factors which affect considerably the socio-psychological dynamics may not be easily reproduced in a different cultural context. The *Shin-ba-lam* cannot blow in other countries. Gestalt psychology formed through the war-time crisis would never be desirable for other countries. But perhaps the implications of the military sub-culture for action-oriented behavior may be worth learning.

The extent of transferability of the Saemaul Undong to other developing countries for their rural development depends on the adaptability of their socio-cultural systems. Even if the Saemaul Undong is transferable, however, some mistakes made by the Saemaul Undong in Korea (Chapter 14) should not be repeated in other countries. They are the excessive intervention and support by the government which in part created a dependency syndrome among rural people, the principle of uniformity of government support ignoring differing local situations and the excessive emphasis on the immediately visible and tangible results of projects. Rural development strategies should be rooted in their own socio-cultural contexts at any point in time.

Chapter 14

FUTURE COURSE OF THE SAEMAUL UNDONG FOR THE 1980's: POLICY IMPLICATIONS*

1. Development Strategies of Korea for the 1980's

The future course of the Saemaul Undong depends on the philosophical foundation of Korea's development strategies during the 1980's. In view of the present magnitude of the national economy as well as the speed of its economic growth and development over the last two decades, the future of Korea in the 1980's should not be viewed as a simple extension of the development pattern of the past. Therefore, development strategies for the 1980's should be reformulated to cope with the changing needs of the country despite the fact that the government strategies have thus far been effective in the sixties and seventies.

Korea's development strategy has been basically a copy of the Western model in the sense that Korea has introduced the wisdom, ideas and technologies from the western industrial countries which have already been tested. However, Korea is

---

*The initial draft was presented at the "Seminar on the Saemaul Undong and Social Development in the 1980's," sponsored by the Ministry of Home Affairs and UNICEF/Seoul, at Sokrisan Hotel, 11-14 July 1979. Otheswise indicated.

now on a threshold of entering a new stage of development which requires a development strategy based on the uniqueness of the socio-economic context in Korea. The western approach has been oriented toward mass consumption of world resources. Political as well as technological factors in the world market during the 19th century enabled Western countries to adopt such strategies for their successful economic growth and development. A resource-saving strategy of development, however, may become an inevitable course of action for the future Korea in view of the international politics surrounding the idea of a New International Economic Order which has been advocated extensively by the Third World countries. The philosophy underlined in the proposed strategy is consistent with world peace over scarce resources such as oil and other raw materials. This reorientation of strategy implies needs for a change in direction with respect to goals, policies, organizations and management behavior in the public sector. The change include reorientation of development goals toward a better quality of life as measured in terms other than economic growth; readjustment of growth targets to an optimal level as opposed to simply pursuing excessively rapid growth; emphasis on the overall harmony of policies rather than the maximization of partial efficiency for growth alone; encouragement of private initiatives and participation with a concurrent decrease in intervention by the government in economic activities; promotion of technological innovation and creativity instead of imitation of Western technologies; local participation and decentralization; utilization of locally available marginal resources; adoption of a donar's point of view with respect to international cooperation rather than a recipient's point of view; and so forth (Whang 1980d, 2).

It is clear that issues related to the philosophical reorientation of Korea's development strategy are a benchmark for reconsidering the objectives and strategies needed for further rural as well as social development in Korea.

Based on KDI's study (1978) on the Korean economy in 1991, Korea will move toward an industrialized, welfare state in which further emphasis will be placed on social development as well as regional development to improve the quality of life of the general public. Gross National Happiness (GNH), Gross National Satisfaction (GNS), and Quality of Life (QOL) will be the basic concepts reflected in the development objectives of the 1980's. The major questions to be addressed are: what should be done to achieve the minimum required level of income? What mechanism should be introduced in order to provide citizens with equal opportunities to improve their standard of living? What is the approach to minimize relative deprivation among the masses who are excluded from the mainstream of rapid economic growth? What policies should be adopted to meet the basic minimum needs of people in rural or underprivileged areas? Solving the problems posed by these questions should be the major concern of any development effort in the coming decade.

From this perspective, the objectives of rural development in the 1980's may be defined as follows:
(a) Continued development of rural communities;
(b) Expansion of women's activities and their increased participation in every aspect of national development both in urban and rural communities;
(c) Development of young human resources in rural areas with respect to education, health, nutrition, mental and intellectual growth and personality; and
(d) An increase in the accessibility of rural people to educational facilities, arts and cultural activities.

The above objectives elevate regional and social development to the status of full partners to economic growth in the 1980's. The Saemaul Undong has proved to be an efficient instrument for achieving these objectives. The Saemaul Undong as a nationwide movement has been activated for the spiritual enlightenment of rural people and ignition of zeal and motivation among them to participate on a voluntary basis, and also for the organization of self-help efforts among community members in the form of physical infrastructure and income-generating projects.

2. Development Potentials of the Saemaul Undong*

What then are the potentials of the Saemaul Undong for rural

---
*Primarily based on Whang(1980a. 207-213), Otherwise indicated.

development and organization? It should be noted that the Saemaul Undong has made a remarkable contribution to rural as well as national development in Korea during the last decade. Aside from the points cited in previous chapters the Saemaul Undong has brought about greater mobility for rural people on the one hand and made local governments which were formerly oriented predominantly toward law and order reoriented toward development support administration. In spite of such contributions, the Saemaul Undong has brought about a dependency syndrome on government assistance among rural people as well as a distorted pattern of consumption among many of rural people. Regardless of its undesirable consequences, however, it is generally accepted that the Saemaul Undong has made a remarkable contribution to rural modernization in Korea.

Nevertheless the future direction of the Saemaul Undong should not remain the same. As the socio-economic and environmental changes which have been brought about by the successful implementation of the Saemaul Undong itself now require a reorientation in the 1980's, changes in national development strategies as well as in the objectives of rural development will require a different role for it. Significant changes will take place in the 1980's which will make Korea move toward: an industrial society; a conspicuous consumption pattern; more demand for protein and vegetable foods; a predominance of middle-class citizens; more extensive political participation of people; small family norms; individualism; greater demand for administrative services and local autonomy; more humanistic consideration in public policy-making; etc. (Whang 1980b, 87–101).

These anticipated changes will be associated with the evolution of the national economy toward (a) an open economy, (b) industrialization with emphasis on heavy and chemical industries, and (c) encouragement of a market economy. This trend has been repeatedly confirmed by studies on the future of the Korean economy (KDI 1978 and KSFS 1970).

Along with economic and social progress, various changes, advantageous and disadvantageous, will also take place in rural communities. Rural villages will tend to become more open communities. Geographical and social mobility among village people will tend to increase. The physical facilities and infrastructure of rural communities will tend to become more urban-like due to the Saemaul Undong; the less productive segment of the labor force including old men and women will tend to remain in the rural sector while young and educated labor will migrate to the urban-industrial sector. Under these circumstances, agricultural modernization and mechanization of large scale farming regardless of land ownership will become a mandate for rural development in the 1980's (Whang 1980b, 141-232).

Another dimension of socio-environmental change concerns the emergence of a new philosophy of rural development in the coming years, a philosophy which will center on the question of whether or not income growth of the rural farmer is the ultimate objective of development. Of course income generation will continue to be viewed as a prime consideration in the eradication of rural poverty. But in addition to this, a philosophical change will take place in favor of improving the quality of rural life in terms of socio-psychological satisfaction with, and accessibility to, educational opportunities, religious activities, museums, arts and other cultural activities beyond income growth itself.

It now seems valuable to consider the extent to which the present mode of organization in the Saemaul Undong will be effective in meeting the series of anticipated changes, challenges, and issues illustrated above. It is generally viewed that the Saemaul Undong will be a limitation unless some major changes in its strategies and orientation are infused. This is because the major thrust of the Saemaul projects has so far been oriented toward improvements in physical infrastructure and/or income growth in farm households. Most projects tend to be initiated by government stimulation. Strictly uniform direction from the central government without any consideration for specific regional needs tends to discourage motivation and creativity on the part of the people. The present system of local administrative support for Saemaul projects has so far been efficient but may not be so when it comes to meeting the changing needs of communities during the coming decades.

Nevertheless, it is generally believed that the development potential of the Saemaul Undong is still great and will continue to grow in the 1980's. The potential role of the Saemaul Undong will only be significant in rural and national development if it is readjusted and readapted to the changing needs of the 1980's.

3. Future Course of the Saemaul Undong for the 1980's

The adaptation and adjustment of the Saemaul Undong to the contextual changes of the 1980's may be described in terms of a series of policy recommendations with regard to following subjects:

A. Definition of Rural Development Objectives

Up until now, improvements in rural income and physical infrastructure have been defined as the major objectives of rural development in Korea. In view of the extent of Korea's industrialization, the objectives of rural development in the 1980's should be redefined in terms of a "better-living rural region," a definition in which each word has its own implications. In pursuit of these broad goals, the specific objectives should be as follows:

(1) The primary unit of development action for the Saemaul Undong should be a "rural region" which includes several villages not just one village. The new dimension may involve reorganization as well as a perceptual change on the part of rural people as well as local administrators.

(2) Positive participation and developmental use of women should be encouraged in order to promote better utilization of marginal resources such as women and children.

(3) Emphasis should be placed on children and youth development in the rural sector for self-sustained development of rural communities and for better distribution of income and development benefits between rural and urban sectors.

(4) Policies should be reoriented toward improvement in the quality of life in the rural sector, in terms of accessibility to facilities and opportunities for education, religious activities, arts, health, welfare, etc.

B. Projects and Activities for the 1980's

The projects and activities to be undertaken in the name of

the Saemaul Undong in the 1980's should be identified in light of the following criteria:

(1) Priority should be given to those Saemaul Projects which are organized for agricultural modernization in order to make the rural sector compatible with more efficient industries in the coming decades. They include projects related to stuctural policy (Dams 1979, 75–86) which encourage the enlargement of cultivating land through innovation in farm organization and also promote the mechanization of farming.

(2) Priority also should be given to policies and projects related to off-farm income including relocation of industrial zones, creation of opportunities for non-farm employment of rural people, and training as well as social insurance for their employment in industries. The multi-dimensonal aspects of rural income policy should be reflected in the organization of specific Saemaul projects.

(3) Greater attention should be paid to improving agricultural marketing systems and flow channels for rural products since these are closely related to increasing rural income.

(4) Emphasis should be placed on projects for expansion and improvement of facilities and opportunities for welfare, education, arts, and other cultural activities.

(5) Activities for encouragement of women's participation should receive greater attention. These include, for example, diploma school for rural housewives, adult education, development of educational and training materials, etc.

(6) Saemaul Undong should cover activities for children and youth development as they are determinants of the future of rural communities. In this connection, emphasis should be given to a child-pampering culture in which desirable inputs will be made available for the planning and operation of day care centers, nursing schools, nutrition and health programs, and so on.

(7) Community-oriented health, education, and nutrition programs should be expanded with a view toward improving the quality of life of rural people.

(8) Utilization as well as accomodation of old men and women

should be another area to be explored in favor of Saemaul projects.
(9) It is again noted that special attention should be given to the enlightenment of Saemaul spirits in terms of co-operation, diligence, self-help, motivation, participation and creativity.

C. Strategy for the Saemaul Undong in the 1980's

For successful implementation of Saemaul projects in the 1980's, strategies in support of the Saemaul Undong should be reformulated. Emphasis should be put on people's initiative in planning and organizing Saemaul projects at the grass-root level. The Government should encourage community people to take part positively in every aspect of the management of Saemaul projects beginning with their initiation. This will require a change in people's attitudes and perceptions on the one hand and a specification of administrators' roles in the Saemaul Undong on the other.

Voluntary participation on the part of the people in planning and implementation of Saemaul projects should be promoted to assure their maximum commitment and contribution to the success of the Saemaul Undong. The current tendency of forced modernization by the government apparatus should not be continued in view of the changing social and political context of rural communities in the 1980's.

D. Reorganization for the Saemaul Undong

It seems natural that any organization of the Saemaul Undong should be redirected in support of those development objectives which are conducive to rural development and mesh well with strategies for action at the local level. The followings are points which should be reflected in the reorganization of activities:
(1) The Saemaul Undong in the 1980's should be reorganized for "work-oriented" cooperative farming, while the contemporary Saemaul Undong is mostly for "village-centered" environmental projects. The major priorities for the 1980's are stimulation of agricultural modernization and farm mechanization through people's cooperative

efforts, creation of employment opportunities in industries at the local level in order to generate off-farm income and implementation of welfare projects for improving the quality of life.

(2) As the spatial boundary of the basic organizational unit of the Saemaul Undong must be expanded from one village to include several villages, rural organization should be redirected from a "village-centered" pattern toward an inter-village "regional organization." This naturally involves enlargement of the average project size as the beneficiaries of a project tend to become broader and more extensive.

(3) As the improvement in the quality of life becomes a focus of rural development, cultivation of the Saemaul spirit among women and children will become a central issue. In other words, Saemaul activities should be reorganized in the form of "family-focused" or "housewife-oriented" activities.

(4) The identification and development of Saemaul leadership should aim at improving their managerial capabilities as well as specialized knowledge and skills necessary for performance of Saemaul projects. Their capacity for political mobilization of community people should be a secondary consideration for leadership development in the 1980's. Within this context, incentive schemes including rewards for leaders and their level of their morale should be instituted according to their leadership performance.

(5) Special attention should also be given to the coordination of interests among community members in order to minimize possible conflicts in the process of rapid social change led by industrialization.

E. Policy and Institutional Innovation

With this background a series of innovations should be introduced in policy support and institutional arrangements for the Saemaul Undong in the 1980's.

One of the areas for significant policy innovation is development of several education centers at the local level which will foster development of local core cities and the embodiment of cultural centers in various regions. The idea of local education centers will eventually contribute to and support activities and projects for the Saemaul Undong in the 1980's. The proposed local education centers could be elaborated in connection with on-going policies such as the Ten-Year Development Plan for Medium-Small Cities which is being drafted by the Ministry of Home Affairs and the current program for Development of Local Universities which is being implemented by the Ministry of Education. Social education concerned with reorientation of values and attitude of adults should also be incorporated into the proposed idea for the development of local education centers. It seems to be inevitable that encouragement of local politics and self-reliant development should be another priority area for the government to emphasize in pursuit of the Saemaul Undong in the 1980's.

F. Local Administration in Support of the Saemaul Undong

It is generally felt that the current local government system has so far been efficient in assisting the Saemaul Undong at the village level. The administrative supports provided by local governments include stimulation and encouragement of voluntary participation of rural people in planning, organization and implementation of Saemaul projects. Technical and financial assistance are provided by different agencies of the government such as extension workers, health centers, etc. Local government plays a coordinating role in providing different input and assistance from various agencies.

Nevertheless, the local administration system should be reformed in support of the new model for the Saemaul Undong which will emerge in the 1980's as described above in terms of objectives, projects, implementation strategy, organization, supportive policies and institutions. Who will be responsible for providing administrative support for community-level action? Should the present system of local administration continue to play the major administrative role or should a new form of rural cooperative be established to replace the present system? It is viewed that complementary functions of both local government and rural cooperatives should be assumed in their institutional rearrangement.

In order to allow the local government system more flexibility in responding to Saemaul needs in the 1980's, a major reform in the local government system should take place in the following areas: (a) structural and functional rearrangement of the comprehensive planning function at county and township levels, functional reallocation between central and local governments, rearrangement of functions and tasks between ministries at the central level, coordination between townships with respect to the Saemaul Undong, etc.; (b) readjustment of the personnel and training system to cope with new demands arising within the Saemaul Undong during the 1980's, which include identification and development of administrative cadets, suitable training programs, and incentive systems such as rewards, promotion, and overseas travel; (c) improvement of administrative management through minimizing red tape, simplifying reporting procedures, providing advanced administrative machineries and tools necessary for processing communication flow, and introducing an appropriate monitoring system and management technique; and (d) self-reliance in local financing to meet increasing administrative demands for implementation of Saemaul projects, which include reclassification of certain national tax items into the category of local taxes and increase in grants-in-aid by the central government to local governments. As a complementary measure for improvement in administrative support function, the capacity of agricultural cooperatives for contributing to the Saemaul Undong should be strengthened at the township level in terms of their credibility, organizational efficiency and relationship with members and clients.

In addition to the local level improvement of the supporting system, administrative support from the central government should not be formalistic but more substantial and consistent. A Saemaul Administration Deliberation Committee consisting of Director-Generals drawn from several ministries is now expected to play a critical role in providing technical and substantive support for local-level actions in the Saemaul Undong. Another important element of the administrative supports will be the Saemaul Leaders Training Program which should be reinforced by introducing new case study materials and other training methods with a view to improving problem-solving capabilities, information analysis, and management and planning skills.

Since the Saemaul Undong in the 1980's will be based on a different development philosophy and strategy, extensive information, education and communication (IEC) activities may have to be organized to promote wider understanding among people in general and thus mobilize political and social support as well.

4. Supplementary Measures: Conclusions

In pursuit of the new strategies underlined in the Saemaul Undong in the 1980's, deliberate preparation should be made. One of the critical issues in the conceptualization of new strategies for the Saemaul Undong as well as the forms of social development in the 1980's is related to the development of indicators regarding the level of people's satisfaction or quality of life (QOL) at the community level. Social indicators provide a useful tool for conceptualizing QOL at the national-aggregate level (Land *et al.* 1975; Morris, 1979). However, a set of relevant indicators to measure the degree of QOL at the community level has yet to be studied and elaborated on. The indicators may have to incorporate concepts related to rural income, educational opportunities and other welfare facilties available in rural areas, improvement in physical environment, and so on. (Whang 1980b, 117–119). It is probable that indicators concerning children, youth, women, and family will be also included among the factors taken into consideration.

The issues and recommendations discussed above are certainly significant and some of them call for drastic changes in critical aspects of the Saemaul Undong in the 1980's. Nonetheless, these measures are not yet ready to be implemented nor systematic enough to be consistent with each other. It should be noted in this connection that the Saemaul Undong in the 1970's was initiated, elaborated, and implemented by administrators and rural people themselves through a process of trial and error. The concepts and strategies have been deliberated in this chapter with the hope of making them consistent with the real context of rural communities in Korea. For efficient management of the complex issues emerging in the coming decade, however, an inter-disciplinary group of experts should develop a master plan for the Saemaul Undong that is relevant to the 1980's. With that in mind, the concepts and strategies discussed in this chapter could serve as a basic framework for that plan.

Appendix One

LIST OF SAMPLE VILLAGES

Chungcheong-Bug-Do
1. Sogyo-Ri, Hwanggan-Myeon, Yeongdong-Gun
2. Seodae-Ri, Ogcheon-Myeon, Ogcheon-Gun
3. Seogsil-Ri, Nami-Myeon, Cheongweon-Gun
4. Naeam-Ri, Gudeog-Myeon, Cheongweon-Gun
5. Byeongwon-Ri, Suchan-Myeon, Boeun-Gun
6. Yeongkyeo-Ri, Dongryang-Myeon, Jungweon-Gun

Chungcheong-Nam-Do
7. Chilsan-Ri, Imcheon-Myeon, Buyeo-Gun
8. Shinsong-Ri, Gobug-Myeon, Seosan-Gun
9. Namseon-Ri Jinjam-Myeon, Daedeog-Gun
10. Sohag-Ri, Gyeryong-Myeon, Gongju-Gun
11. Yeomjag-Ri, Dunpo-Myeon, Asan-Gun
12. Samgeo-Ri, Eumbong-Myeon, Asan-Gun

Jeonra-Bug-Do
13. Bongchon-Ri, Dunnam-Myeon, Imsil-Gun
14. Wagseon-Ri, Sanseo-Myeon, Jangsu-Gun
15. Woncheon-Ri, Baegsan-Myeon, Buan-Gun
16. Ibseog-Ri, Weolchon-Myeon, Gimje-Gun
17. Bujeol-Ri, Sandong-Myeon, Namweon-Gun
18. Sanwol-Ri, Daeya-Myeon, Oggu-Gun

Jeonra-Nam-Do
19. Dodeog-Ri, Samdo-Myeon, Gwangsan-Gun
20. Seonpyeong-Ri, Seo-Myeon, Seungju-Gun
21. Namseog-Ri, Nampyeong-Myeon, Naju-Gun
22. Keumnae-Ri, Toji-Myeon, Gurye-Gun
23. Mansu-Ri, Neungju-Myeon, Hwasun-Gun
24. Seungbeop-Ri, Ogog-Myeon, Gogseong-Gun

Gyeongsang-Bug-Do
25. Gajang-Ri, Sangju-Eub, Sangju-Gun
26. Wolcho-Ri, Cheongri-Myeon, Sangju-Gun
27. Gopyeong-Ri, Hwayang-Myeon, Cheongdo-Gun
28. Chasan 1-Ri. Punggag-Myeon, Cheongdo-Gun
29. Jueung 1-Ri, Daesan-Myeon, Yeongdeog-Gun
30. Yeonpyeong 2-Ri, Yeonghae-Myeon, Yeongdeog-Gun

Gyeongsang-Nam-Do
31. Songjeong -Ri, Sanin-Myeon, Haman-Gun
32. Naegog-Ri, Yeohang-Myeon, Haman-Gun
33. Geonam-Ri, Ibang-Myeon, Changnyeong-Gun
34. Seog-Ri, Daeji-Myeon, Changnyeong-Gun
35. Daedong-Ri, Mari-Myeon, Geochang-Gun
36. Daehyeon-Ri, Namsang-Myeon, Geochang-Gun

BIBLIOGRAPHY

ADB (Asian Development Bank), (1977), *Rural Asia: Challenge and Opportunity,* (Singapore: Federal Publications).

Adelman, I. and C. Morris (1967), *Society, Politics and Economic Development,* (Baltimore: Johns Hopkins U. Press).

Ahmad, Yusuf J., (1975), "Administration of Integrated Rural Development Programmes: A Note on Methodology," *Internation Labor Review,* Vol. 3, No. 2 (Feb.), pp. 119–142.

Apter, David, E., (1963), "System, Process, and Politics of Economic Development" in Bert F. Hoselitz and Wilbert E. Moore, (eds.), *Industrialization and Society* (The Hague, UNESCO, Mouton), pp. 135–158.

Arnstein, Sherry, (1971), "Eight Rungs on the Ladder of Citizen Participation," in E. Chan and B. Passett (eds.), *Citizen Participation: Effecting Community Change,* (N.Y: Praeger Publishers), pp. 69–91.

Ban, S.; P. Moon; and D. Perkins, (1980), *Rural Development,* (Cambridge: Harvard Univ. Press).

Banerjee, Inayatullah, & Whang (1976), "The New International Economic Order: An Overview of Issues and Implications," A paper presented at ACDA Round Table Discussion on Major Implications of New International Economic Order, Singapore,

15-17 March.
Baum, W.C., (1978), "The World Bank Project Cycle," *Finance and Development*, 15 (Dec.): 10-17.
Bertalanffy, Ludwig (1968), *General System Theory*, (Penguin Books).
Boyer, Willam W. and Byong Man Ahn, (1977), "The New Communtity Movement (Saemaul Undong) in South Korea," *Journal of Korean Affairs*, Vol. VI, No. 3/4 (Oct. 1976/Jan. 1977), pp. 48-61.
Brandt, Vincent, (1977), "Why Rural Korea was Transformed," *Asian Wall Street Journal*, (14 Jan)
Brandt, Vincent and Man-Gap Lee, (1977), "Community Development in South Korea," Seoul, Seoul National Unviersity, mimeo.
Caroll, T., et al., (1969), *A Review of Rural Cooperation in Developing Areas* (Geneve: UNRISD).
Choe, Yang-Boo, (1978a), "The Korean Model of Rural Saemaul Undong: Its Structure, Strategy, and Performance," Seoul: Korea Rural Economics Institute, Working Paper No. 4 (mimeo.).
_____, (1978b), "Saemaul Undong eui Sahoejeog Pyeongga" (Social Performance of the Saemaul Undong: An Interim Report), (Seoul: Korea Rural Economics Institute, mimeo.).
Chee, Stephen and Khong Kim Hoong, (1977), "The Role of Rural Organization in Rural Development in Peninsular Malaysia," A paper presented at ACDA Seminar on Role of Rural Organization in Rural Development, Kuala Lumpur, 20-28 June.
Cheema, Shabbier, et al., (1977), "Rural Organizations and Rural Development in Malaysia," A paper presented at ACDA Seminar on Role of Rural Organization in Rural Development, Kuala Lumpur, 20-28 June.
Cheong, Ji-Woong, (1980), "Information, Education and Training in the Saemaul Movement," presented at the International Research Seminar on the Saemaul Movement, Seoul, 8-13 December.
Chung, Kyung Kyoun, (1980), "Role of Women in Saemaul Undong," presented at UNICEF Regional Saemaul Undong Study Seminar, Seoul, 9-22 June.
Clayton E. and F. Petry (ed.), (1980), *Monitoring Systems for Agricultural and Rural Development Projects* (Rome: FAO).
DHC (Dag Hammarskjold Center), (1976), *Development Dialogue* (New York: United Nations).
Dams, Theodor, (1980), "Development from Below and People's Participation as Key Principles of Integrated Rural Development," presented at Seoul National University, International Re-

search Seminar on the Saemaul Movement, Seoul, 8–13 December.
_____, (1979), "Agricultural Structural Policy in the Framework of Regional Development," *Journal of Rural Development*, II, No. 1, pp. 75–86.
Deutsch, Karl W., (1961), "Social Mobilization and Political Development," *American Political Science Review*, LV, 3, pp. 493–514.
DeVris, Egbert, (1961), *Man in Rapid Social Change*, (Toronto, Doubleday)
Emrich, Keith (1979), "Evaluation and Participation," presenged at UN/APDAC, Expert Group Meeting on Monitoring and Evaluation of Rural Development, 7–13 November.
EPB (Economic Planning Board), (1978), *Major Indicators*, Seoul.
____, (1960), (1966), (1970), (1975), *Population and Housing Census Report*, Seoul.
____, (1955), (1965), (1970), (1975), (1979), *Statistical Yearbook*, Seoul.
____, (1979), *Annual Report on Economically Active Population Survey*, (Seoul).
____, (1980), *Handbook of Korean Economy* (Seoul).
ESCAP, (1976), "Report of Bangladesh/ESCAP/Inter-agency Workshop on Integrated Rural Development," (Bangkok: PLO/EGM/IRD/4, Dec.).
Esman, Milton, (1978), "New Directions in Rural Development: The Changing Role of Officials," in Whang, In-Joung (ed.), *Training Strategies for Integrated Rural Development*, (Kuala Lumpur, UN/APDAC), pp. 28–47.
____, (1976), "NIEO and Domestic Development Strategies," *International Development Review*, (March) pp. 21–22.
Etzioni, Amitai (1961), *A Comparative Analysis of Complex Organizagion*, (New York: Free Press).
FAO, (1977), *Inter-Regional Symposium on Integrated Rural Development*. Berlin, 19–23 Sept.
____, (1979a), Summary Report of the Inter-Agency Technical Workshop on Monitoring and Evaluation of Rural Development Projects and Programmes, Rome, 1–3 February.
____, (1979b), Review and Analysis of Agrarian Reform and Rural Development in the Developing Countries. Rome, mimeo.
FEC (Federal Electric Corporation) (1963), *A Programmed Introduction to PERT*, (New York: John Wiley).
Griffin, Keith, (1974), *The Political Economy of Agrarian Change*, (London: Macmillan).
Hag, Mahbub Ul, (1976), *The Poverty Curtain :Choice for the Third*

World (New York: Columbia U. Press).

Hag, M. Nurul, (1973), *Village Development in Bangladesh* (Colombia, Bangladesh Academy for Rural Develyment).

Haque, W., M.; A. Rahman and P. Wignaraja, (1975), *Toward a Theory of Rural Development,* (Bangkok: Asian Development Institute, Prepublication copy: mimeo.).

Humble, John W., (ed.), (1970), *Management by Objectives in Action,* (London; McGraw-Hill).

IBRD, (1974), *Rural Development and Bank Policies: A Progress Report,* Washington.

____, (1975), *The Assault on World Poverty: Problems of Rural Development, Education and Health,* (Baltimore, Johns Hopkins Univ. Press).

Iglesias, Gabriel, (1976), "Marcos' Rice Self-Sufficiency Program: Leadership Role in Implementation," Iglesias (ed.), *Implementation: The Problem of Achieving Results* (Manila: EROPA), pp. 1–34.

Inayatullah (ed.), (1976a), *Strategies of Rrual Development in Asia: A Discussion* (Kuala Lumpur, Asian Center for Development Administration).

_____, (1976b), "An Analysis of the Emergence of a Rural Development Innovation in Comilla, Bangladesh," *Journal of Developing Areas* II, (Oct.), pp. 79–80.

_____, (ed.), (1978), *Rural Organizations and Rural Development* (Kuala Lumpur, APDAC).

_____, (ed.), (1979), *Approaches to Rural Development: Some Asian Experiences,* (Kuala Lumpur, APDAC).

Inkeles, Alex, and Smith, David H., (1974), *Becoming Modern: Individual Change in Six Developing Countries,* (Harvard Univ. Press).

Johnson, R.A., Kast, F.E. and Rosenzweig, J.E., (1973), *The Theory and Management of Systems,* 3rd ed. (Tokyo: McGraw-Hill Kogakusha).

Kada, R., (1980), "Employment Creation in Rural Areas" presented at Seoul National University, International Research Seminar on the Saemaul Movement, Dec. 7–14.

Katz, D. and R. Kahn, *The Social Psychology of Organization,* (New York, John Wiley, 1966).

Kaul, Mohan, (1979), "Monitoring and Evaluation Systems for Rural Development in India," presented at UN/APDAC, Expert Group Meeting on Monitoring and Evaluation of Rural Development, Kuala Lumpur, 7–13 November.

KDI (Korea Development Institute), (1978), *Long-Term Prospect for Economic and Social Development, 1977–91,* (Seoul).

Keim, Willard D., (1974), "The Attitudes of Korean Peasants," *Journal of East & West Studies*, Vol. III, No. 1, pp. 65-100.
Kim, Ho-Jin, (1979). "Development Leadership: A Comparative Study Two Korean Villages" (Ph.D. Dissertation), Univ. of Hawaii.
Kim, Hyung-Hyo, (1978), "Hangugjeog Gieobmunhwa eui Changjo wa Gyeongyeongga eui Yeoghal" (Manager's Role in Creation of the Korean Business Culture), Korea Human Development Institute, *Hangugjeog Nosagwangye* (The Korean Style of Labor-Industry Relations), pp. 321-330.
Kim, Il-Chul, (1971), "A Study of Value-Interest Dichotomy," *Seoul National University Paper*, Vol. 1 (B), Oct., pp. 174-182.
Kim, Jong-Ho, (1977), "The Saemaul Undong gwa Jido Inyeom" (The Saemaul Undong and Its Guiding Ideology), Suwon: Saemaul Leaders Training Institute, (mimeo.).
Kim, Kyong-Dong (1966), "Tasks of Value Studies in Modernization Process," *Dong-A Munwha*, Vol. 6, pp. 226-228.
———, (1967), "Gongeobhwa reul Wihan Junbi" (Preparedness for Industrial Development) in *Korean Journal of Public Administration* Vol. 5, No. 1, pp. 179-200.
———, (1971), "Industrialization and Industrialism: A Comparative Perspective on Values of Korean Workers and Managers," ILCORK Working Paper (mimeo.).
Kim, Taekil, John A Ross, G.C. Worth, (1972), *The Korea National Family Planning Programs*, (NY: Population Council).
Kluckhohn, Clyde, (1962), "Values and Value Orientation in the Theory of Action," in Parsons and Shils (eds.), *Toward A General Theory of Action*, (Cambridge: Harvard University Press).
KOIS (Korean Overseas Information Service), (1979), (1977), *Saemaul Undong*, Seoul.
KRIPDC (Korea Rural Industrial Products Development Center), *Status of Saemaul Factories 1980* (Seoul, mimeo).
KSFS (Korean Society for Future Studies), (1971), *Korea in the Year 2000*, (Seoul: Ministry of Sciences and Technology).
Kuitenbrauwer, J., (1977), "People's Rural Organization in China," presented at ACDA Seminar on Role of Rural Organization in Rural Development, Kuala Lumpur, 20-28 June.
Kunkel, John H., (1965), "Values and Behavior in Economic Development," *Economic Development and Cultural Change*. Vol. XIII, No. 3. (April).
Kwon, Soon-Jong, (1978), "Saemaul Leaders Training Programs in Korea," presented at the Consultative Meeting on Monitoring and

Evaluation of Social Development Programmes, Manila, 15–23 February.

Land, Kenneth C., et al., (1975), *Social Indicator Models,* (New York: Russel Sage Foundation).

Lee, Hahn-Been, (1968), *Korea: Time, Change and Administration,* (Honolulu: East-West Center Press).

Lee, Jil-Hyun, (1978), "Saemaul Training for Rural Development: A Korean Perspective," "Whang In-Joung (ed.), *Training Strategies for Integrated Rural Development,* (Kuala Lumpur, APDAC), pp. 112–126.

Lee, Man-Gap, (1973), *Hangug Nongcheon Sahoe eui Gujo wa Byeonhwa* (The Structure of Korean Rural Communities and Its Change), (Seoul: Seoul National University Press).

Lee, Manwee, (1980), "Education and Training on the Saemaul Undong," presented at the Regional Saemaul Undong Study Seminar, Seoul, 9–22, July.

Lee, S.W., (1980), "Land Reform in South Korea: Macro-level Policy Review," Inaytullah (ed.), *Land Reform,* (Kuala Lumpur, UN/APDAC), pp. 319–349.

Lerner, Daniel, (1958), *The Passing of Traditional Society,* (Princeton: Princeton Univ. Press).

Litchfield, E.N., (1956), "Notes on a General Theory of Administration," *Administrative Science Quarterly,* Vol II. No. 1, pp. 1–29.

Macklin, David B., (1969), "A Socio-Psychological Perspective on Modernization," in Allan R. Holmberg (ed.), *Modernization by Design,* (Ithaca, New York: Cornell Univ. Press), pp. 85–146.

McClleland, David C. (1961), *The Achieving Society,* (Princeton: Van Nostrand)

MOAF (Ministry of Agriculture and Fisheries), (1980), *Nong-Jung-Soo-Chup* (Handbook of Agricultural Administration), Seoul,

MOE (Ministry of Education), (1955), (1965), (1970), (1975), (1979) *Annaul Statistical Report on Education* (Seoul).

MOHA (Ministry of Home Affairs), (1979a), (1978), (1977), (1976), (1974), (1973), *Saemaul Undong: Sijag Buteo Oneul Ggaji* (Saemaul Undong: From Beginning to the Present), Seoul.

____, (1979 b), *1979 Saemaul Jonggyeol (Overall Evaluation of Saemaul Undong for 1979),* Seoul, mimeo.

____, (1980), *Ten Year History of Saemaul Undong,* Vol. II, (Seoul).

Moon, P.Y., (1980), "Nongsanmul Gagyeog Jeongchaeg eui Jeongae (Development of Agricultural Products Price Policies," in KREI, *Hangug Nongeob eui Geundaehwa Gwajeong* (Modernization Process of Korean Agricutre), Seoul, 1980, pp. 99-155.

Morris, Charls, (1956), *Varieties of Huamn Values*, Univ. of Chicago Press

Morris, Morri David (1979), *Measuring the Conditions of the World's Poor: The Physical Quality of Life Index*, (New York: Pregamon Press).

Mosher, A.T., (1976), *Thinking About Rural Development* (New York: Agricultural Development Council).

Myrdal, G., (1968), *Asian Drama: An Inquiry into the Poverty of Nations* (New York: Pantheen, 3 Vols.).

Ness, Gayl D., (1967), *Bureaucracy and Rural Development in Malaysia*, (Berkeley, Calif: U. of California Press).

Onate, Burton T. (1977), "Indicators for Monitoring Rural Area Development Projects," presented at the Symposium on Programs for Rural Development of the Philippines at Los Banos, Philippines, 23-24 June.

Pak, Ki-Hyuk, *et. al.*, (1966), *A Study of Land Tenure System in Korea*, (Seoul: Korea Land Economic Research Institute).

Park, Chung Hee, (1979), *Saemaul: Korea's New Community Movement*, (Seoul, Korea Textbook Co.).

Park, J.H., (1978), "Integrated Rural Development: The Case of Saemaul Undong in Korea," Whang (ed.), *Training Strategies for Integrated Rural Development*, (Kuala Lumpur: APDAC), pp. 13-26.

_____, (1980), "Process of Saemaul Undong Project Implementation in Korea," presented at International Research Seminar on the Saemaul Movement, Seoul, Korea, 8-13 December.

Parsons, Talcott, (1960), *Structure and Process in Modern Societies*, (Glencoe, Ill.: Free Press).

Perrow, C., (1967), "A Framework for the Comparative Analysis of Organization," *American Sociological Review*, 32: pp. 194-208.

_____, (1970), *Organizational Analysis*, (London: Tavistock).

Price, James, (1968), *Organizational Effectiveness* (Homewood, Ill.: Richard Irwin).

Pye, L., (1962), "Armies in the Process of Political Modernization," in Johnson (ed.), *The Role of the Military in Underdeveloped Countries*, (Princeton University Press), pp. 80-90.

_____, (1965), "The Concept of Political Development," *The Annuals of the American Academy of Politics and Science*, 358 (March), pp. 1-13.

Rajandra, M., (1976), "The Rajangana Colonization Project: A Study of the Implementation of a Development Project," Iglesias (ed.), *Implementation: The Problem of Achieving Results*, (Manila: EROPA),

pp. 62-94.
Raper, Arthur, F., (1970), *Rural Development in Action*, (Ithaca, New York: Cornell University Press).
Riggs, Fred (1964), *Administration in Developing Countries: Theory of Prismatic Society*, (Boston: Hougton Muffin).
Rogers, Everett M. (1969). *Modernization among Peasants*, (Holt Rinehart Winson).
_____, and Shoemaker, F.F., (1971), *Communication of Innovations*, (New York: Free Press).
_____, (1973), *Communication Strategies for Family Planning*, (New York: Free Press).
Rondinelli, D.A., (1975), "Preparing and Analysing Case Studies in Development Project Management," Honolulu: East-West TDE, Working Paper, mimeo.
_____, (1977), "Local Organization for Integrated Rural Development," *International Review of Administrative Sciences*, Vol, SLIII, No. 1, pp. 20-30.
_____ and K. Ruddle (1978), *Urbanization and Rural Development*, (New York: Prager Pub.).
Selznick, Philip, (1957), *Leadership in Administration*, (New York, Harper & Row).
Singer, Hans W. and Baster Nancy O., (1980), *Young Human Resources in Korea's Social Development*, (Seoul, Korea Development Institute).
_____, (1980), "The Role of Human Capital in Development" A lecutre note delivered at Bristol University on 22 December, reprinted by UNICEF, Seoul.
Shin, Yun-Pyo, (1979), *Jiyeog Gaebal Ron* (Regional Development Theories), (Seoul, Beob-Jeong-Sa)
Skinner, W.G., (1958), *Leadership and Power in the Chinese Community of Thailand*, (New York: Cornell University Press).
SLTI (Saemaul Leaders Training Institute), (1974), Saemaul Jidoja Hunryeon Jichim (Guide to the Training Program for Saemaul Leaders) Suwon; mimeo.
Suchman, Edward A. (1967), *Evaluation Research*, (New York: Russel Sage Foundation).
Sutcliffe, Claud R., (1974), "Achievement Motivation & Economic Development among Peasants," *Rural Sociology*, Vol. 39, No. 2.
Thompson, J., et al., (1959), *Comparative Studies in Administration*, (Pittsburgh: University of Pittsburgh Press).
Tinker, Irene and Hyung Cho, (1980), "Women's Participation on Community Developmment in Korea" presented at International

Research Seminar on the Saemaul Movement, Seoul, Korea, 8–13 December.
UN, (1975), *Popular Participation in Decision-Making for Development*, (New York: Dept. of Economic and Social Affairs).
UNAPDI, UNCRD, UNICEF, (1978), *Monitoring and Evaluation of Social Development Programs, Summary Report of A Consultative Meeting*, Manila, 15–23 February.
Waller, John, *et al.*, (1976), *Monitoring for Government Agencies*, (Washington: The Urban Institute).
Wanasinghe, Shelton, (1977), "Rural Development Policies, Bureaucracies, and Rural Organizations," A paper presented at ACDA Seminar on *Role of Rural Organization in Rural Development*, Kuala Lumpur, 20–28 June.
Weber, Max, (1958), *The Protestant Ethic and the Spirit of Capitalism*, (Trans. by T. Parsons) (New York: Charles Scribner's Sons).
Weise, Carol H. (1972), *Evaluative Research*, (Prentice-Hall).
Whang, In-Joung, (1970a), *Haengjeong gwa Gyeongie Gaebal* (Public Administration and Economic Development in Korea), Seoul; Seoul National University Press.
____, (1970b), "Hangug Gyeongje Gyehoeg eui Inyeomjeog Jeonje, (Ideological premise of Economic Planning in Korea), *Korean Journal of Public Administration*, Vol. 8, No. 1, pp. 165–198.
____, (1972), "A Guideline for Evaluation of Educational Projects," *Korean Journal of Public Administration*, Vol. 10, No. 1, pp. 247–254.
____, (1974), "Integration and Coordination of Population Policies in South Korea," *Asian Survey*, 19 (Nov.) pp. 985–999.
____, (1975), "Systems Approach to Training: An Overview," Lecture note for the United Nations Asian Center for Development Administration, Maragement Development for National Training Directors, Jakarta, Indonesia, 6–25 November.
____, (1976), *Framework for Coordination in Implementation of Family Planning Programme*, (K. Lumpur, ACDA).
____, (1978a), *Administrative Feasibility Analysis for Development Projects: Concept and Approach*, Kuala Lumpur: UN/APDAC.
____, (1978b), "Training Strategies for Intergrated Rural Development," *Journal of Rural Development* 1 (Nov.) pp. 111–131.
____, (1978c), "Introduction: Concepts of Integrated Rural Developjment," in Whang, In-Joung (ed.) *Training Strategies for Integrated Rural Development*, Kuala Lumpur, UN/APDAC, pp. 1–15.
____, (1980a), *Hangug eui Jonghab Nongcheon Gaebal* (Integrated Rural

Development in Korea), (Seoul: Korea Rural Economics Institute), Research Series No. 2.

———, (1980b), *Godo Saneob Sahoe e Bueunghaneun Nongcheon Kaebal Jeonryag* (Rural Development Strategies Compatible with Advanced Industrial Society in Korea), Seoul: Republic of Korea, National Council of Economy and Sciences.

———, (1980c), "Transferability of the Saemaul Undong for Rural Development in Other Developing Countries," presented at the Seoul National University, International Research Seminar on Saemaul Undong, 8–13 December, Seoul, Korea.

———, (1980d), "Gaebal Jeonryag eui Gijo Jeonhwan" (Shift in Foundation of Development Strategies in the 1980's), *KREI Newsletter* Vol. I, No. 3, (March), p. 2.

Wildavsky, A. and J. Pressman, (1973), *Implementation*, (Berkeley: Univ. of California Press).

INDEX

Achievement motivation, 217–220
Ad hoc visit, 153
"Administration by identification," 45, 50
Agrarian reform (see Land Reform)
Agricultural Cooperatives, 66
Agricultural labor force, 197
Agricultural production mix, 190–192
Attitudinal pattern, 222–236
Authoritarian innovation, 123
Authority decision, 122

Balanced regional development, 182
Behavioral pattern, 79–88
Better-living rural region, 261
Big-push, all-out training, 176
Bottom-up, 92

Budget Speech, 43
Budgetary support, 51
Bureaucratic subculture, 232

Case study, 135
Change orientation, 210–213
Citation Law, 86
Closed oven situation, 247
Collective commitment, 247
Collective decisions, 122
Comilla experiment, 14
Common village, 209
Communal kitchen utensils, 109
Communication skill, 232
Confucian ethic, 225
Consultative Council, 48, 119–120
Content analysis, 44
Cooperation and solidarity, 225–231
Coordination, 133–134

and integration, 21
of training program, 174–175
Creativity, 48

Daycare center, 108
Deputy County, Chief, 48,121
Development projects, 15–16, 245
"Down-to-village" movement, 164, 171
Dynamics of political systems, 247–250

Economy of scale, 10, 231
Educational drive, 99–101, 251
Efficiency, 48
Elite, 20, 171–172,
Empathy, 102
Employment (see Rural employment)
opportunities, 196-201
Entrepreneurship, 218
Evaluative research, 135
Export promotion, 183

Factory Saemaul Undong, 25–26
Family-focused activity, 264
Farm household income (see Income redistribution)
Farm mechanization, 190
Farmers' value system, 240
Financial support, 31–36
Field visit, 135
Follow-up activity, 170
Foot-loose industry, 205
Future orientation, 214–217

Gantt chart, 134–135, 147, 149
General Assembly, 119
General Government Sector Budget, 51
Geographical affiliation, 67

Godly wind (see *Shin-ba-lam*)
Government commitment, 41
mobilization, 92
support, 16–19
Grass-root democracy, 234, 242
Green Revolution, 253
Gross National Happiness (GNH), 258
Gross National Satisfaction (GNS), 258

Hangul, 99
Hierarchical authority, 94
High rice price policy, 54, 257
High-yielding variety (HYV), 55, 250
Horizontal coordination, 133
Housewife-oriented activity, 264

Ideological specialization, 94
diffuseness, 94
Ideology of equal opportunity 199
IEC (see Information-education-communication)
Incentives and supporting policies, 249–250
Income redistribution, 179–180
Income-increasing projects, 26
Individual motivation, 92
Industrial development, 252–258
Information-education-communication, 13, 202, 205, 267
Innovation, 122
Institutional
arrangement, 173
innovation, 264–265
reform, 48
Integrated process, 21
Integrated rural development,

3–5, 126–129
  definition, 261
  model of, 20–21
Integration
  horizontal and vertical, 4
  coordination and, 21
Interdisciplinary approach, 7
Intervention
  maximum vs. minimum, 5
Intervillage joint project, 230
Investment,
  amount and pattern of, 25–31

Japanese colonial rule, 233

Korean War, 97, 251

Land ownership, 97–99
Land reform, 11, 98, 250
Land Reform Act, 97
Land utilization, 192
Leadership
  commitment, 92
  pattern, 79–81
  Training Center, 52, 56, 116
  Training Course, 12, 20, 146
  development, 116
Local administration, 265–267
Local Administration Training Institute, 52
Local government system, 49–51

Management by objectives, 124
Management techniques, 125, 254
Manpower development, 52
Marketing linkages, 15
Mass participation, 94
Mechanization (see Farm mechanization)
Military service, 70–71
  influence, 251
  subculture, 72
Mobilization system, 94
Modernizing autocracy, 94
Monitoring and evaluation, 134
Monitoring
  assessment of, 157–158
  definition of, 134, 138
  of project performance, 138
  system, 140–153
Monthly Economic Situation Report, 45
Morale, 84–85
Mother's Bank, 108
Mother's Club, 104
Motivation, 82–84

National economy, 178, 242–243
National Conference of Saemaul Undong Leaders, 41, 45
New Year Press Conference, 41, 43
Non-farm income (see Village income)

Observatory evaluation, 135
Off-farm employment, 200
On-going evaluation, 139, 153–157
Operational strategy, 52–54
Organization defined, 114
Organizational behavior, 240–242
  reform, 48
  strategies, 243–247
  technology, 126
Output, 48
Outstanding village, 209

Participation
  definition, 95
  induced, forced, voluntary, 94

PERT technique, 135, 149
Planning, 132
   and rationality, 220–221
Planning-mindness, 220
Planned Parenthood Federation, 104
Political commitment, 40–47
   leadership, 40
   support, 19–20, 247
Presidential Award, 242
Principle of observability, 115
Private savings, 180–181
Process and technology, 48
Project
   cycle, 134
   income-increasing, 26
   management, 129–131
   production infrastructure, 26
   spiritual enlightment, 26
   welfare-environment, 25
Project-specific criteria, 157

Quality of Life (QOL), 258, 267

Rationality, 221
Reconciliation system, 94
Regional organization, 264
Resources, 47
   mobilization, 246
Responsiveness, 48
Role performance, 72–79
Rural development (see Integrated rural development)
Rural employment, 195–203
Rural region, 261

Saemaul factory, 183, 199
Saemaul flag, 41
Saemaul Fund, 180
Saemaul leader
   background, 62–72
   election, 59
   identification, 61
   incumbency, 58
Saemaul Leaders Training Institute, 116
Saemaul leadership training, (see Training)
Saemaul Planning Division, 48
Saemaul projects, 117
Saemaul song, 41
Saemaul spirit, 45, 54
Saemaul Technical Service Corps, 55, 185
Saemaul Undong Bureau, 48
Saemaul Undong
   objectives, 114
Saemaul Women's Association, 235
School attendance, 194
School Saemaul Undong, 25
Selective-sequential approach, 182
Sequential order of training course, 172
"Service men or women," 19, 50
Shin-ba-lam, 253, 259
Social mobilization, 217
Social Transformation, 250–254
Spiritual enlightenment, 115, 126
Societal support, 19–20, 247
Standard of living, 192
Step-by-step approach, 182
Strategic mixture of clients, 171
Structure, 47
Systems' criteria, 157

Tactical flexibility, 94
Technical improvement, 183
Ten-Year Development Plan for Medium-Small Cities, 265

"The better village the first support," 33, 53, 250
Top-to-down and bottom-up, 92
Total allegiance, 94
Township Promotion Committee, 48
Training
  institutions, 164–165
  methods, 168–171
  needs, 159–164
  program content, 167–168
  target groups, 165–167
Trickle down effect, 252
Transferability, 254–255

Unit of rural community, 9–10
Unitarism, 94
Urban Saemaul Movement, 25–26

Value orientation, 210–222
Values and perception, 208
Value system, (see Farmers' value system)
Vertical coordination, 133

Vicious circle of poverty, 2, 42
Village, 248
  co-op store, 108
  economy, 186, 242
  income, 186–190
  kitchen project, 108
  reclassification, 184
Village-centered pattern, 263–264
Village Development Committee, 49, 119
Village Head, 81
Village leadership, 61
Village leader (see Saemaul leader)

War-time catastrophe 251
Wage-earning project, 198
Welfare-environment project, 25
Well-to-do villages, 220
Women's participation, 103
Work-oriented cooperative farming, 263

Yi Dynasty, 233

ABOUT THE AUTHOR

Dr. In-Joung Whang is presently working with the Korea Rural Economic Institute, Seoul, as Research Director (since 1978). He is also associated with the Institute of Social Sciences, Seoul National University as a Senior Visiting Fellow. Prior to these, he served with the United Nations as a Senior Expert in Policy Analysis and Development at the Asian and Pacific Development Administration Centre (APDAC) in Kuala Lumpur, Malaysia (1973–1978). He was Professor of Development Administration at the Graduate School of Public Administration, Seoul National University in Seoul (1968–1976). Dr. Whang also served as Consultant to the East-West Technology and Development Institute in Honolulu (1971), the U.N. Asian Institute for Economic Development and Planning in Bangkok (1972) and recently to the U.N. Asian and Pacific Development Center (APDC) for development of research programs(1981). He was a Senior Economic Planner of the Economic Planning Board (1962–1964) and Chief of the Budget Reform Unit, Bureau of Budget, the Republic of Korea (1960–1961).

He completed his B.A. in Political Sciences (1958) and M.A.

of Public Administration (1961) at the Seoul National University, and his Ph.D. in the field of economic and social development at the Graduate School of Public and International Affaris, University of Pittsburgh, Pennsylvania, U.S.A. (1968). In 1966, Dr. Whang received the *Traknath Das Award* at the University of Pittsburgh "for his outstanding studies on Asian organization, society and development."

He has published a number of books and articles including *Public Administration and Economic Development in Korea* (Seoul: Seoul National University Press, 1970); "Elites and Economic Programs," *The Korean Journal of Public Administration* (April, 1969); "Comparative Analysis of PPBS and Line-Item Budgeting from Sociological Perspectives," *ibid* (October 1969); "Ideological Premise of Economic Planning in Korea," *ibid* (April 1970); "Leadership and Organizational Development," *Asian Survey* (October 1971); "Integration and Coordination of Population Policies in Korea," *Asian Survey* (November 1974); *A Framework for Coordination in Implementation of Family Planning Programme* (Kuala Lumpur: ACDA, 1976); *Administrative Feasibility for Development Projects: Concept and Approach* (Kuala Lumpur: APDAC, 1978); "An Integrated Perspective of Food Policies: Identification of policy Alternatives" *Journal of Rural Development* (1979) and "Role of UNICEF in Korea for the 1980's" (Seoul: UNICEF, 1979, mimeo).

Dr. Whang has also edited several books among them—*Korea in the Year 2,000* (Seoul: Korean Society for Future Studies, 1970); *Management of Family Planning Programmes in Asia :Concepts, Issues and Approaches* (Kuala Lumpur: ACDA, 1976); and *Training Strategies for Integrated Rural Development* (Kuala Lumpur: APDAC, 1978); and *Child Development Policies in Korea* (Seoul: Korea Development Institute, 1981).